Marketing Through Search Optimization
How people search and how to be found on the Web

Second edition

Alex Michael and Ben Salter

ELSEVIER

AMSTERDAM • BOSTON • HEIDELBERG • LONDON • NEW YORK • OXFORD
PARIS • SAN DIEGO • SAN FRANCISCO • SINGAPORE • SYDNEY • TOKYO

Butterworth-Heinemann is an imprint of Elsevier

Butterworth-Heinemann is an imprint of Elsevier
Linacre House, Jordan Hill, Oxford OX2 8DP, UK
30 Corporate Drive, Suite 400, Burlington, MA 01803, USA

First edition 2003
Second edition 2008

British Library Cataloguing in Publication Data
A catalogue record for this book is available from the British Library

Library of Congress Control Number: 2007932103

ISBN: 978-0-7506-8347-0

For information on all Butterworth-Heinemann publications
visit our web site at http://books.elsevier.com

Typeset by Integra Software Services Pvt. Ltd., Pondicherry, India
www.integra-india.com
Printed and bound in Slovenia

08   09   10   11   12   10 9 8 7 6 5 4 3 2 1

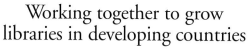

Working together to grow
libraries in developing countries

www.elsevier.com | www.bookaid.org | www.sabre.org

ELSEVIER   BOOK AID
International   Sabre Foundation

Contents

Contents

Acknowledgements

We would both like to thank Sprite Interactive Ltd for their support with this book.

Introduction

Search engines provide one of the primary ways by which Internet users find websites. That's why a website with good search engine listings may see a dramatic increase in traffic. Everyone wants those good listings. Unfortunately, many websites appear poorly in search engine rankings, or may not be listed at all because they fail to consider how search engines work. In particular, submitting to search engines is only part of the challenge of getting good search engine positioning. It's also important to prepare a website through 'search engine optimization'. Search engine optimization means ensuring that your web pages are accessible to search engines and are focused in ways that help to improve the chances that they will be found.

How search engines work

The term 'search engine' is often used generically to describe both crawler-based search engines and human-powered directories. These two types of search engines gather their listings in very different ways.

This book provides information, techniques and tools for search engine optimization. This book does not teach you ways to trick or 'spam' search engines. In fact, there is no such search engine magic that will guarantee a top listing. However, there are a number of small changes you can make that can sometimes produce big results.

The book looks at the two major ways search engines get their listings:

1 Crawler-based search engines
2 Human-powered directories

Crawler-based search engines

Crawler-based search engines, such as Google, create their listings automatically. They 'crawl' or 'spider' the Web and create an index of the results; people then search through that index. If you change your web pages, crawler-based search engines eventually find these changes, and that can affect how you are listed. This book will look at the spidering process and how page titles, body copy and other elements can all affect the search results.

Human-powered directories

A human-powered directory, such as Yahoo! or the Open Directory, depends on humans for its listings. The editors at Yahoo! will write a short description for sites they review. A search looks for matches only in the descriptions submitted.

Changing your web pages has no effect on your listing. Things that are useful for improving a listing with a search engine have nothing to do with improving a listing in a directory. The only exception is that a good site, with good content, might be more likely to get reviewed for free than a poor site.

The parts of a crawler-based search engine

Crawler-based search engines have three major elements. The first is the spider, also called the crawler, which visits a web page, reads it, and then follows links to other pages within the site. This is what it means when someone refers to a site being 'spidered' or 'crawled'. The spider returns to the site on a regular basis, perhaps every month or two, to look for changes. Everything the spider finds goes into the second part of the search engine, the index.

The index, sometimes called the catalog, is like a giant book containing a copy of every web page that the spider finds. If a web page changes, then this book is updated with new information. Sometimes it can take a while for new pages or changes that the spider finds to be added to the index, and thus a web page may have been 'spidered' but not yet 'indexed'. Until it is indexed – added to the index – it is not available to those searching with the search engine.

Search engine software is the third part of a search engine. This is the program that sifts through the millions of pages recorded in the index to find matches to a search and rank them in order of what it believes is most relevant.

Major search engines: the same, but different

All crawler-based search engines have the basic parts described above, but there are differences in how these parts are tuned. That is why the same search on different search engines often produces different results. Some of the significant differences between the major crawler-based search engines are summarized on the search engine features page. Information on this page has been drawn from the help pages of each search engine, along with knowledge gained from articles, reviews, books, independent research, tips from others, and additional information received directly from the various search engines.

How search engines rank web pages

Search for anything using your favourite crawler-based search engine. Almost instantly, the search engine will sort through the millions of pages it knows about and present you with ones that match your topic. The matches will even be ranked, so that the most relevant ones come first. Of course, the search engines don't always get it right. Non-relevant pages make it through, and sometimes it may take a little more digging to find what you are looking for. But by and large, search engines do an amazing job. So, how do crawler-based search engines go about determining relevancy, when confronted with hundreds of millions of web pages to sort through? They follow a set of rules, known as an algorithm. Exactly how a particular search engine's algorithm works is a closely kept trade secret. However, all major search engines follow the general rules below.

Location, location, location . . . and frequency

One of the main rules in a ranking algorithm involves the location and frequency of keywords on a web page – let's call it the location/frequency method, for short. Pages with the search terms appearing in the HTML title tag are often assumed to be more relevant than others to the topic. Search engines will also check to see if the search keywords appear near the top of a web page, such as in the headline or in the first few paragraphs of text. They assume that any page relevant to the topic will mention those words right from the beginning. Frequency is the other major factor in how search engines determine relevancy. A search engine will analyse how often keywords appear in relation to other words in a web page. Those with a higher frequency are often deemed more relevant than other web pages.

Spice in the recipe

Now it's time to qualify the location/frequency method described above. All the major search engines follow it to some degree, in the same way that cooks may follow a standard chilli recipe. However, cooks like to add their own secret ingredients. In the same way, search engines add spice to the location/frequency method. Nobody does it exactly the same, which is one reason why the same search on different search engines produces different results.

To begin with, some search engines index more web pages than others. Some search engines also index web pages more often than others. The result is that no search engine has the exact same collection of web pages to search through, and this naturally produces differences when comparing their results.

Many web designers mistakenly assume that META tags are the 'secret' in propelling their web pages to the top of the rankings. However, not all search engines read META tags. In addition, those that do read META tags may chose to weight them differently. Overall, META tags can be part of the ranking recipe, but they are not necessarily the secret ingredient.

Search engines may also penalize pages, or exclude them from the index, if they detect search engine 'spamming'. An example is when a word is repeated hundreds of times on a page, to increase the frequency and propel the page higher in the listings. Search engines watch for common spamming methods in a variety of ways, including following up on complaints from their users.

Off-the-page factors

Crawler-based search engines have plenty of experience now with webmasters who constantly rewrite their web pages in an attempt to gain better rankings. Some sophisticated webmasters may even go to great lengths to 'reverse engineer' the location/frequency systems used by a particular search engine. Because of this, all major search engines now also make use of 'off-the-page' ranking criteria.

Off-the-page factors are those that a webmaster cannot easily influence. Chief among these is link analysis. By analysing how pages link to each other, a search engine can determine both what a page is about and whether that page is deemed to be 'important', and thus deserving of a ranking boost. In addition, sophisticated techniques are used to screen out attempts by webmasters to build 'artificial' links designed to boost their rankings.

Another off-the-page factor is click-through measurement. In short, this means that a search engine may watch which results someone selects for a particular search, then eventually drop high-ranking pages that aren't attracting clicks while promoting lower-ranking pages that do pull in visitors. As with link analysis, systems are used to compensate for artificial links generated by eager webmasters.

Chapter 1

Introduction to search engine optimization

To implement search engine optimization (SEO) effectively on your website you will need to have a knowledge of what people looking for your site are searching for, your own needs, and then how to best implement these. Each SEO campaign is different, depending on a number of factors – including the goals of the website, and the budget available to spend on the SEO. The main techniques and areas that work today include:

- Having easily searchable content on your site
- Having links to and from your site from other high profile websites
- The use of paid placement programs
- Optimized site content to make site users stay after they have visited.

This book will teach you about all this, but initially Chapter 1 will take you through the background to search optimization. First of all we will look at the history of search engines, to give you a context to work in, and then we'll take a look at why people use search engines, what they actually search for when they do, and how being ranked highly will benefit your organization. Next we will provide a critical analysis of choosing the right SEO consultancy (if you have to commission an external agency).

The history of search engines on the Web

Back in 1990 there was no World Wide Web, but there was still an Internet, and there were many files around the network that people needed to find. The main way of receiving files was by using File Transfer Protocol (FTP), which gives computers a common way to exchange files over the Internet. This works by using FTP servers, which a computer user sets up on their computer. Another computer user can connect to this FTP server using a piece of software called an FTP client. The person retrieving the file has to specify an address, and usually a username and password, to log onto the FTP server. This was the way most file sharing was done; anyone who wanted to share a file had first to set up an FTP server to make the file available. The only way people could find out where a file was stored was by word-of-mouth; someone would have to post on a message board where a file was stored.

The first ever search engine was called Archie, and was created in 1990 by a man called Alan Emtage. Archie was the solution to the problem of finding information easily; the engine combined a data gatherer, which compiled site listings of FTP sites, with an expression matcher that allowed it to retrieve files from a user typing in a search term or query. Archie was the first search engine; it 'spidered' the Internet, matched the files it had found with search queries, and returned results from its database.

In 1993, with the success of Archie growing considerably, the University of Nevada developed an engine called Veronica. These two became affectionately known as the grandfather and grandmother of search engines. Veronica was similar to Archie, but was for Gopher files rather than FTP files. Gopher servers contained plain text files that could be retrieved in the same way as FTP files. Another Gopher search engine also emerged at the time, called Jughead, but this was not as advanced as Veronica.

The next major advance in search engine technology was the World Wide Web Wanderer, developed by Matthew Gray. This was the first ever robot on the Web, and its aim was to track the Web's growth by counting web servers. As it grew it began to count URLs as well, and this eventually became the Web's first database of websites. Early versions of the Wanderer software did not go down well initially, as they caused loss of performance as they scoured the Web and accessed single pages many times in a day; however, this was soon fixed. The World Wide Web Wanderer was called a robot, not because it was a robot in the traditional sci-fi sense of the word, but because on the Internet the term robot has grown to mean a program or piece of software that performs a repetitive task, such as exploring the net for information. Web robots usually index web pages to create a database that then becomes searchable; they are also known as 'spiders', and you can read more about how they work in relation to specific search engines in Chapter 4.

After the development of the Wanderer, a man called Martijn Koster created a new type of web indexing software that worked like Archie and was called ALIWEB. ALIWEB was developed in the summer of 1993. It was evident that the Web was growing at an enormous rate, and it became clear to Martijn Koster that there needed to be some way of finding things beyond the existing databases and catalogues that individuals were keeping. ALIWEB actually stood for 'Archie-Like Indexing of the Web'. ALIWEB did not have a web-searching robot; instead of this, webmasters posted their own websites and web pages that they wanted to be listed. ALIWEB was in essence the first online directory of websites; webmasters were given the opportunity to provide a description of their own website and no robots were sent out, resulting in reduced performance loss on the Web. The problem with ALIWEB was that webmasters had to submit their own special index file in a specific format for ALIWEB, and most of them did not understand, or did not bother, to learn how to create this file. ALIWEB therefore suffered from the problem that people did not use the service, as it was only a relatively small directory. However, it was still a landmark, having been the first database of websites that existed.

The World Wide Web Wanderer inspired a number of web programmers to work on the idea of developing special web robots. The Web continued growing throughout the 1990s, and more and more powerful robots were needed to index the growing number of web pages. The main concept behind spiders was that they followed links from web page to web page – it was logical to assume that every page on the Web was linked to another page, and by searching through each page and following its links a robot could work its way through the pages on the Web. By continually repeating this, it was believed that the Web could eventually be indexed.

At the end of December 1993 three search engines were launched that were powered by these advanced robots; these were the JumpStation, the World Wide Web Worm, and the Repository Based Software Engineering Spider (RBSE). JumpStation is no longer in service, but when it was it worked by collecting the title and header from web pages and then using a retrieval system to match these to search queries. The matching system searched through its database of results in a linear fashion and became so slow that, as the Web grew, it eventually ground to a halt. The World Wide Web Worm indexed titles and URLs of web pages, but like the JumpStation it returned results in the order that it found them – meaning that results were in no order of importance. The RBSE spider got around this problem by actually ranking pages in its index by relevance.

All the spiders that were launched around this time, including Architext (the search software that became the Excite engine), were unable to work out actually what it was they were indexing; they lacked any real intelligence. To get around this problem, a product called Elnet Galaxy was launched. This was a searchable and browsable directory, in the same way Yahoo! is today (you can read more about directories in Chapter 4). Its website links were organized in a hierarchical structure, which was divided into subcategories and further subcategories until users got to the website they were after. Take a look at the Yahoo! directory for an example of this in action today. The service, which went live in January 1994, also contained Gopher and Telnet search features, with an added web page search feature.

The next significant stage came with the creation of the Yahoo! directory in April 1994, which began as a couple of students' list of favourite web pages, and grew into the worldwide phenomenon that it is today. You can read more about the growth of Yahoo! in Chapter 4 of this book, but basically it was developed as a searchable web directory. Yahoo! guaranteed the quality of the websites it listed because they were (and still are) accepted or rejected by human editors. The advantage of directories, as well as their guaranteed quality, was that users could also read a title and description of the site they were about to visit, making it easier to make a choice to visit a relevant site.

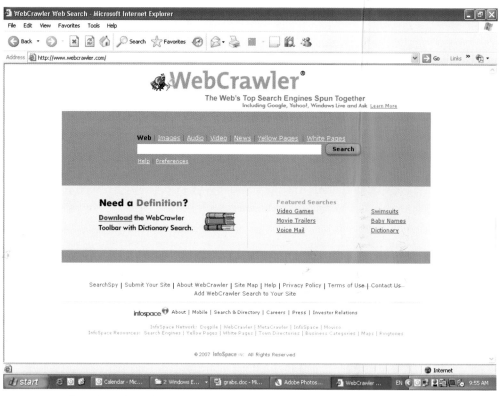

Figure 1.1 *The WebCrawler website*

The first advanced robot, which was developed at the University of Washington, was called WebCrawler (Figure 1.1). This actually indexed the full text of documents, allowing users to search through this text, and therefore delivering more relevant search results.

WebCrawler was eventually adopted by America Online (AOL), who purchased the system. AOL ran the system on its own network of computers, because the strain on the University of Washington's computer systems had become too much to bear, and the service would have been shut down otherwise. WebCrawler was the first search engine that could index the full text of a page of HTML; before this all a user could search through was the URL and the description of a web page, but the WebCrawler system represented a huge change in how web robots worked.

The next two big guns to emerge were Lycos and Infoseek. Lycos had the advantage in the sheer size of documents that it indexed; it launched on 20 July 1995 with 54 000 documents indexed, and by January 1995 had indexed 1.5 million. When Infoseek launched it was not original in its technology, but it sported a user-friendly interface and extra features such as news and a directory, which won it many fans. In 1999, Disney purchased a 45 per cent stake of Infoseek and integrated it into its Go.com service (Figure 1.2).

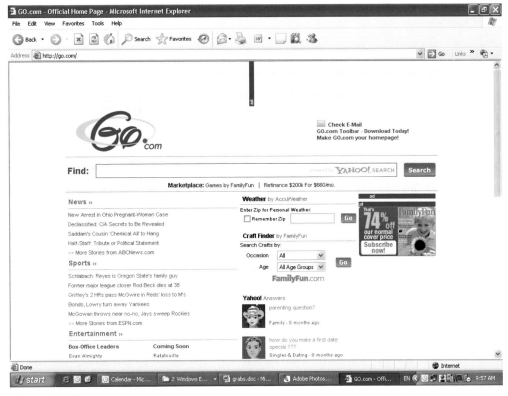

Figure 1.2 *Go.com*

In December 1995 AltaVista came onto the scene and was quickly recognized as the top search engine due to the speed with which it returned results (Figure 1.3). It was also the first search engine to use natural language queries, which meant users could type questions in much the same way as they do with Ask Jeeves today, and the engine would recognize this and not return irrelevant results. It also allowed users to search newsgroup articles, and gave them search 'tips' to help refine their search.

On 20 May 1996 Inktomi Corporation was formed and HotBot was created (Figure 1.4). Inktomi's results are now used by a number of major search services. When it was launched HotBot was hailed as the most powerful search engine, and it gained popularity quickly. HotBot claimed to be able to index 10 million web pages a day; it would eventually catch up with itself and re-index the pages it had already indexed, meaning its results would constantly stay up to date.

Around the same time a new service called MetaCrawler was developed, which searched a number of different search engines at once (Figure 1.5). This got around the problem, noticed by many people, of the search engines pulling up completely different results for the same search.

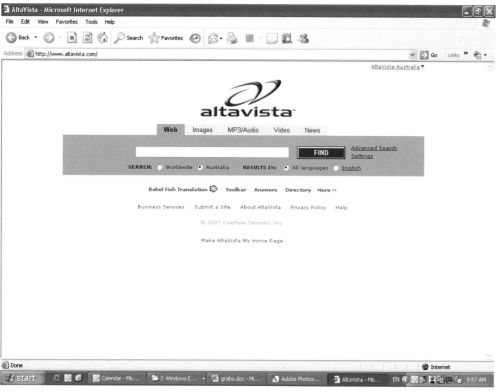

Figure 1.3 *The AltaVista website (reproduced with permission)*

MetaCrawler promised to solve this by forwarding search engine queries to search engines such as AltaVista, Excite and Infoseek simultaneously, and then returning the most relevant results possible. Today, MetaCrawler still exists and covers Google, Yahoo! Search, MSN Search, Ask Jeeves, About MIVA, LookSmart and others to get its results.

By mid-1999, search sites had begun using the intelligence of web surfers to improve the quality of search results. This was done through monitoring clicks. The DirectHit search engine introduced a special new technology that watched which sites surfers chose, and the sites that were chosen regularly and consistently for a particular keyword rose to the top of the listings for that keyword. This technology is now in general use throughout the major search engines (Figure 1.6).

Next, Google was launched at the end of 1998 (Figure 1.7). Google has grown to become the most popular search engine in existence, mainly owing to its ease of use, the number of pages it indexes, and the relevancy of it results. Google introduced a new way of ranking sites, through link analysis – which means that sites with more links to and from them rank higher. You can read more about Google in Chapter 4 of this book.

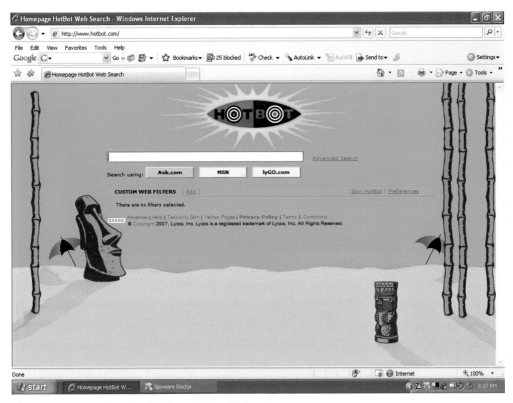

Figure 1.4 *HotBot (reproduced with permission of Inktomi)*

Another relatively new search engine is WiseNut (Figure 1.8). This site was launched in September 2001 and was hailed as the successor to Google. WiseNut places a lot of emphasis on link analysis to ensure accurate and relevant results. Although the search engine is impressive it hasn't managed to displace any of the major players in the scene, but is still worth taking a look. It is covered in more depth in Chapter 4 and can be found at www.wisenut.com.

More recently we have seen the launch of Yahoo! Search, as a direct competitor to Google. Yahoo! bought Inktomi in 2002 and in 2004 developed its own web crawler, Yahoo! Slurp. Yahoo! offers a comprehensive search package, combining the power of their directory with their web crawler search results, and now provides a viable alternative to using Google. MSN Search is the search engine for the MSN portal site. Previously it had used databases from other vendors including Inktomi, LookSmart, and Yahoo! but, as of 1 February 2005, it began using its own unique database. MSN offers a simple interface like Google's, and is trying to catch Google and Yahoo!

Other notable landmarks that will be discussed later in the book include the launch of LookSmart in October 1996, the Open Directory in June 1998 and, in April 1997, Ask Jeeves, which was intended to create a unique user experience emphasizing an intuitive easy-to-use system.

Figure 1.5 *The MetaCrawler website (©2003 InfoSpace, Inc. All rights reserved. Reprinted with permission of InfoSpace, Inc.)*

Also launched around this time was GoTo, later to be called Overture, which was the first pay-per-click search engine (see Chapter 9).

There we have it, a brief history of search engines. Some have been missed out, of course, but the ones covered here show the major developments in the technology, and serve as an introduction to the main topics that are covered in a lot more detail later in this book.

Why do people search?

Having a page indexed is the first stage of being recognized by search engines, and is essential – we can go as far as to say that until it is indexed, your site does not exist. Unless the surfer has seen your web address on a piece of promotional material or as a link from another site, they will try to find your website by using a search engine – most likely Google or Yahoo!. If your site is not listed in the index of a search engine, then the surfer cannot access it. Many URLs are not obvious or even logical, and for most searches we have no idea of the URL we are trying to find. This is why we use search engines – they create an index of the World Wide Web and build a giant database by collecting keywords and other information

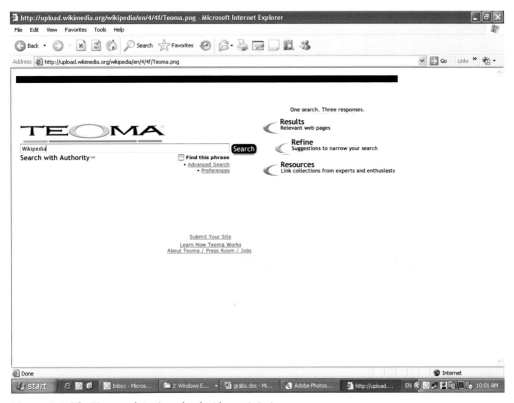

Figure 1.6 *The Teoma website (reproduced with permission)*

from web pages. This database links page content with keywords and URLs, and is then able to return results depending on what keywords or search terms a web surfer enters as search criteria.

Our research shows that around 80 per cent of websites are found through search engines. This makes it clear why companies want to come up first in a listing when a web surfer performs a related search. People use search engines to find specific content, whether a company's website or their favourite particular recipe. What you need to do through your website SEO is ensure that you make it easy for surfers to find your site, by ranking highly in search engines, being listed in directories, and having relevant links to and from your site across the World Wide Web. Essentially, you are trying to make your website search engine-friendly.

Search engines have become extremely important to the average web user, and research shows that around eight in ten web users regularly use search engines on the Web. The Pew Internet Project Data Memo (which can be found at www.pewinternet.org), released in 2004, reveals some extremely compelling statistics. It states that more than one in four (or about 33 million) adults use a search engine on a daily basis in the USA, and that 84 per cent of American Internet

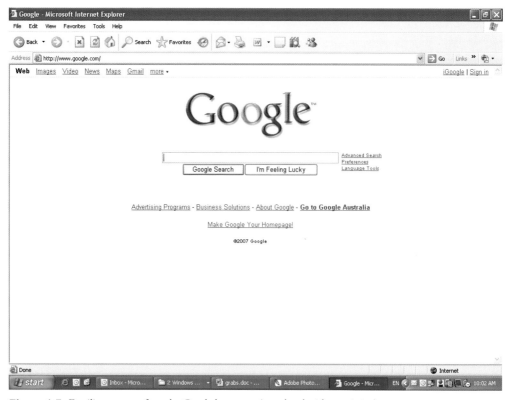

Figure 1.7 *Familiar to most of us, the Google homepage (reproduced with permission)*

users have used an online search engine to find information on the Web. The report states that 'search engines are the most popular way to locate a variety of types of information online'. The only online activity to be more popular than using a search engine is sending and receiving emails. Some other statistics that the report revealed were:

- College graduates are more likely to use a search engine on a typical day (39 per cent, compared to 20 per cent of high school graduates).
- Internet users who have been online for three or more years are also heavy search engine users (39 per cent on a typical day, compared to 14 per cent of those who gained access in the last six months).
- Men are more likely than women to use a search engine on a typical day (33 per cent, compared to 25 per cent of women).
- On any given day online, more than half those using the Internet use search engines. And more than two-thirds of Internet users say they use search engines at least a couple of times per week.
- 87 per cent of search engine users say they find the information they want most of the time when they use search engines.

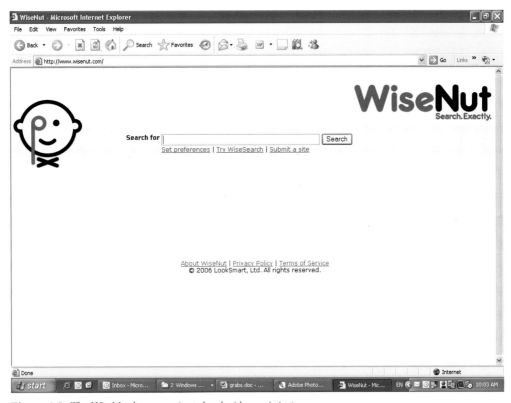

Figure 1.8 *The WiseNut homepage (reproduced with permission)*

If you are not convinced already of the importance of SEO as part of the eMarketing mix, here are some more interesting statistics:

- The NPD Group, a research group specializing in consumer purchasing and behaviour study, has shown that search engine positions are around two to three times more effective for generating sales than banner ads (http://www.overture.com/d/about/advertisers/slab.jhtml).
- 81 per cent of UK users find the websites they are looking for through search engines (Source: UK Internet User Monitor. Forrester Research Inc., June 2000).
- According to a report published by the NPD Group, 92 per cent of online consumers use search engines to shop and/or purchase online.
- A study conducted by IMT Strategies found that search engines are the number one way (46 per cent) by which people find websites; random surfing and word-of-mouth were ranked equal second (20 per cent each).

Finding out what people search for

Sites that allow you to see what people are searching for are listed at the end of Chapter 5. As well as being a bit of fun, these sites can be quite revealing; they let you see the top search terms for particular searches across various search engines, and the terms that are doing the best overall. Just to give you an idea of some results, here is a list taken from www.wordtracker.com of the top twenty ranking searches across the top metasearch engines on the Internet (including the Excite and MetaCrawler search engines) on 25 February 2007:

5027 myspace
4944 google
3852 yahoo
3772 ebay
3711 anna nicole smith
3498 games play
3469 britney spears
3361 myspace.com
3043 akon
2881 antonella barba

This is interesting reading – particularly the fact that people are actually searching on search engines for 'Google' and 'Yahoo!'. This goes to show that even if web surfers know a company's name (in the case of the 1411 searches for 'Yahoo.com' they knew practically the whole web address), they will still search for it on a search engine. These searchers were using one particular search engine in order to find another. If Google and Yahoo!, therefore, do not have good search engine positioning, then they will lose a lot of users who cannot find their site in searches from other engines. The same will, of course, happen to your site if it is not listed.

So what's so great about being ranked highly?

Getting listed in a search engine doesn't do you much good if you're number 298 of 900 524 results, and it also doesn't help much if you rank at number eleven. Most search engines display ten results per page, and this is where you have to be aiming for. So once your site is indexed, you will need to turn your attention to ranking. Realistically, you want to be aiming for the top ten to twenty positions on any given search engine, and these are the most treasured positions by webmasters. You will learn more about positioning on specific engines and directories as you read through this book, but take the top ten as a general rule of thumb. Some webmasters go as far as to employ 'dirty tricks' to get their site into the top positions, but why do they do this?

To find the answer, you need to put yourself into the position of a searcher. When searchers are confronted with a page of results, their immediate reaction is to look down that list and then stop looking when they see a relevant site. No major studies exist regarding the importance of top ranking, but common sense dictates that searchers will visit the first two or three relevant sites found rather than trawling through pages of search results to find your site listed at position 298. Our own research shows that around 50 per cent of search engine users expect to find the answer to their query on the first page, or within the top ten search engine results. Another 20 per cent revealed that they would not go past the second page of search results to find the site they were looking for. Therefore, if your website is not ranked towards the top you will essentially be invisible to most search engine users. Most search engine software uses both the position and the frequency of keywords to work out the website ranking order – so a web page with a high frequency of keywords towards the beginning will appear higher on the listing than one with a low frequency of keywords further down in the text. Another major factor that is taken into account is link popularity. All these topics are covered in more detail in Chapter 3.

Today's search engine promotion requires a multifaceted approach. To achieve a site's full potential, site promotion must incorporate target audience research and analysis, competitor analysis, pay-per-click optimization, and professional copywriting. SEO also requires a sharp eye and an ear to the ground; search engine technology is constantly changing, so you will need to keep up with the changes and reassess your search engine strategy accordingly.

Should you use an SEO consultancy or do it yourself?

By buying this book you have already taken the first steps towards DIY SEO, but for some of you the use of an SEO consultancy will be unavoidable and perhaps you have chosen this book to arm you with the knowledge you need to approach an SEO company confidently. In any case, if you do decide to use an SEO consultant there are a number of issues that you will need to be aware of.

Specialist marketing firms, like Sprite Interactive, live and breathe search engine marketing and understand fully what it takes to generate traffic for your site and to achieve a top ranking. By investing in the services of one of the many highly skilled SEO consultants available, you can reap considerable rewards, but you need to have the knowledge to choose the company that is right for you. There are a number of companies who will use underhand tactics to attempt to promote your site, or who will not promote your site well at all. You should start with the basics when you approach an SEO company. Ask the consultant to explain the difference between a directory and a search engine (which you, of course, will know after reading this book). Then ask what type of approach will be taken when the company optimizes your site – which should be done within the site's existing structure. SEO consultants should be able to explain to you how the different search engines find their content, and have a good working knowledge of web design and development – including HTML and Flash. You should be able to ask them questions about the site architecture (see Chapter 7) and expect answers, as this information is essential to any SEO campaign.

Credible SEO consultants should outline a plan where they will spend time working with you to develop the relevant site keywords and phrases that you expect people to use when searching for you. Consultants should also be skilled in writing quality concise copy. Building link popularity for your site is another important service provided by SEO consultants, as it will boost your ranking on certain search engines – in a nutshell, you should make sure any links you exchange with other sites are relevant and that the consultant does not use automated linking software (see Chapter 3). Be very wary of consultants who advocate 'spamming' techniques, such as using hidden text on your web pages or submitting your site multiple times over a short period of time. They will only be found out by the search engine in question, and thus run the risk of getting your site banned altogether. Legitimate SEO consultants will work well within the rules set by the search engines and will keep up to date with these rules through industry sources.

An investment in professional SEO consultancy is likely to be cheaper than one month of a print advertising campaign. For your investment your site will be optimized across three to five key phrases. Your contract will probably last from six months to a year, as it will take this long for the optimization to take full effect. Expect your chosen SEO consultants to be able reliably to inform you about the latest rates on all the pay-for-placement engines. If you choose correctly, your SEO consultant can save you a considerable amount of time and effort, and will generate quality targeted traffic for your site.

Watch out for companies that offer guarantees against rankings achieved. Many of these are pretty worthless and generally have a number of 'let-out' clauses. There is no guarantee of success, but there are ways to greatly increase the odds of being ranked highly. The main factor in measuring the success of an SEO campaign is the increase in traffic to your website.

You need to ask yourself a few questions when choosing an SEO professional. Is it the consultant's job to increase your sales? Is the consultant there to increase your traffic, or just to get you a high ranking? Most SEO professionals would agree that they are there to get their client's site ranked highly, and many will state up front that this is their main aim; however, generally speaking the first two options will result as a knock-on effect of having a highly ranked site. What happens if this is not the case? The client will often assume that high rankings will immediately result in extra traffic and additional sales, but in some cases this does not happen, and the finger of blame is pointed. So who is to blame? The answer will lie in what the original agreement and expectations were between the SEO consultant and the client.

There are a number of reasons why sales or traffic might not increase, and these may be the fault of either the SEO company or the client. For example, it would be the SEO company's fault if the wrong keywords were targeted. A client's website may be listed highly but for the wrong keywords and search terms, and therefore would not generate any relevant traffic, or any traffic at all. So make sure you agree on what keywords you are going to use first, to avoid any conflicts later on. There is no real excuse for an SEO professional to target the wrong keywords, especially after having consulted you and doing the necessary research.

There are two immediate ways in which the client could be in the wrong. First, the client may decide that they know best, fail to pay attention to the SEO advice offered, and choose unrelated keywords for the website. It is up to the client to follow the advice of the SEO consultant. Second, a client may have a badly designed site, which does not convert visitors into sales; an SEO consultant can advise on this, but in the end it is down to the client to act and to commission a site redesign.

It's important to know exactly what you'll be getting from your SEO company right from the start, so here is a checklist of questions to ask a potential SEO consultant:

1 How long have you been providing search engine optimization services?
2 Are you an individual consultant, or are you part of a team?
3 How long have you and your team been online?
4 What types of websites do you *not* promote?
6 Can you describe and/or produce recent successful campaign results?
7 Do you have website design experience?
8 What are your opinions with regard to best practices for the SEO industry, and how do you try to keep to these?
9 How many search engine optimization campaigns have you been involved with? What was your role for those projects? How many are still active? How many are inactive? If inactive, why?
10 Are there any guarantees for top search engine positions? (The answer to this question will depend on whether or not you choose a pay-per-click program; see Chapter 9 for more information.)
11 Do you have experience managing bid management campaigns?
12 What strategies would you use to increase our website's link popularity?
13 Explain to me how Google's PageRank software works, and how you could increase our website's rating. (The answer to this will involve building quality inbound links to your website.)
14 How would you orchestrate a links popularity campaign?
15 What changes can we expect you to make to our website to improve our positioning in the search engines?
16 Will there be changes in the coding of our website to make it rank better?
17 What type of reporting will you provide us with, and how often?

This checklist provides a useful starting point for you when approaching an SEO professional. At Sprite we make sure that all the consultants can answer these questions, and more, whenever they are approached for new SEO business. Most importantly, however, if you choose to use SEO professionals, be patient with them. You need to remember that SEO is a long-term process, and it will take around six months before you have any real measure of success. If you are not happy with the results after this time, then it is probably time to move on. Appendix A provides an example SEO presentation; although this is more of an internal presentation, it will give you an idea of some of the issues you should be looking out for.

White hat or black hat SEO?

There are considered to be two main areas of SEO methods and tactics in use: white hat and black hat. Many of the search engines and directories have a set of unwritten guidelines that site managers must conform to for their site to be indexed. These are put in place to ensure a level playing field for the websites that are indexed by that search engine; however, many site owners try to bypass the guidelines without the website knowing, with varying levels of success. As these guidelines are not generally written as a set of rules, they can be open to interpretation – an important point to note.

A technique is 'white hat' when it conforms to the submission guidelines set out by a search engine and contains no kind of deception in order to artificially gain higher rankings. White hat SEO is about creating a compelling user experience and making the content easily accessible to search engine spiders, with no tricks involved.

'Black hat' SEO techniques are efforts to try to trick search engines into ranking a site higher than it should be. There are many black hat techniques, but the more common ones are 'hidden text' that a site user cannot see but a search engine spider can, or 'cloaking', which involves serving one page up for search engine spiders and another page up for site visitors. Search engines have and will penalize and even ban sites they find using these techniques; one recent example occurred in February 2006, when Google removed the BMW Germany site from its listings for use of doorway pages.

White hat search engine techniques present a holistic view of search engine optimization – the search engines are viewed as a necessary part of the whole web marketing mix – whereas many black hat practitioners tend to see search engines as an enemy to be fought in order to get higher listings. When using black hat SEO the content on a page is developed solely with the search engines in mind. Humans are not supposed the see the black hat content on a page (such as hidden links and text). The content may be incomprehensible to humans and if they do see it then their experience of using the site will be considerably diminished. White hat techniques produce content for both the search engines and the site user, usually focusing primarily on creating relevant interesting content that is also keyword-rich for the search engine spider. Even without the presence of a search engine, white hat pages will still be relevant.

Another area of concern should be your domains. There is always the risk of a search engine removing your domain from their listings, due to a change in algorithm or some other related cause, but in general by following white hat techniques you can reduce this risk. Black hat techniques, on the other hand, will positively increase the risk. Many black hat practitioners view domains as disposable, which can be especially hazardous if they are working on your primary domain name. Black hat techniques may get you quick results, but these are more often than not short-term gains, as the domains are quickly banned from the search engine indexes. White hat techniques on the other hand will generally take longer to implement and be ingested by the search engines, but they will provide you with a long-term stable platform for your website.

So the question is: how do I make sure I am following white hat techniques and search engine guidelines? The one point to bear in mind is to make sure your site and its content makes sense to humans! That is all you need to do to follow white hat guidelines. The only time you should really have to consult search engine guidelines is if you are working on an element of your site that is not related to the user experience, such as META tags, code placement and site submission.

Natural traffic

If you are going to use an agency for SEO, then you will also need to tap into your site's natural traffic. Your natural traffic is web traffic that will develop outside of the optimization services provided by an SEO company. It is not traffic that is 'directed' to your site by good search engine ranking and positioning; it is traffic that will find your site in other ways, such as through printed advertising or through having a shared interest in your website. You need to bear this in mind throughout your SEO process, as it is part of the full marketing mix that will result in quality traffic for your website. Make sure your print advertising (and any other promotional material for that matter) features your web address in a prominent position. Target relevant publications with your advertisements, and make sure that any groups that share an interest in your website are well informed.

If you want to track the success of a print campaign, one technique you can use is to feature an alternative URL; you can then track the amount of hits to this URL, which will tell you how successful the print ad or campaign has been. Tapping into your site's natural traffic may take more thought and planning than just optimizing your site and hoping that people will find it by searching for it, but the hits that you will receive from 'natural' traffic will be of a higher quality, and will be more likely to spend longer on your site than those coming from search engine results alone. Another way to increase your 'natural' traffic is by building your site's link popularity (see Chapter 3).

In conclusion

This chapter has been designed as a basic introduction to some of the concepts surrounding SEO. It is clear from reading the statistics quoted that getting listed on search engines is essential to promote your website effectively, and that ranking highly is essential if you want your site to be noticed by surfers performing searches. If you do choose to use an SEO consultancy, then be sure to follow the guidelines outlined above, and read this book first to give you the knowledge to approach an agency confidently and make sure you are able to get the most out of them. Remember that SEO is a long-term process; it cannot happen overnight, and is something that you need to commit to fully to get the most out of.

Chapter 2

How people search

Power searching

Before commencing a search engine marketing campaign it is important to understand how the search engines work and become a power searcher yourself. This will give you important background knowledge into the area you are entering. Power searching means using all the tricks at your disposal in your chosen search engine to get the most relevant results for you. Modern search engines are generally pretty good on relevancy, but there are still pages that are not particularly well optimized, but that will contain the information you're after that can only be accessed by using power search techniques. Learning power searching will also give you a good background on what works and what doesn't when optimizing your site.

It is worthwhile starting with the basics. The most important rule of any searching is that the more specific your search is, the more likely you are to find what you want. Try asking Google 'where do I download drivers for my new Motu sound card for Windows XP', more often than not this technique works to deliver relevant results. Here is a very brief summary of basic search engine terms.

The + symbol

The + symbol lets you make sure that the pages you find contain all the words you enter. If you wanted to find pages that have references to both Brad Pitt and Angelina Jolie you could use the following query:

+Pitt +Jolie

You can string as many words together as you like, and this technique is especially useful for narrowing down results when you have too many to check through.

The — symbol

The — symbol simply lets you find pages that have one word on them but not another. If you wanted to find a page with Brad Pitt but not Angelina Jolie then you would simply type:

Pitt—Jolie

Again, you can use this technique to filter your results as much as you like and it is useful to focus your results when you get too many unrelated pages.

Quotation marks

You can use quotation marks around a phrase to be sure that that phrase appears as you have typed it on the page, so a search for Ben Salter may return results with the two words appearing separately on the page; if you typed in 'Ben Salter' then you would be guaranteed to return that exact phrase which would lead to much more relevant results. Another example would be the book title 'Marketing Through Search Optimization'; without the quotation marks you would be more likely to be presented with SEO consultancy websites, but with the quotation marks the book title is much more likely to appear as one of the top search results.

These symbols can be added to each other in any way you please, and you can create some quite elaborate search strings with them. For the most part these are the only ways most search engine users will enhance their results — Boolean commands are not covered here as on the whole they are not widely used by a typical search engine user.

Power search commands

These commands are usually located on the 'advanced search' page of a search engine; have a play with them and see how they affect your search results. There are a number of commands that are also very useful for marketing professionals to track their sites on the search engines. The examples below will work on most search engines, but we have used Google commands as the basis.

- *Match Any* — this lets you find pages that contain any of your search terms. Usually when this is selected the search engine will first display results with both terms.
- *Match All* — this is similar to the + command and makes the search engine return results that include all the terms you have specified.
- *Exclude* — similar to the — command, this lets you exclude words from the search if you don't want them to appear in the results that are returned.
- *Site Search* — this is a powerful feature that lets you control what sites are included or excluded in a search. If you wanted to see all the pages in the Sprite Interactive website you could type:

site:www.sprite.net

This would return all the pages in the search engine's index for www.sprite.net. This is a useful tool to see what pages from your site have been indexed and what versions of the page are in the search engine directory, and whether it has picked up any recent updates you have done.

You can also add other terms onto the end of the search query to see pages from that site that have specific content, for example:

Site:www.sprite.net search engine marketing

This returns the search engine marketing page from the Sprite Interactive website. You can also use all the other search terms (+, −, '') to refine your search further.

Title search

If you want to find pages that just mention certain terms in the title you can use the ':allintitle' command and the resulting pages will be restricted to those containing just the terms you specified in the title. Again, this is useful for finding certain pages in a site to see if they have been indexed. You can also use 'intitle:' to return results that just have the first query in the title rather than all the search terms; for example 'intitle:sprite interactive' would return pages with 'Sprite' in the title, but with 'Interactive' in the body copy.

Info search

This is a great way to find out more information on your, or your competitors', sites. It returns all of the information Google has on the site you search for. If you typed 'info:www.sprite.net' you are given the following options from Google:

- Show Google's cache of www.sprite.net
- Find web pages that are similar to www.sprite.net
- Find web pages that link to www.sprite.net
- Find web pages from the site www.sprite.net
- Find web pages that contain the term www.sprite.net

Link search

Perhaps the most useful power search tool for the SEO professional, this lets you see all the sites linking into a particular URL; the search query would look like 'link:www.sprite.net'. This is a great way to see who is linking into your competitor sites to see if you can also benefit from those links. It also lets you see if Google has indexed pages linking to your site – if it hasn't then you can submit them to Google yourself.

Personalization

The major search engines are now looking into personalized search, the main players currently being Google, Yahoo!, MSN and Amazon's a9.com service. Microsoft is seen as having the advantage due to its ability to access the files on your computer (for PC users). The concept of personal search is that the more a search engine knows about your likes and dislikes, your history, your search patterns and your interests, the better search results it can provide you with. Not only can personal search base results on the terms you enter in the search query, it can also use your personal info to work out what you really mean by those terms and suggest other results that may be relevant or interesting to you.

Many commentators have cited personalization as the 'Holy Grail' for search engines, and the search engines are certainly 'in bed' with the concept. It is easy to see that the more data they can collect on their users, the more they can target their results, and also the more they can charge for targeted advertising. Here are a couple of examples of simple searches that can 'benefit' from personalization: if you are searching for 'beatles' are you after the band or the insect? If you search for 'rock' are you interested in music or geology, and so on. Of course, using the information provided at the start of this chapter you could narrow your search engine results down to the same as these particular personalized search results.

Google Homepage, My Yahoo! and My MSN also offer personalized versions of their homepages, with services like email, chat and calendars readily available.

The essence of personalized homepages is a technology called Really Simply Syndication (RSS). This allows content to be distributed through the Web very efficiently, so a news organization like the BBC will use RSS to plug their headlines in to any site also using the technology. RSS can be used for a wide range of content, like weather reports, star signs, traffic and road information, and so on. RSS feeds can be seen on the Google homepage screenshot (Figure 2.1).

The search engines can use the information a user decides to display on their personal homepage to then create the user profile. This profile enables them to serve up more relevant advertising.

One of the more negative features of personalized search is that once a search engine thinks it knows what you want to be searching for it will narrow your results, thus narrowing the amount of information you can access. Though getting narrow search results can be a good thing, searching is also about broadening your mind, and search results regularly lead users off on tangents into information that they may not necessarily have considered. Is ending this a good thing? Should there be an option to turn personalization off?

Another problem that people seem concerned about is privacy. What is to stop search engine operators tracking everything a user does on the Internet? Though there is clearly going to be an issue of privacy with any kind of personalization, this may be less of an issue than many have made it out to be. The search engines can track users anonymously, setting a cookie in your browser that simply contains an ID that gives you a profile, without having to enter anything

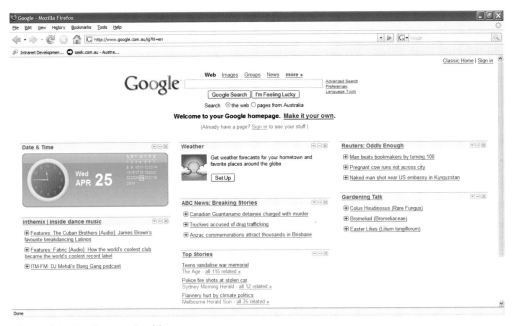

Figure 2.1 *Google personalized homepage*

that will identify you as an individual. All they need to know is that you like the Beatles; they don't need your name or address. This system is being developed by the major search engines, most notably Google.

There is another important side effect of personalization that is only just starting to be realized, and that is the effect it will have on the SEO industry. If a user can filter results personally then this change could lead to whole new profiles. What profile did they have? Where were they located? This change could lead to whole new profiles being developed for different sets of search engine users, and personal profiling would become commonplace. You would no longer be tracking your site for a search on a particular keyword, you would be tracking your site by a particular user demographic (London IT Worker, 25–30, for example). So this could lead to the job of the SEO consultant becoming more complicated, but if you are creating useful relevant sites aimed at people rather than search engines, you will be well on the way to benefiting from personalized search.

Mobile search

With the increased use of the Web on mobile devices, the major search engines are now providing support for mobile devices. The mobile Internet is developing in much the same way as the Internet developed. In the early days of the Internet users were restricted to select content via portals such as Netscape and Compuserve. These are reflected by the mobile operator portals today (Vodafone, Orange Three, to name a few), who carry a very small selection of the mobile content available, but are the first stop for many mobile users. Some of these operators have even put a walled garden around their portal, so users cannot access any content outside those they have chosen for them (as some of the early Internet portals did). As the Internet developed, and the depth of content developed, the portal sites were unable to provide the necessary coverage, and search engines such as Google and AltaVista provided a way for users to find this content. This is now happening in the mobile space, as the search engines are starting to tap into the huge amount of mobile content available that cannot be found on the operator portals.

Google provides search interfaces for devices such as Palm PDAs, i-mode phones and WAP and xHTML enabled devices. Google also supports facilities that let users use their numeric keypad to enter search terms and keywords. Yahoo! provides a directory of WAP-enabled sites and delivers personalized data to mobile devices, such as sports scores, news and entertainment and travel information, as well as the ability to use Yahoo! email and messenger on your device. MSN's strategy focuses on the pocket PC and smartphone devices, which have windows software installed on them, and which deliver up web content through Pocket MSN.

Research from Bango (www.bango.com) indicates that the most popular mobile content services are:

- Music (including ring tones) 32 per cent
- Pictures 15 per cent
- Adult services 22 per cent
- Video 7 per cent
- Games 14 per cent
- Information services 10 per cent

Personalized mobile search

Personalization is possibly more important for mobile search than it is for web search. A mobile screen can only display a few results at a time, probably ranging from two to four, while on a desktop you will typically see the top 10 results. It is critical, therefore, that the results are accurate and relevant.

Location aware mobile search

One of the most interesting features of mobile search, which continues on from the personalization discussion, is location-based search. Technologies such as GPS and wireless networks can detect the location of a mobile user, which can then send additional data to a search engine to narrow down its results. There are two main types of location-based search available for mobile users:

- Real time searches for local landmarks, such as restaurants, ATMs, specific shops.
- Predefined search, which can pull up preset data on what is available in a local area.

Local search needs to be quick and accurate for it to be successful. For more detail on mobile search and the mobile Internet see Chapters 6 and 8.

Social networks

A basic social network is a collection of people you know and stay in contact with. You swap ideas and information, and recommend friends and services to each other. This leads your network to grow. Sharing in a social network is based on trust; if the recommendation is unbiased and is from a known source then you are more likely to trust it than not. The best recommendations are therefore those that come from unbiased and trustworthy sources.

In the past few years social networks on the Web have become some of the most popular sites around. Sites like Myspace, YouTube, Friendster and Linkedin have all become big business, and there are ways you can benefit from their popularity and user-base. The key to all these networks is the sharing of ideas and information, and the way that they open up this area to web users who would previously have to have had knowledge of web development to be able to do what they are able to do through these sites now, i.e. share photos, publish journals and create their own personal web page.

Social networks open great new opportunities for viral and word-of-mouth marketing, and provide huge marketing potential for your business. They make viral marketing and word-of-mouth marketing much easier than before. The best use of social networks is not to make money 'directly' off them, but to harness their marketing potential and to use them to market your own business. Each social network has its own unique language: YouTube is for uploading and commenting on videos; Myspace is for finding interesting new 'friends' and leaving comments for them.

Make your message unique

If you want your message to succeed on these networks the best thing you can do is to make it unique – social networks are full of very samey content, particularly a site like YouTube. To stand out from the crowd your message has to be interesting, easy to understand, memorable, and easy to spread around (including being easy for someone to describe). Being funny also helps a great deal. If you get the right mix for your content then you have the potential to spread your idea through thousands of people without spending any money at all.

Today's SEO understands that standard manipulation of websites only achieves results in the most non-competitive of markets. To profit from the Web you must cover the social connected aspect of the Internet and make it work for you. This is partly covered through link building, but also through tapping into social networks to bring traffic to your sites.

Social Media Optimization

Social Media Optimization (SMO) was a phrase coined by Rohit Bhargava, who said:

> The concept behind SMO is simple: implement changes to optimize a site so that it is more easily linked to, more highly visible in social media searches on custom search engines, and more frequently included in relevant posts on blogs, podcasts and vlogs.

This quote encompasses all the social aspects of the Web. SMO understands that people are the Internet, and optimizes your website and your promotional content for people as well as for the search engines. SMO feeds into SEO – the links you build will benefit your site's organic search engine results and will naturally increase the profile of your site and content, and drive targeted traffic through a whole new network that does not rely on the major search engines.

Bhargava, Jeremiah Owyang and Loren Baker have identified 13 rules between them to help guide thinking when conducting SMO:

1 Increase your linkability: using blogs, 'sticky' content and aggregation.
2 Make tagging and bookmarking easy: make it clear and easy for users to tag and bookmark your content and recommend it to sites like digg.com.
3 Reward inbound links: if someone links to you, list them on your links page or in your blog. Make it worth someone's while to link to you.
4 Help your content travel: use formats such as PDFs to allow people to easily download and redistribute your content.
5 Encourage the mashup: let others use your content or your tools to create something new, don't be precious.
6 Be a user resource, even if it doesn't help you: add outbound links to your site. Even if this doesn't help you in the short term by driving traffic away from your site, it will help in the long term by making your site friendly.
7 Reward helpful and valuable users: give people who contribute or use your site regularly something back in return.
8 Participate: get out there and participate in discussions, don't just read them.
9 Know how to target your audience: understand how you can appeal to the people you are targeting and focus on this.
10 Create content: create content that works for you.
11 Be real.
12 Don't forget your roots, be humble: keep your feet on the ground and respect those that helped you along the way.
13 Don't be afraid to try new things, stay fresh: keep up with new tools, sites and content in your area.

Having a large social network is what will turn your site content into 'linkable' content and increase its 'link factor'; for more on linking see Chapter 3. It is important to build links, but it is also important to build the network that will give you the links into the future. If you want something to spread virally it has to have a network to be seeded into. If your network takes it on and the content is good, then it might spread into other networks, who might then link to you too. As well as understanding the raw elements of SEO, such as site architecture, keyword choice and keyword placement, SEO today is very much about making the social Web work for you, as it will build the profile of your site in a way you never could on your own.

Social network sites to check out
- Myspace – http://www.myspace.com
- Friendster – http://www.friendster.com
- YouTube – http://www.youtube.com
- LinkedIn – http://www.linkedin.com
- Orkut – http://www.orkut.com
- Flickr – http://www.flickr.com

Weblogs

A weblog (blog) is a personal website where the site owner makes regular entries, which are presented to the viewer in reverse chronological order. Blogs are often a commentary on a specific subject, such as politics, food or films, and some take the form of a personal diary, where the author records their thoughts on a range of subjects. Blogs can feature text and graphics, and links to other blogs and other websites. 'Blogging' is also a term that means to add an entry or a comment to a blog.

Blogs evolved from the concept of the online diary, where writers would keep an online account of their personal lives. Early blogs were usually manually updated sections of websites but with the advance of technology and the introduction of blogging software, such as Blogger and LiveJournal, the availability of blogging has been opened up to a much wider, less technically minded audience. Blogging had a slow start, but it rapidly gained popularity. The site Xanga, which was launched in 1996, featured only 100 diaries by 1997; this had leapt to 50 000 000 by December 2005.

Blogging makes building your own simple web page easy. It also makes linking to other web pages easy, with tools such as:

- Permalinks – this is a URL link that points to a specific blog entry even after the entry passed from the front page into the blog archives.
- Blogrolls – these are collections of links to other weblogs. They are often found on the front page of a blog, on the sidebar.
- TrackBacks – these are ways for webmasters (blog owners) to be informed when someone links to one of their articles.

Blogs and blog posts are naturally search engine-friendly as they are full of keywords and links. They use style sheets and CSS (Cascading Style Sheets), and generally have very clean HTML formatting. Optimizing your blog is very similar to optimizing a web page, but depending which software you use the results may look different. There are a number of simple rules, however, that you can follow that will boost your blog ranking and perhaps rank it higher than many websites. Once you have a blog ranked highly you can use its positioning to link to your websites; there is more on using a blog to increase your link factor in Chapter 3.

Tips to increase your blog's search engine ranking:

1 *Pick a blog domain name that includes your keywords*
   This is pretty straightforward. If you have keywords in your domain name you will increase your chances of being ranked highly. Even if your blog is a subdomain of your main website, try to include relevant keywords in the subdomain URL.
2 *Make sure your blog tags include your primary keywords*
   If you have identified your primary keywords as 'running shoes' make sure these appear in the header tags throughout the blog (more on identifying keywords in Chapter 5). Make sure all your blog titles also include the keywords.
3 *Use your keywords throughout the body copy and link text*
   Make sure that all your keywords are used throughout each post on your blog, but not so much that it doesn't read naturally. Use your keywords throughout links on your page and link your keywords as they appear in your posts.
4 *Make your blog search engine spider-friendly*
   Set up your blog so that the navigation is present on every page and make sure that all your posts, including your archives, are available from every page.
5 *Get other blogs and sites to link to yours*
   Submitting to blog search engines and directories is a great way to get quality links into your blog. Check out sites such as:
   - Blogdigger
   - Bloglines
   - Feedster
   - Google Blog Search
   - IceRocket
   - PubSub
   - Technorati
   Find similarly themed blogs and approach them to swap links into your content.
6 *Keep your content fresh*
   Search engine spiders love fresh content, so keep your blog up to date with relevant and interesting articles. Write posts that people will want to read as well; if they enjoy reading your posts people will reward you by returning to your blog and possibly recommending it to their friends and colleagues.

Chapter 3
Linking strategies and free listings

So you've built a great site and you have great content; all you now need is an audience. However, there is a problem: there are around 100 million web pages out there and well over a million unique domains. Of these, the top 10 per cent receive around 90 per cent of the overall traffic. The Web is a very tough place for small sites to get exposure, particularly those without a large budget for promotion. In this chapter we'll look at how you can build a presence for your site and increase your traffic, even if you have little or no site promotion budget.

Free mass submission services – do they work?

There are only two ways to increase a website's traffic: you have to increase the number of new users coming to the site, or you need to get your current users to look at more pages when they are surfing your site. One of the main ways that the site is advertised is through the use of mass submission services. Many people have lost money on lower priced, poor quality services that guaranteed top search engine placements. If they had taken more time and invested the little money they had in more relevant services, then they could have done a lot better.

The first method discussed here of getting your site listed for free is one that should be avoided, and one that is readily available across the Web. This is the mass submission service. There are a number of companies offering this; just type 'free search engine submission' into Google and this will become evident (Figure 3.1).

When you sign up for one of these services you will generally pay a low monthly fee and in return the company will submit your site to what they describe as 'thousands' of search engines. Don't be fooled! Some services even offer submission to as many as 250 000 engines, although there are not 250 000 search engines in existence. Many of these companies will take your money

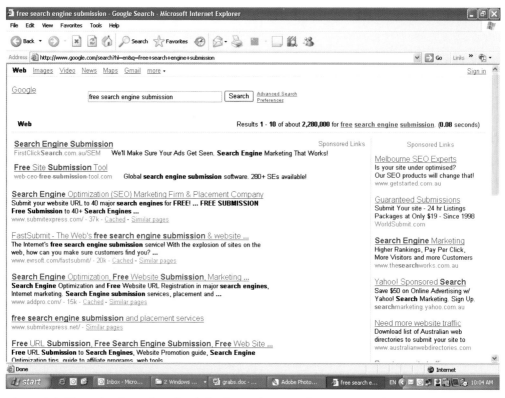

Figure 3.1 *The results of a search on Google for 'free search engine submission'; notice the sponsored links (reproduced with permission)*

and then generate spam email, which will give you no benefit and clog up your inbox. You only need to concentrate on the top eight to ten search engines. Many of the top search engines will not accept automatic submission of this kind and, even if your site does get listed, if it has not been optimized in the first place it is very unlikely that it will rank well. When you next come across a service that offers guaranteed top ten positions or submissions within a certain time (say ten or fifteen days), it is worth remembering a few things. First, let's take the previous example. If eleven people apply to get the guaranteed top ten positions, what will happen then? Logic dictates that it will be first come, first served, which is not very fair on the eleventh person, who has also been guaranteed top ten placement. Anyway, submitting your URL to search engines does not guarantee anything (see Chapter 4).

If you are going to use a mass submission tool, then use a recognized one such as Submit It. This engine is so good and came so highly recommended that Microsoft bought it, and it is now a part of their bCentral suite of site promotion tools. The service is not free, however, and there is a charge to submit your site. For this, Submit It promises to get you a prominent listing on a number of top search engines.

Free submission to major search engines

Many of the major search engines still include a free submission section for their listings. Paid inclusion is always the faster choice, but if your budget is limited you may want to consider submitting and waiting the six to eight weeks (or more) that it often takes to see your listings show up. Bear in mind that if you have no budget it is still well worth submitting to the major search engines, as your site will be listed eventually.

Major search engines providing free submissions include:

- Google
- AltaVista
- Yahoo!.

Building links

Another great way to get traffic to your site for free is to have other sites link to it. This is one of the most powerful tools you can use to promote your site. It's the online equivalent of word-of-mouth advertising and, just like word-of-mouth, it's the most effective way to get new business.

It's like one of your neighbours recommending a good plumber; a recommendation carries more weight than if a person just stumbles across your website using a search engine – and, for the purposes of this chapter, it can also be free or come at a very low cost. One of the best ways to find sites to approach to link to yours is to use the search results for terms that are important for your site. Do a search at Google for phrases that you wish to be ranked first for, and then treat all the top listed sites as potential linking partners. Some of the sites listed may be competitors, and you will not realistically be able to trade links with them, but there should be a number of sites that do not sell competitor products to you – the only thing you are competing for being the same search terms.

Now you need to visit the sites that are not competitors and see how it would be possible for your site to get a link from them. If they have a links page, this is an obvious place for your site to be linked from; if they have an ezine that users subscribe to then you could place a text link in this, maybe in return for promotion on your own site or for a small fee. An example of this in action would be a nutritionist who has written a book on 'living better through healthy eating'; these words would therefore be very important to the nutritionist on a search engine. Instead of trying to rank first for these results, he or she could try to exchange links with those sites listed first – which would mostly be stores advertising vitamins and nutritionist services. The technique is a cost-effective way of getting your site to the top, and is known as 'piggybacking'. You are using the fact that some sites will be ranked highly for a specific search phrase, and will not compete with you. It can take you a very long time to get to these positions, especially if you have little or no budget, so the next best solution is clearly to have a link from their site onto yours. In time, if you have links from the top ten sites for a particular term or phrase you will receive a lot of traffic, as these sites will receive a lot of traffic anyway as a result of their high listing. However, it is not quite this easy, and you have to work out why these sites would want to give you a link.

There are a number of possible options:

- You could make them an affiliate of yours if you sell products
- If you already have a number of high-ranking pages, then you could simply swap links between your sites in a mutual fashion – some sites actually have a reciprocal links page, in which case you'll have got lucky and will usually be able to place a link in return for a link from your site.

In any case, it's the research that goes into analysing sites and identifying how you can link from them in the first place that makes all the difference. You need to seek solutions where both parties win, and you can secure for your site a cheap and plentiful supply of valuable traffic. You need to take the time to visit any sites you are asking for links from, then find out who runs the sites and send a polite email – addressing them by name so it is clear that your email has not come from a piece of link generating software. Tell them your name and demonstrate that you have seen their site and taken the time to analyse it. Explain to them why you think a link exchange makes sense and, if they have a links page already, let them know you have been to see it and ask for a link from it. When you send another webmaster a link request or reciprocal linking offer, you should also state what you would like your link to say. It is suggested that you include a piece of HTML code in your email, such as the following:

```
<a href=''http://www.yoursite.com''>Your Keywords</a>
```

Finally, you should offer to talk by telephone. This may seem like a lot of effort, but it works – and is the only way that does. The goal is to leave zero doubt in the site owner's mind that you are a real person who has been to the site and taken the time to evaluate it and find out where a link can fit in.

Increasing your link factor

Linking from one website to another is, in essence, why the Internet was created. Researchers needed a way to link their documents together, and the Internet was how the academics were able to achieve this. This section of the chapter is about increasing the link factor of your site – both to make other sites link to yours more readily, and to give you the knowledge to be able to identify sites that are worth linking to.

A site's link factor is determined by having certain elements that will encourage other sites to want to link to it, which in turn will inspire users to visit it more often and thus earn more overall coverage for the site. At the top end of the link-factor scale are sites such as the British

Library website, which contains links throughout the site to vast amounts of data as well as a number of off-site links; there are also hundreds, possibly thousands, of websites that link into the British Library. This is because it has extremely rich content that is organized efficiently and with a lot of care.

Sites with a low link factor include those that have little or no relevant content, or rely on databases or a lot of Flash content. This is not to say that Flash content or databases are a bad thing, but these do reduce a site's link factor. In the case of Flash content, the text in a movie is all pre-rendered and a movie exists under only one URL. Database-driven content constantly changes, so there are no static pages to link to and URLs in a database can change for every page load, which negates the power to link to these pages. In some cases a database may be absolutely necessary to organize a large amount of information, but when considering whether to implement one into your site you should bear this major factor in mind. For example, a magazine with a number of articles on the Web can have a very high link factor; however, if the articles have been organized as a database this link factor suddenly goes down because if a user wants to link to one, a direct link will not work.

The main issue in increasing your link factor will always be the quality and relevancy of content and the architecture to support it. For every website there are many other sites or venues (such as search engines, directories, web guides, discussion lists, online editors, and so on) that will link to it, and your challenge is to identify these and contact them. As mentioned above, building links to your site can be a great free or low-cost exercise to increase your traffic and, as we will see below, your site's ranking.

A good way to get people to notice your site, thus increasing its link factor, is to use guerrilla marketing techniques. There are a number of tactics and methods that can be used to increase the visibility of your website, but if you are operating on a small budget you need to remember one major factor when using these techniques: set realistic goals and keep to them. You can still achieve big results with a small budget, but this has to be done in a realistic and clear manner, otherwise you can end up concentrating all your resources on one area only to find that it is not working. Make sure that you analyse the media related to your industry or trade, and learn about which trade shows to attend and who the respected figures are, etc.; you need to know all about your target audience, and this will give you the knowledge to create targeted campaigns that really appeal to them. One great guerrilla tactic for promoting your site is using newsgroups and chat forums. Most email clients now include a newsreader that will allow you to access thousands of newsgroups on a range of topics. You need to subscribe to these in order to contribute, and you can subscribe to as many different newsgroups as you wish.

You should be aware that each newsgroup is governed by a strict set of rules that generally apply to the posting of messages on the board and to members' conduct. You should make sure you read this before posting, as if you break the rules of a particular group you run the risk of being banned. Using newsgroups as a marketing tool is much the same as using a web forum

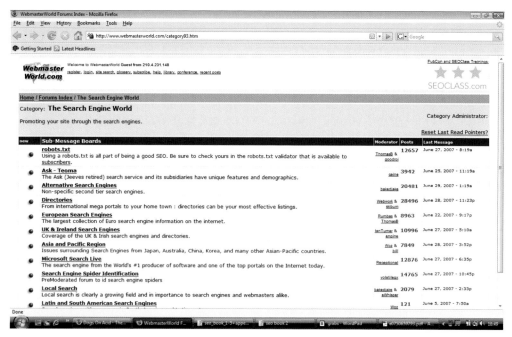

Figure 3.2 *A search engine optimization forum*

(Figure 3.2), so you can take these lessons and use them elsewhere. The main aim is to attract more visitors to your site, and in turn more places that link to your site. The overall aim of this type of guerrilla marketing is to increase your site's link factor.

The first rule to remember when using newsgroups as a marketing tool is that you should never post 'in your face' postings or adverts, or any kind of classified sales adverts. You will almost certainly get 'flamed' for this, i.e. other users of the newsgroup will abuse you through posting. It may even get you banned. The way to approach newsgroup marketing is to get involved in the discussions, and gradually to become seen as an informative contributor. You should offer advice and tips on problems to the other contributors and become an accepted member of the group. If you offer well thought-out advice, then people will naturally want to find out more about you – which will involve visiting your website. Many newsgroups allow you to have a signature, which is usually a small graphic or message that you attach to the bottom of your posts; make sure you include your web address in here, as any time you post people will see the link and some of them may follow it.

Here are a few tips on conducting yourself in newsgroups and discussion forums:

- Before you post to a newsgroup, spend a bit of time reading others' posts so you can become comfortable with the posting style of the group.
- Read the rules before you begin to post.
- Never post 'in your face' postings or adverts, or any kind of classified sales adverts.

- Don't post the same message to multiple newsgroups; this will probably be noticed by somebody.
- Make sure you use a signature file if you are given the opportunity, and keep it short and to the point.
- Don't post messages that have nothing to do with the topic of the message.

Content that can increase your link factor

Here are a few ideas regarding basic site content that can increase your link factor. These are all free ways to promote your site, requiring only the time it takes to implement and integrate them.

1 *Email to a friend link.* Make it easy for people to send pages of your site to their friends. You need to make your site easily accessible by all, and you can do this by putting a link at the bottom of a page to recommend the page to a friend. You can take this one step further by having e-cards that are related to your product or website, which site users can send to a friend with a personalized message. You can also collect users' email addresses using this technique, and these can then be used to send out targeted ezines.

2 *Offer free tools.* You can try offering to your users a free trial version of your product if you are a software company, or perhaps free games or useful software for download. Make sure that whatever you offer is useful to your audience, and that it has links to your website contained within the software. You could perhaps create a high quality screensaver, featuring your company or products, for download. This has the extra benefit of advertising your site on the computer screen of whoever installs the screensaver.

3 *Newsletter/ezine.* Newsletters and ezines are great tools when used effectively. You need to offer an incentive for site users to subscribe, such as exclusive promotions and special offers, or the chance to be kept fully up to date with the latest site developments – make them think they will be the first to know. Your newsletter should be delivered to a subscribers' inbox regularly, and should always carry relevant, useful content. Make sure you provide a number of special offers and promotions relating to your products that the user cannot find anywhere else. To take part in the special offers from your ezine a user should have to visit a page on your website; this will increase hits to your site and essentially increase the number of links you have pointing to you. At Sprite we have integrated successful ezines into a number of our clients' sites, and use them to promote our range of mobile software (Figure 3.3).

4 *Fresh content.* This is one of the most important considerations. Make sure that your site always offers relevant and fresh content, as this will encourage users to return to it. If the content you are offering is topical or exclusive news that they might not find anywhere else, such as breaking industry news, then this will encourage them further.

5 *Link page.* Create a page on your site that showcases or recommends your favourite websites, and offer reciprocal links to other webmasters from this page. It seems simple, but having a clear links page will make people far more likely to approach you for links, and in turn link to your site.

Figure 3.3 *The Kitty the Kitten mobile pet ezine*

Publishing an article

As regular contributors to *Computer Arts and Computer Arts Special*, as well as other top design magazines such as *Create Online*, we at Sprite know the power of an article to promote. This is true for printed articles, but is also particularly so for online articles. Identify magazines and other periodicals that relate to your product or service, and that feature articles on their websites. Articles also serve the purpose of increasing your credibility; if you or your company can be seen to be the authority on a certain topic, then people will visit your site to find out more about your subject. Allowing your articles to be freely published, and submitting them to as many sources as possible, means that they can potentially be viewed by literally thousands of web users.

Building links to improve your search engine ranking

Link popularity refers to the number and quality of the incoming links that are pointing to your site. In search engine optimization, 'off page' factors have become more and more important as they relate to rankings. If other sites consider your site important enough to link to, then so will the search engines. One of the most difficult areas of search engine optimization is building link popularity, because there are no easy ways to do this.

Building links to your site will improve your ranking in certain search engines. The main engine that does consider links to your site when working out rankings is Google, so there are clear advantages to building links – above and beyond the fact that they are a free way to promote your site. However, Google knows that not all links are equal, and that FFA (Free-For-All) links are worthless. Google actually measures the quality of links, taking into account each link's importance – so it's not only the amount of links to your site but also the relevancy of these links that is measured. Google actually lets you view the link popularity of any particular page, using its PageRank engine. To use this you have to download the Google Toolbar and install it into your Internet Explorer; it can be found at http://toolbar.google.com/ (Figure 3.4).

Once the toolbar is installed, you will notice that there is a small green bar with the words 'PageRank' next to it. This is the PageRank meter, and it tells you how important Google considers a site to be. The PageRank actually refers to the current page you are viewing, and if

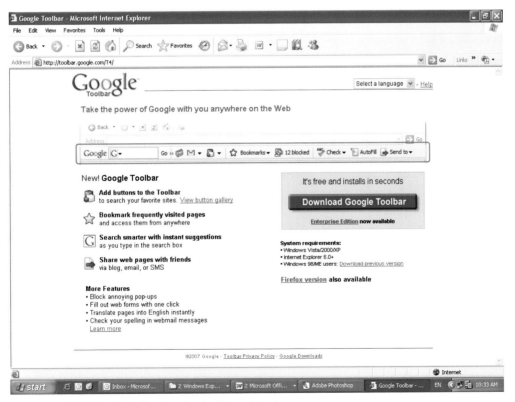

Figure 3.4 *The Google Toolbar (reproduced with permission)*

you place your mouse over the meter you will be given a ranking of one to ten. This is a very useful tool in deciding whether a site (including your own) has a high link factor. Sites with high PageRanks are the ones that you should approach to link to your site, as they will help increase your PageRank the most – which will in turn increase your ranking within Google.

It can be hard to understand exactly what Google mean when they talk about PageRank, but the best definition is that it is an indication of how popular a web page is. If you have a high PageRank then you have a more popular web page. Google PageRank ranges from 0 – for a page that has too few inbound links to be rated, or that is too new to have been ranked – to 10, which is only awarded to an exclusive few sites on the Web. Here are a few examples:

http://www.yahoo.com – 9
http://www.google.com – 10
http://www.msn.com – 9
http://www.microsoft.com – 10
http://www.nike.com – 7
http://www.myspace.com – 8

PageRank is not just an indication of how many web pages point to your site; it is also an indication of how important those sites are. A page with a smaller number of pages with a high PageRank linking into it will generally have a higher PageRank than a page with hundreds of low PageRanked pages linking into it. There are a number of factors that will determine your Google PageRank, the most important ones are:

- Incoming links to your site.
- The relevancy of the pages linking to your site and their PageRank.
- The keywords in the links to your site and how these relate to the main keywords on your website.

Google created quite a storm when it launched its PageRank bar, and many webmasters became obsessed with increasing their site's ranking, and getting high PageRank sites to link into them. A link from a high PageRank site has been known to increase a site's PageRank by one or even two whole numbers, also increasing the site's search engine ranking. PageRank can be deceptive, however; the green bar on the Google Toolbar is only updated quarterly and your site's PageRank will change from day to day, so if you use the Google Toolbar to work out your PageRank you will most of the time be looking at an out-of-date representation of your pages.

Unfortunately there is a degree of randomness to PageRank. There have been instances of sites having little or no inbound links, but a high PageRank, which can be baffling for the webmaster trying to build their ranking. Having a higher PageRank also does not necessarily mean that you will have a higher search engine placement; pages with low PageRank consistently rank higher in the search engine results than those with high ranks, so there are obviously many other factors at play in determining site ranking. The best PageRank strategy to pursue is to forget about it and get on with developing the factors that control it. Build a strong website and focus on developing links from sites with content relevant to your website, as this will naturally increase your PageRank and the number of visitors to your site. Don't forget – its quality traffic you're after before a high PageRank. Don't waste your time chasing only links from highly ranked sites, build your link-base naturally and your PageRank will increase by itself.

The PageRank is a useful tool, but it is not the only thing to be considered. You should also bear in mind that the site must hold relevant content, otherwise it is not worth being linked with in the first place. The key to ranking well on Google is not just the amount of links you have to and from your site, but also having content-rich pages in the first place. Taking all the above information into account, here is a step-by-step guide to building free links to your website. All these steps are supported by the link planning charts and tables which can be downloaded from Sprite Interactive (http://www.sprite.net/linkcharts).

1 *Set yourself a goal and a schedule to keep to.* Set a goal for the number of links you want, as a way to stay motivated. Use a 'site link chart' to help you stay on top of the amount of sites you are linking to. You should set the amount of sites you are approaching at about three times the amount you hope to get. Some sites will not want to trade links, so you need to set yourself realistic targets to keep your motivation up. Put aside around 30–60 minutes for link building each day, so you work consistently on the project; it is easy to spend too much or too little time on it and to lose focus.

2 *Make your site worth it.* Your site needs to offer something of value to those sites you are hoping will link to it. You need to make sure you have a lot of linkable content. If all you do is sell products, then you need to have some content (such as articles, news, reviews or tips) that is exclusive to your site and that will be tempting for other sites to link to. Having this content on your site will increase your link factor. It will also improve the quality of your site, so it is worth doing anyway. If you create enough linkable content, then you will find that people will approach you to link to their sites. Make sure you write about something that you know about or, if you cannot write, add some kind of unique software tool or download.

3 *Work out which types of site you want to trade links with.* This will take some thought. You are not actually finding the sites at this stage, but are working out the types of site to contact, so create a plan regarding which type of site to approach. For example, a site that sells tennis rackets might approach sites that sell tennis shoes and tennis clothes, but not tennis rackets. Once links from these sites have been accumulated, the tennis racket site can then develop a new section on playing tennis, and ask for links from sites that give tips on playing tennis. This will result in a significant number of links from sites related to the target market, and new pages of rich content for the website, to make the user experience more fulfilling.

4 *Locate quality link partners.* The best way to do this, as explained previously, is to type a search for the key terms or phrases you want to be listed for into Google, and choose your potential

partners from there. The higher such potential partners are listed the better, as you do not want to be linking to sites that are not ranked highly by Google. You can extend your search to the other major search engines; Yahoo! and the Open Directory are particularly good, as sites selected to be listed on these directories will already have been through a strict selection process (see Chapter 4).

5 *Evaluate.* You don't want to waste your time on link partners who are not relevant or who will not increase your search engine rankings, so you should use the Google PageRank software to evaluate your potential linking partners before you contact them. You should try to link up with sites that are ranked as highly or higher than your own.

6 *Organize your findings.* Keeping your findings organized is one of the most important things you can do when building links. Record:
- The full name of the site owner or webmaster
- The email address of the site owner or webmaster
- The home page URL of the link partner
- The URL of the page where you think your link belongs, and why you think it belongs there
- The PageRank of the page
- The date of the initial link request.

7 *Create a link exchange letter.* This letter requests a link exchange with your site, and should be directed to each of the sites you have noted in your list. Make sure you've come up with at least 50 good quality content, non-competitive sites with a decent PageRank. Take great care in writing your reciprocal links letter, as this will be the most memorable point of contact. Make sure it's the best it can be before sending it out. Remember, you're asking for a favour, so be polite and respectful in your letter – otherwise you'll get nowhere fast.

8 *Contact the webmaster.* You now need to go through your list of websites and send a personalized email to each of the webmasters. Make sure you compliment their sites, refer to them by name (if you have it), and state which page you would like to be linked from and why. You should also include in the email some HTML that contains the link, so they can easily put it into their page. Always have a link already put on your own site before you ask for a link in return, and give the location of the link. It is harder for the other sites to say they will not link to you if you already have a link to them. When you do this, make sure you give them the exact link text to use; however, probably the most important thing is to make sure that they have some kind of linking policy or even a links page. Whatever information you give, make sure it's easy for them to link to you. If they have a big site that's divided into sections, give them the exact URL of where your site would fit in, and then provide the HTML for the link to your site.

9 *Follow up.* Check at each of the websites where you requested a link to see if your request has been fulfilled. If not, contact the webmaster concerned, asking why your offer has been rejected. Remember that these people are human and they may have simply forgotten to put your link in, so sometimes a polite reminder can work wonders. At Sprite, initial contact is always by telephone instead of email. More people are inclined to respond to your request when you introduce yourself by telephone and let them know that you have been visiting their site.

Linking campaigns never really end, so you will constantly need to update the above information and renegotiate deals. To do this well requires a lot of time. Chapter 7 provides advice on different types of software that can help you with this part of the process. It is difficult to manage this type of project if you're using an external agency, and the main problem is assessing performance. If you pay the agency on a per link basis, then you will probably get lots of poor links. Therefore, if you opt to pay based on the numbers of links generated, agree quality control standards up front and always reserve the right of approval for any link deals. You then need to police and assess the quality of these links. You will have to take control of your inbound-linking strategy and execution, because nobody cares about your site as much as you do.

Automated link-building software – beware

If you have ever received an email that looks like the one below, then you have been the target of a piece of automated link-building software:

> Hi, I was just looking at your website and think we should exchange links. Exchanging links will be a brilliant way to . . .

This email will have been generated by a piece of automated link-building software. This is another way to build your links, and can be free or inexpensive, but you should be very wary of using such software. Most of these pieces of software work in the same way: they prompt you to do a search using a specific search engine for a specific term, and then the software visits each site in the results and looks for email addresses in the HTML. It then sends every email address an automatically generated email like the one above. Automatic link generators are used by hundreds of novice webmasters who do not know what they are doing, but just from reading the description above you can see that the software is essentially flawed and most of the emails will be written off as spam. The most you can hope to achieve is a couple of worthless links and loads of spam in your inbox from the link generator provider.

Link generators are a cheap and nasty way of doing a job that it should take you a couple of days to do properly. Finding a site to link to should be totally personalized, and most experienced webmasters will delete link requests as soon as they receive them – many of them will be insulted that you have used link-building software to attempt to link to their site. This software is totally indiscriminate, and contacts sites that are totally irrelevant or don't even have a links page in the first place. Also, a site may contain six different contact addresses and if those six people in the company received the same email, this would look a bit suspect.

Free-for-all links – a warning

Free-for-all links are another way by which webmasters can supposedly build up the amount of links going to their pages. You might also hear an FFA link page being referred to as a link farm.

They have been in existence since around 1995, and are pages that anyone can drop a link onto – normally through using some kind of submission software or website. Novice webmasters are lured in by the promise of having their site submitted to 3000 FFA links; this may sound impressive but actually is not, and the links do not generate any real traffic. FFA links also ask you for an email address to confirm your entry; entering a valid address here will mean that you will get an inbox full of junk mail, generated by the FFA's autoresponders. This steady stream of junk mail can cause many people to have to close their email account because of the sheer quantity they are receiving.

Another problem with FFA links is that they are temporary; they receive new links all the time, and your link will quickly be outdated by new submissions. If you plan to use FFA sites, resubmit often. Also consider submitting the URL of the FFA page containing your link to search engines to make sure the new link is indexed. If you are going to use FFA pages, you should also make sure you set up a dummy email account to catch all the junk mail you will undoubtedly receive. There is one minor benefit to FFA links, and that is that if your page stays on an FFA link for a bit it will look a little more popular when you submit to search engines. However, some search engines, most notably Google, see FFA links as an artificial and illegitimate way to increase your link popularity – which they essentially are – and consider them spam. You run the risk of having your site banned from their listings for participating in an FFA scheme.

Business directories

If you are a small business, then a great way to get free listings is to seek out business directories to submit to – particularly those directly related to your business. Have a look in Yahoo! and the Open Directory, and you should find directories relevant to your industry. For example, Sprite targets online SEO consultants directories, getting the site listed in as many as possible (Figure 3.5).

Many people who are wanting to find out about your industry will tend to visit industry-wide sites first, and you will find that many of these hold targeted lists of suppliers. A number of them offer free listings, so getting your site listed is an economic way to get your site out to a targeted audience.

Get a link in an appropriate category from an About.com guidesite. The popularity of About.com, and the extent of its quality links, positions the network as an important stop in a marketing campaign. Look hard for industry association sites, as the amount of links you need to point to your site is invariably more than your competition. Look for themed directories. When you find a directory, make sure that it is already in Google, has a good PageRank, and doesn't use dynamic script in the address. Look out for directories, hubs, portals and vortals. Once you are listed, it's good to have a page on your site that you use to feed the spiders.

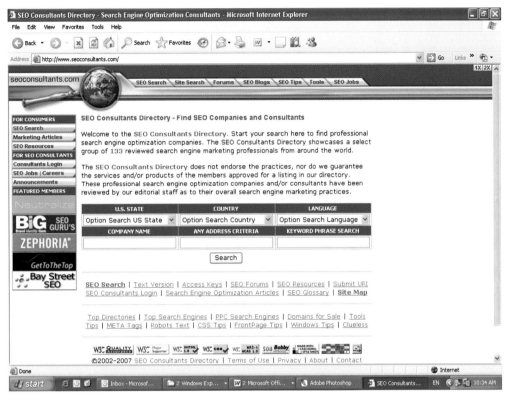

Figure 3.5 *An example SEO directory (reproduced with permission of SEO Consultants)*

Which method should I use?

Search engine optimization on a budget is not easy. You can of course submit to all the major search engines that still offer free submission; your site will be listed eventually, but it will take time. Since search engines are now discouraging the use of FFA sites and link-exchange programs, it is strongly suggested that you focus your efforts on contacting webmasters with link requests and on building up a network of free links to your website. Not only will this give you a number of new avenues for visitors to come to your site, it will also help to increase your ranking in Google and other search engines that measure link popularity.

Building up links in related business websites will also help your site. Although FFA sites may have been effective in the past, they are now considered to be 'spam' by some search engines, and it is not worth even dabbling in them because you run the risk of being banned from major search engines. As for mass submission tools, these are even worse than FFA sites and should be avoided. You can go some way to promoting your website with little or no budget, and still get quality traffic to it. The path is slightly more laborious and time-consuming than with a large budget, but it is worth it, and many of the techniques outlined in this chapter – especially those for link building – are useful to any webmaster, whether they have a budget or not.

Weblog linking strategies

Adding a blog to your website can be a great way to increase your site's link factor. Blogs can play a powerful role for most websites and, as a linking strategy for attracting new incoming links to your site and as a way to facilitate link exchange, they are one of the most powerful tools available to you. Blogs attract many incoming links; these links will encourage a high Google PageRank and will be highly relevant to you. Managers of blogs are generally pretty generous with their links, and will be keen to set up reciprocal links to your blog, which you can then link back into your website. Most blog links are to interesting content, and to the keen blogger that means that fresh links will be updated pretty much on a daily basis. Links from blogs will nearly always be relevant to your site content as bloggers tend to read blogs on similar themes. The majority of bloggers will swap links and aren't concerned with the value of the links they swap; blog links will generally benefit both partners.

There are a few rumours circulating in the SEO community that search engines give blog links less weight; this is not true. Do a search on Google and you will find blogs with a high PageRank appearing in top places in the listings; this is proof enough. Search engines like blogs, as there is constant addition of relevant content to the blog; this is a great example of how writing for your target audience and keeping site content fresh can get you high search engine rankings. Successful blogs have daily updates of at least one article; this combined with lots of inbound relevant links is search engine spider heaven. Fresh content, including breaking news, interesting commentary or funny content, is a magnet for inbound links.

Once a blog writer has uploaded a new article to their blog, this will appear on the homepage of the blog, and other blog managers will add a link to the unique URL of the blog (which is called a permalink). In addition to this they will usually add a link to the homepage of the blog, as a courtesy, providing the blog with two incoming links. The linking blog is likely to be relevantly themed which adds to the power of these links, and the links will be behind keyword-rich anchor text. All these factors add up to make blog links very powerful and explains why many blogs rank highly in the search engines.

Bloggers also trade links all the time; while many reciprocal link programs for static websites are generally not worth getting involved in, blog link exchanges tend to be between related blogs, leading to relevant links and high PageRank scores. The main motivation behind blog link exchanges is for traffic building and development, rather than for SEO, and should therefore be approached as such.

There are a number of Internet directories that are only available for blogs. The Open Directory and the Yahoo! Directory have opened up an exclusive blog section on their sites. Some other blog-exclusive directories to check out are:

Blog Search Engine – http://www.blogsearchengine.com
Blogwise – http://www.blogwise.com
Eatonweb portal – http://www.portal.eatonweb.com

Blog Universe – http://www.bloguniverse.com

Popdex – http://www.popdex.com

Blogarama – http://www.blogarama.com

Blogdex – http://www.blogdex.com

Blo.gs – http://www.blo.gs/

Globe of Blogs – http://www.globeofblogs.com

Blizg – http://www.blizg.com

Online Marketing Links – http://www.onlinemarketinglinks.com

In conclusion

Getting your site listed for free is possible; however, it can be time-consuming and you may not see the results for a number of months on the main search engines. If your website is non-profit making, you stand a much better chance of being able to get it listed for free or at least at a lower cost. Probably the main way to promote your site for free is by building up reciprocal links with other related sites.

Developing a link strategy

A link strategy is made up of three parts:

1 Linking to the directories, search engines and industry websites
2 Harnessing link suppliers, friends and associates
3 Creating mini sites.

Linking to the directories is what most people mean by linking. This entails finding the main web directories and paying to be in them. In addition to that you can focus on industry portals and offer them a free search optimization service for a particular engine in return for a link from their site for a period of time. You can also register your appropriate association site to all the Web crawlers in return for a link. This is easy to do, and can increase both your stature in the industry and, most importantly, your link popularity.

The second part of the strategy is to create a list of all the people who fall into the categories of suppliers, friends and associates, and agree a link strategy and a links policy across the group. Once all the sites are fully linked, representatives of each site then register or subscribe (budget allowing) to all the directories and search engines they can in a given time. Over a short period of time, you will notice a continual improvement of search engine rankings.

Directories can help you to identify directories, informational sites and complementary businesses that may be interested in exchanging links with your website. Make use of directory listings as part of an ongoing link-building campaign. Yahoo! has categories listing regional and topic directories, which are often willing to link to any website that submits information.

The third part of the strategy is to build mini sites around your service or product offering. When searching for information, people tend to start generally and get more specific as they narrow down their search. Therefore, if your first page has a lot of general links this should work better than a few very specific links. However, if each of your mini sites covers a product offering, you are creating a bigger target for the search engines.

Maintaining a links strategy is very important. Chances are, your site will not answer all the readers' questions off the front page. This means that your first page needs to be a good starting point for your readers to find what they need, because if they can't find a good starting place they'll leave immediately. This means that the links on all your landing pages should give your readers an excellent idea of what they will get if they click on them.

Link tips

- Review your search engine logs to see what people are looking for
- Make sure that your links are clear and that the appropriate landing pages go where you imply they will go
- Avoid cute links or links that are there just for the sake of a link
- Try to create links that go to content. Lists of links are useful, but the information that is the goal is usually found on content pages, and not on lists.

How to locate quality link partners

There are many ways of finding partners, but the easiest way to find quality link partners quickly is to start at Open Directory and Yahoo!. You are really looking for two types of links from these directories: the first is one that is going to gain you popularity in the search engines stakes, and the other is going to drive business your way. The Open Directory and Yahoo! are good places to start, as these directories are both so difficult to get listed in that each potential link partner found there is likely to be of a higher quality than those found elsewhere. Yahoo! and the Open Directory greatly boost a site's link popularity when they list it, and your site will receive a little bit of that boost each time someone from one of those directories links to you. The links you build don't help your link popularity in the search engines unless the engines know about the link, and since the search engines crawl the sites listed in Yahoo! and the Open Directory on a regular basis, you can be sure that the search engines will find you new links quickly.

Increasing link popularity is very much about building one step at a time. One good link is better that ten mediocre links. You are certainly going to get good links from your mini sites, so build them first and then start linking and promoting your site. Doing things this way will make a tenfold difference to the success of your mission. The worst thing you can do is to start a campaign when the linking out is just not there.

Use the guerrilla marketing techniques outlined in this chapter to promote your site in related forums and newsgroups; you will find that you can attract a lot of traffic in this way.

Writing articles and adding interesting 'sticky' content to your site will also increase its link factor and make people more likely to return to it.

It's worth researching the various business directories that exist on the Web, and joining the directories and associations that are relevant to your industry. Avoid using any mass submission software, particularly free-for-all link farm pages. Search engines are wise to these techniques, and you may end up getting your site banned from major search engines for using them. These forms of site promotion will usually just leave you with a clogged inbox and no results.

In short, by using the techniques outlined above you can get your site noticed for free. This requires a bit more thought than merely submitting your website via paid submission programs, but for the webmaster who is on a tight budget it is very worthwhile.

Chapter 4
Web crawlers and directories

Web crawlers

A web crawler is a program that automatically surfs the Internet looking for links. It then follows each link and retrieves documents that in turn have links, recursively retrieving all further documents that are referenced. Web crawlers are sometimes referred to as web wanderers, web robots, or spiders. These names give the impression that the software itself moves between sites, although this is not the case. A crawler simply visits sites by requesting documents from them, and then automatically visits the links on those documents.

Unlike directories, where you subscribe a URL, with a crawler you are likely to have several (if not many) pages listed. Crawler-based search engines automatically visit web pages to compile their listings. This means that by taking care in how you build your pages, you can rank well in crawler-produced results.

Web crawlers start from a list of URLs, such as server lists. Most indexing services also allow you to submit URLs manually, which will then be visited by the crawler. Crawlers can select URLs to visit and index, and to use as a source for new URLs. Robots may index the HTML titles, or the first few paragraphs, or parse the entire HTML and index all words, prioritizing the HTML constructs (see Chapter 7 for more on HTML construction and page architecture). Some parse the META tag, or other special hidden tags. To register your site with a robot, you need to find the link to a URL submission form on the crawler's search page. Fortunately you don't have to submit your URL manually to every service: Submit-it <URL: http://www.bcentral.com/products/si/default.asp> will do it for you.

You can always check to see if a crawler has visited your site by looking at your server logs. If your server supports user-agent logging, you can check for retrievals by looking at the user-agent header values. If you notice a site repeatedly checking for the file '/robots.txt', chances are it is a robot. You will notice lots of entries to 'robots.txt' in your log files. This is because the log files are automatically generated by your server robots, which are trying to see if you have specified any rules for them using the Standard for Robot Exclusion. If you don't care about robots and want to prevent the messages in your error logs, simply create an empty file called robots.txt in the root level of your server (see Chapter 7 for more information regarding robots.txt files).

The alternative to using robots.txt is a new standard for using HTML META tags to keep robots out of your documents. To learn more about META tags, refer to Chapter 7. It is true that listing pages or directories in the robots.txt file may invite curiosity as to why you are keeping people out. So, you can put all the files you don't want robots to visit in a separate subdirectory and make it unlistable, then list only the directory name in the robots.txt. A robot can't traverse that directory unless a link is placed from a file on the Web.

We will run through submitting your site to a number of the search engines that you can perform a manual submission for. The small selection of search engines covered in this chapter is only the tip of the iceberg, and there are many others that do not allow manual submission, but will find your site if it is properly optimized and listed in the index of sites such as Google and Yahoo! Many of the lessons here can be transferred to all your search engine submissions.

Submitting to Google

Arguably the most important crawler-based search engine is Google. The best way to get listed with Google is to build links to your website – in fact, this is the way to get listed for free with all the major crawlers on the Web. Crawlers' only purpose in life is to follow links, so the more links you have pointing to your site, the more likely it is that the crawlers will find and include your pages. This of course means that if you have submitted your site to the major directories, then Google and other crawlers will almost certainly have found the URL that was listed – thus you can benefit in two ways from subscribing to the directories. You can 'Add URL' in Google,

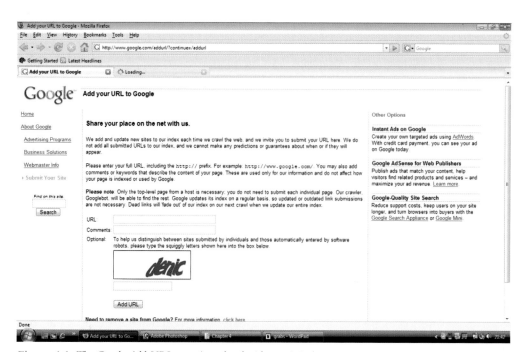

Figure 4.1 *The Google Add URL page (reproduced with permission)*

which lets you submit a URL directly to its crawler: http://www.google.com/addurl.html. Figure 4.1 shows you the page and its contents.

Whilst you cannot guarantee that Google will include a URL submitted to it in this way, it is the only means by which you can submit your site details. If you do submit, then you should submit your homepage and perhaps one or two other URLs from 'inside' your website via the Add URL page. The main reason for submitting some of your inside pages is that this increases the target for the crawler, which may miss your homepage, and gives Google a number of alternate routes into your site. It could take up to a month before Google lists the Web pages of a new site, and because of this you might consider making use of its paid placement program (see Chapters 9 and 10).

Submitting to Yahoo!

Until 2004 Google powered the Yahoo! non-directory search results. In 2002 Yahoo! bought Inktomi and in 2004 Yahoo! launched their own web crawler, called Yahoo! Slurp. Yahoo! and Google had become each other's main competitors. There are several ways to submit your site to Yahoo! Search links to all of them can be found on http://search.yahoo.com/info/submit.html; Yahoo! offers a very comprehensive submission service.

Like Google, Yahoo! Crawler will crawl the Web and eventually find your site, but there is also no harm in submitting your site to the search engine, and they offer a number of different

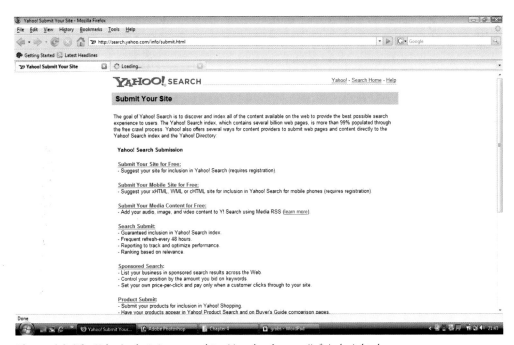

Figure 4.2 The Yahoo! submission page – http://search.yahoo.com/info/submit.html

submission criteria and even fast-track paid submission. Once you have registered with Yahoo! you can then submit a website or web page, in much the same way as you would with Google. Yahoo! also gives you the option to submit a site feed in the following formats:

- RSS 0.9, RSS 1.0 or RSS 2.0, for example, CNN top stories
- Sitemaps, as documented on www.sitemaps.org
- Atom 0.3, for example, Yahoo! Search Blog
- A text file containing a list of URLs, each URL at the start of a new line. The filename of the URL list file must be urllist.txt; for a compressed file the name must be urllist.txt.gz.

Yahoo! has also made it easy to submit your mobile sites, in xHTML, WML, or cHTML format at http://search.yahoo.com/free/mobile/request. If you have media, such as images, videos and audio, Yahoo! also lets you submit these via Media RSS; you can read the specification for Media RSS at http://search.yahoo.com/mrss.

Submitting to Ask.com (Teoma)

Teoma is an important crawler-based search engine because it powers the Ask Jeeves website. The Teoma algorithm is now known as ExpertRank, which ranks sites on how important they are, not necessarily how big they are or how many inbound links they have. Teoma has no free Add URL page; it creates its index from crawling the Web, so if you have links pointing at your website you will get included naturally some time down the line. However, Teoma will guarantee to include your pages if you use its paid inclusion program, and it has been known to list sites within three days. This appears to be the only feasible route for a commercial website. For a small fee, the page will be revisited each week for up to a year. It's possible that your page could be dropped if you don't renew, but this is highly unlikely to happen to a homepage. To sign up for the program, visit http://ask.ineedhits.com/

Teoma's underlying technology is an extension of the HITS algorithm developed by researchers at IBM. Teoma seeks out 'hubs' and 'establishments' related to your query terms using a 'social network' of related content that forms a 'community' about the topic. This approach differs from Google's, which uses a similar but more static ranking system. It's also unlike the approach taken by Northern Light and other engines that classify web pages based on predefined categories. The 'refine' result is Teoma's exceptional feature. These links are automatically generated labels that 'define' a community for the query words entered by the user. So even if an initial query doesn't provide good results, the 'refine' links allow the user to 'drill down' into a community, revealing information that would never be found using other search engines. This dynamic approach to content means that Teoma can find the beginnings of a new community for new or obscure pages. This is an alternative approach to that used by other search engines (including Google), which tend to rely on lots of links pointing to pages. Teoma is a new type of hybrid between a search engine and a directory, incorporating the best features of both. Like most search engines, Teoma's scope is large enough to satisfy even the most obscure information need, but without overwhelming the user.

WiseNut

WiseNut was launched in September 2001, and was seen in the media as a potential 'Google killer'. When San Francisco-based LookSmart purchased the search engine in April 2001, industry watchers wondered how a search engine using crawler-based technology fitted in with LookSmart's business model of using human editors to compile directories of the Web. Like Google and most of the other major search engines, WiseNut puts a lot of emphasis on link analysis, but adds a few other ingredients for calculating relevance. In addition to link analysis, WiseNut also emphasizes the proximity of search terms in underlying documents, computing results in real time, based on specific queries.

WiseNut automatically categorizes results into 'wiseguides', which are semantically related to the words in your query. You can open up a wiseguide category by clicking its link, or click on an icon next to the category to conduct a new search automatically using the category as your query. WiseNut offers links for related queries, and clusters results from individual sites. Its clustering is unique; instead of the usual 'more results' from this site link, WiseNut lists the exact number of pages on a site that it has determined are relevant to your query. It also offers a 'Sneak-a-Peek' function, which lets you preview a page without leaving the WiseNut's result page (see Figure 4.3). This eliminates a lot of 'mouse traffic' between the results page and the back button.

WiseNut's indexing technology has been designed to scale up to 1 trillion (a million million million) URLs. While this may seem like overkill given the current estimates of two to four

Figure 4.3 *The WiseNut homepage*

billion pages on the Web, it means that WiseNut is serious about staying in the game as the Web continues to grow. WiseNut's public search engine is just one part of its overall business, and is expected to generate only about 20 per cent of revenues. WiseNut's main emphasis is on providing site search to large websites, and enterprise search for intranets. This is where the real money and profit potential for search technology lies.

The root page advantage

Breaking up a website into multiple sites gives you more 'root' – sometimes described as multiple homepages that collectively tend to be more highly ranked than any other single homepage. That's due both to search engine algorithms, and because root pages tend to attract the majority of links from other websites.

The root page is whatever page appears when you enter the domain name of a site. Usually, this is the same as your homepage. For instance, if you enter www.sprite.net into your browser, the page that loads is Figure 4.4 – both the Sprite homepage and the 'root' page for the

Figure 4.4 *The Sprite interactive homepage*

Sprite web server. However, if you have a site within someone else's web server, such as http://www.ellenzak.com/mysite/, then your homepage is not the root page. That's because the server has only one root page, the page that loads when you enter 'ellenzak.com' into your browser. In our example there used to be only one root page – the one that appeared when someone went to 'sprite.net' – and this page had to focus on all different product terms. Now, each of the new sites also has a root page – and each page can be specifically about a particular product type. Breaking up a large site might also help you with directories. Editors tend to prefer listing root URLs rather than long addresses that lead to pages buried within a website. So to some degree, breaking up your site into separate sites should give each site the same possibility of a ranking while collectively having a greater hit area.

Submitting to the major search engines

Depending on the search engine, there is not always an advantage in submitting multiple pages from your website. All crawler-based engines will send out a crawler to your site and gather what they find of interest independently of your submission. With some search engines, directly submitting a page greatly increases the odds that the page will be listed. It is important to remember that there is usually no reason to submit each page from your website to search engines where the listing is not tied to submission. Our experience at Sprite is that the closer you approach the limit for submission, which is usually 50 URLs (unless otherwise stated) per day, the more likely it is that you may attract a review of your site.

It is almost impossible to be certain how up-to-date a search engine's data is. In fact the best guideline is to take what the search engines say and double it for all mission critical content. There have been situations where pages on certain crawler sites were out of date by at least twice the amount that the search engines would normally allow.

After all the effort invested in your favourite search engine, will it ever pay off? Is the search engine likely to be around tomorrow? For searchers, such losses could mean less diversity in search results. For web marketers, it could mean less likelihood of being found. The demise of Go was dramatic and simple – Open Text faced the search engine question of whether it should develop its technology as a product for businesses, concentrate on its consumer website, or try to do both. The company ultimately decided to concentrate on software, and the Web search site was allowed to die slowly. Magellan was a rival to Excite, and was finally consumed in the mid-1990s. Magellan has never closed; it is just withering away essentially unsupported. Excite also acquired WebCrawler in 1996. WebCrawler is far more popular than Magellan, but it is no longer one of the Web's major search services. There haven't been service enhancements for ages; nor does Excite position the service toward users. Lycos acquired Point in 1996, and this never survived.

To survive, the search engines need content and services to keep users visiting their sites, and thus boost ad revenue. A big turnabout came in July 1997, when Amazon announced a landmark deal to be a preferred book merchant carried by Excite and Yahoo!. All the big search engines were making online retailing deals; this apparently saved the search industry. By 1998, instead of the expected shakeout, the future of search engines seemed bright owing to their transformation into portals. Investors loved them. Searching was only a small part of what search engines offered.

In addition to the loss of big retailing deals, the search engine portals also suffered from the decline in more ordinary banner advertising as a result of the crash of dotcom stocks in 2000. Both Go and AltaVista pulled back from wanting to be all-purpose portals in September 2000. The consolidation that had long been predicted was finally here. Visit the LookSmart site today, and you'll only find the non-profit submission form after a struggle. In contrast, Yahoo!'s system of limiting mandatory fees to commercial categories makes sense. Perhaps we'll see a hybrid approach – some categories may cost more than others, allowing non-profits to pay a smaller fee while letting search engines capitalize further on what they charge to appear in popular commercial categories. Google has been the shining example of a service offering a good search facility and that has attracted users without needing to spend large advertising budgets. The long-term strategy for all the search engines is to provide great search products to an ever more sophisticated market.

There are three main tips to achieve better ranking on search engines:

1 Register your site on all the engines, using commercial and non-commercial registration
2 Build good architecture for your site
3 Have a clear strategy for link building, and make sure it works.

Directories

Here we'll be looking at the two major search engine directories on the Web – Yahoo! and the Open Directory. As well as gaining an understanding of how each of these engines works, you will learn the best way to get your site listed at both, and tips on how to improve your site listing. There is a marked distinction between how a directory-based search engine works and how a crawler-based search engine works, and this is discussed first.

What is a directory?

A directory is an approach to organizing information – one of the most common types of directory is a telephone directory. On the Web, a directory is essentially a subject guide, typically organized by major topics and subtopics. Results in a directory are taken from websites that have already been submitted to that directory, and have been listed through some kind of screening process. Many directories have web crawlers as a part of their service (most notably Yahoo! and Google), but directories are generally maintained and updated by humans, and to get your site listed you will have to go through some kind of approval process – so your site has to be both relevant and good (especially in the case of Yahoo!).

Yahoo! – www.yahoo.com

Yahoo! (Figure 4.5) is the oldest search service on the Web, and is the most important place to begin site submission. There are a number of distinct advantages that sites on Yahoo! have, and this will be covered later.

Yahoo! is the perfect example of an idea that blossomed into something bigger than its founders could have hoped, and is now the brand name most associated with the Internet. For some users it *is* the Internet, owing to the portal-like services Yahoo! now offers. Yahoo! was started in 1994 by two electrical engineering students, David Filo and Jerry Yang. They began by building a list of their favourite websites, but it soon became evident that they needed more than their own personal time to manage the information they had accumulated.

To accommodate all the information and resources they required, Filo and Yang moved Yahoo! over to the Netscape facilities in early 1995. Netscape was a very large portal in its own right, and had vast technical resources. Yahoo! continued to grow, and today is a public company with over 1 million sites in its directory. Yahoo! has acquired a number of companies, including Geocities and Rocketmail, in order to provide free web pages and email to its subscribers. Yahoo! continues to grow, and is now one of the biggest portal sites in existence.

As mentioned above, it is important to remember that Yahoo! is not just a search engine but also a directory that is edited and maintained by humans; therefore, when you submit a site to

Figure 4.5 *Screen grab of yahoo.com (reproduced with permission)*

the Yahoo! directory it will be reviewed by a human and not by a piece of software. Yahoo! employs a number of full-time professional editors, whose job it is to visit the thousands of sites that submit to the directory and decide if they should be listed. Yahoo! is also not the biggest directory service on the Internet; the Open Directory (see below) holds this crown, with around 2 million sites indexed.

The Yahoo! directory

Yahoo! holds its own database of over 1 million web pages. Being listed with the Yahoo! directory poses advantages to site owners for a number of reasons. First, if you are listed in the directory then you stand more chance of being noticed by users browsing through or detouring through the directory listings after or before performing a search. Second, being listed in the directory can help your listing in the Web matches results. Third, being listed may help your link analysis rating in search engines such as Google.

Before you learn about techniques for actually getting your site listed in the directory, it is important to delve a bit further into how the directory is put together and how the human editors decide where sites are placed in it. Websites that are featured on Yahoo! are either found by its human editors, or are reviewed and then submitted. Sites are placed into one or more of Yahoo!'s categories. If you browse around Yahoo!, you will see that each of the categories is a stand-alone web page, with the websites featured in that category listed in alphabetical order. Pages are only in the Yahoo! directory if they can be found in these alphabetical listings; many people think that just because their site has been listed in the 'web matches' section of the results page they are listed with Yahoo!, but this is not always the case. In each category there is also usually a 'most popular' section, which contains the most popular websites in that category. This is useful if you are browsing around Yahoo! and want to know what the best or most popular website is in a particular category, but it is a major disadvantage if your site is not listed in this section, because these are the sites that are the most frequently visited. Yahoo! uses an automatic system to select which sites are listed in this section and will not reveal its criteria, but it is most likely through the use of link analysis.

Preparing your website for submission

Websites listed on Yahoo! are chosen by humans, and therefore the listing criteria are a lot stricter than if your site were being selected by a spider. Yahoo! will not index sites that are not of the highest quality for their particular category, and this means no broken links, spelling mistakes or 'under construction' signs. One good method for seeing how much of a chance your site has of being listed is to view the other sites in the category to which you're applying. If these sites are poorly designed and unattractive and yours is not, then you have a better than average chance of being listed. This technique is relative, and you will find that certain categories (such as heavyweight scientific sites) will feature poorer quality websites (which contain a lot of relevant content) than categories such as 'soft drink companies', where manufacturers will have invested a lot of money in developing their online presence.

It is important to make sure that your website is consistent with the description you submit to Yahoo!. If the editors visiting your site expect one thing and then actually find another, this is a sure-fire way not to be listed. Also, be careful about using frames.

Click-through   An important feature of Yahoo!'s listing system is that it tracks click-through behaviour as part of the ranking system. This means that when you click on a link in Yahoo! it will count the click-throughs on that page. It will also log the fact that the user chose that page after searching with a particular keyword, and as more people select the site using the same keywords its ranking will rise. This can lead to some sites being listed above others that have more relevant keywords in their descriptions. Yahoo! is also now tracking 'click away' behaviour; this means that it times how long a user stays at a site before returning to Yahoo! – and the longer the user stays, the better it is for the site's ranking. This means that sites that have high quality, relevant content and design are more likely to fare well.

Submitting your website to the Yahoo! directory

It is important to have a plan before actually submitting your site to Yahoo!, so make sure you follow the subsequent instructions and create a strategy. This means when you do submit your site you will know exactly what to do and will thus ensure the best possible results. Throughout this section we're going to refer to a fictional 'sports shoes' website as an example.

Keywords   First you need to decide what search terms are the most important to people searching for your website. You need to be careful when you are doing this, and perform a number of searches on Yahoo! to test the words and phrases you have chosen – are they returning the same kind of website as yours? You need to use these keywords to write a site description that is no more than 25 words in length and will be submitted to Yahoo! later. It is important to make sure this description is appealing; it's very tempting to submit a list of keywords to Yahoo!, but if you submit something that reads well and describes your product effectively and succinctly it is more likely to be looked at by both editors and searchers, and also to generate a higher click-through rate – which in turn will lead to a higher ranking. Bearing all this in mind, choose four or five top keywords and phrases to describe your site. For our fictional sports shoes site these could be:

1 Sports shoes
2 Sports trainers
3 Running shoes
4 Shoes.

Decide which of these is the most important, as it will help you when choosing which category to submit to.

Choose the right category   Your website will be placed into one of Yahoo!'s categories, so it is helpful to have researched which category to submit your site to before starting the submission process. On Yahoo!'s search page a few categories will typically be listed at the top of the page, and users frequently detour into these categories when searching for sites. To research which is the best category for your site, you should go to Yahoo! and search for the terms by which you hope to be found. Then look at the categories Yahoo! returns on its results page, and choose the most appropriate one. It also helps to visit the categories you have short-listed to check the other sites there. Check whether your competitors are listed in that category, and whether the other sites listed are similar businesses to yours. You will probably find about six or seven relevant categories for your site; you need to choose the one that is the most 'obvious', bearing in mind that if the category you choose is not sufficiently relevant Yahoo! can either reject your listing or put your site in a different category altogether. If your web page seems appropriate for two or more categories then you'll need to pick one, but you can suggest one of the others (this is covered in more detail later). If you have decided to use the Yahoo! Express submission program, you don't need to choose a category; the editors will choose it for you.

Submission methods

To begin the submission process, you need to go to the category you have chosen and click on the 'suggest a site' link at the bottom of the page. The Yahoo! Express service was introduced in February 1999 because Yahoo! had received a number of complaints that certain sites were not being listed. For a fee, Yahoo! will guarantee to review your submission and give you a yes or no answer within seven working days. It is very important to remember that this does not guarantee that your site will be listed; all you are getting is a yes or no answer. The service also does not guarantee where or how you will be listed. You are not given a refund if your site is not accepted.

Although this process may seem quite harsh, most of the sites that do submit via Yahoo! Express are accepted, and by following the tips outlined in this chapter you can vastly increase your chances of being listed in your preferred category. A year after submitting your site you will be sent a renewal notice by Yahoo!, prompting you to pay the annual fee. One feature of Yahoo! Express is that you can leave the choice of category up to the editors at Yahoo! However, it is recommended that you choose your own category. If you choose it you are more likely to select somewhere that is relevant, and you will probably have done a lot more research than the Yahoo! editor before choosing it. It is worth putting in the effort and research necessary to select the category that is relevant for you.

Choosing a title   You are going to have to choose a title for your site when you get to 'Step 2: Site and contact information'. The title of your site is crucial to how it is ranked in the directory listings, and you want to choose a title that reflects the most important search terms and keywords associated with it. Your site title should not exceed 60 characters, and it is worth bearing in mind that Yahoo! ranks sites alphabetically. Being towards the beginning of the alphabet is therefore advantageous; people are more likely to look at your site, as the typical user does not take the time to scroll down a page to check out all the results, but clicks on the first few sites that appear. If your company name is not high in the alphabet, try choosing one of your brands or products that is; however, do not be overt with your use of letters. If you choose something like 'A1 Sports Shoes' this will not go down well with the Yahoo! editors, and they will likely use your real business name instead. If you are submitting your site for free you should be especially careful, as editors tend to ignore sites that use these tactics in favour of getting through the backlog of sites that have submitted properly.

There are exceptions to this rule, where sites are allowed to use alphabetical and numerical games to influence their listing. One high profile case is the 'Viagra' category, where there are plenty of sites whose name begins with symbols and numbers. You will see in this section a lot of the sites begin with '!'; this is because of the way Yahoo! ranks ASCII characters.

Your site description   The main mistake that people make when submitting to Yahoo! is to create a 25-word description that is merely a list of relevant keywords, making no attempt to arrange these into a meaningful paragraph. If you do this the Yahoo! editor can and will cut down your description, and in the process you will lose some of your valuable keyword phrases. A good start to defining your site is to look at the description of other relevant sites in the category to which you are submitting. If there is a prevailing trend in the site descriptions, then follow this – for example, all the descriptions might begin with the word 'Provides'. This means that the particular editor for the category likes that type of language, and as it is this editor you have to impress, it helps to use the kind of language they like. Do all you can to make sure your description sounds like those in your chosen category, and if your main keyword is not listed in any of the site descriptions, then chances are that the editor does not like that keyword. If you use it it's likely it will be removed, so choose another word instead.

You need to make sure your site description reads well; if it is a 'clunky' paragraph that does not flow, then the editor is likely to alter it to make it read better. It is worth getting an experienced copywriter or editor to look at your description and make sure that it is written well. Your main aim is to create a site description that will not be edited by Yahoo!, and something that is going to be enticing for someone surfing Yahoo!'s directory.

Additional category   The submission form also has an 'Additional information' box, and you can use this box to suggest one additional Yahoo! category for your site. For example, if you sell running shoes but also provide information on health and running, then you could ask to be listed in a non-commercial category about health and fitness. You will need to provide a short explanation as to why Yahoo! should include your site in the additional category, and there is no guarantee that you will be listed, but at the same time there is nothing to lose by trying.

If your site could be listed in both the business-to-business and the business-to-consumer sections of Yahoo!, you should select the most appropriate of these when you submit, and put the other in the additional category box, with an explanation as to why you should be in both. Yahoo! should then comply and list you in both.

The listing

Yahoo! will notify you via email within seven days regarding whether your site has been listed. You will not, however, know how it is going to be described until you see the listing in the directory. If Yahoo! has not listed your site, has put you in a category that is not suitable for your site, or has given your site a poor or misleading description, you can appeal against the decision. Yahoo! will then tell you why your site was not listed; if it was due to something repairable, like broken links, you should fix the problem and then resubmit. If the rejection was caused by something else, you should deal with this the best you can. If your site description was edited so much that you feel it no longer describes your site, Yahoo! suggests that you change the URL form to update your listing. You need to have a good reason to change your listing, other than just making your site rank better. Reasons, if relevant, may include a change of company name, or that your business has shifted its focus. If your site has not appeared within seven days, Yahoo! advises that you resubmit once. If after two weeks your site has still not appeared, then contact Yahoo! support services at url-suport@yahoo-inc.com to find out what's wrong.

Special tactics to get listed

You can take advantage of the way Yahoo! lists characters and letters; it indexes characters and word phrases rather than whole words, which means that if you search for 'run' you will also find 'running' and 'runner'. You should make sure that you use the longest variation of the most important keywords to describe your site. If you use the word 'runner', you can be certain that this will return results for 'runner' and 'run'; you should therefore think about how you can fit the longest variations of words possible into your site description.

The Open Directory – http://dmoz.org

The Open Directory is a human-compiled directory of websites. It works in the same way as Yahoo!, meaning you find a category for your website, and then submit to it with a short description of your site. The Open Directory was set up in June 1998 by Rich Skrenta, and was originally called GnuHoo. The idea was that editors would pick a topic that they were interested in and begin editing. It is now staffed by nearly 30 000 volunteer editors, who act in much the same way as Yahoo!'s editors, but the sheer number of them means that they can get through and list far more sites. The Open Directory sees itself as a part of the open source movement, and this is reflected in the fact that it is staffed by volunteers and that companies are free to use its search results. It actually provides search data to many other high profile search engines, including

Figure 4.6 *The Open Directory homepage*

AOL search, Netscape search and Lycos. The Open Directory says the following about its services:

> The Web continues to grow at staggering rates. Automated search engines are increasingly unable to turn up useful results to search queries. The small paid editorial staffs at commercial directory sites can't keep up with submissions, and the quality and comprehensiveness of their directories has suffered. Link rot is setting in and they can't keep pace with the growth of the Internet.

> Instead of fighting the explosive growth of the Internet, the Open Directory provides the means for the Internet to organize itself. As the Internet grows, so do the number of net-citizens. These citizens can each organize a small portion of the Web and present it back to the rest of the population, culling out the bad and useless and keeping only the best content.

This gives you a good idea of why the Open Directory was set up; it is essentially a search engine community of enthusiastic individuals, and because of this is the largest existing directory of websites on the Internet.

Search results

When you perform a search on the Open Directory you will see that the results are broken down into two sections, and the search page looks quite similar to that of Yahoo! before it introduced its Web results in October 2002 (Figure 4.7). The first section of the results is the Open Directory category matches; only the top five will be shown here. Below this are the Web page matches, where individual websites are listed by their relevance.

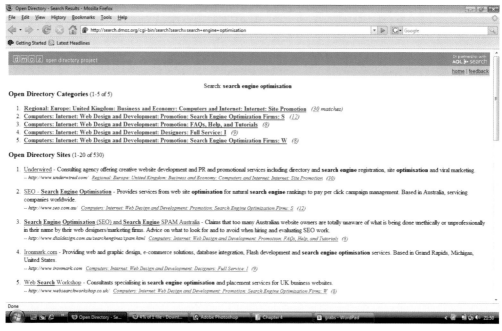

Figure 4.7 *The Open Directory results page*

Getting listed

As with Yahoo!, you first need to find the right category to submit your site to, and again the easiest way to do this is to search for the keywords that you would use to describe your site and pick the most appropriate category from those returned on the results page. If your search does not return any specific categories at the top of the page, look under each website that is returned and you will see the name of the category it has come from in italics next to the Web address.

At the top of each category page you'll find an 'add URL' link; click on this to add your website to that particular category. If this is not at the top of the page you'll be in a top-level category, and will therefore need to go down another level in that category before you can submit. Submitting is done in much the same way as to Yahoo!, and if you have already submitted to Yahoo! you should already have a decent website with a relevant targeted description to submit.

Site descriptions for the Open Directory should not be longer than 25–30 words. It usually takes around four weeks to index your site, but it could take more or less time depending on how many editors there are for the category you have submitted to and how efficient they are.

Submitting to multiple categories   The Open Directory does let you submit to more than one category, but you can't submit your site twice to the same directory. The directories that you choose have to be relevant. The best way to submit to multiple directories is first to submit your homepage to the most relevant category you can find, and then submit other pages from your site to other relevant categories. If these pages are relevant and individual enough, they will be accepted into that particular category. It's worth coming up with a new description for each page you submit, summarizing each individually. The Open Directory editor responsible for the category you submit your homepage to will decide if your homepage should be submitted to multiple categories. You should be careful, however, when submitting to multiple categories, as if you are too insistent and forceful the editor may think you are spamming the directory and not list your site. One good tip is to spread your submissions out over a period of time, as submitting them all at once (if you have a lot) will create the wrong impression – it is even worth waiting until one page has been accepted before going on to submit the next. Do not submit doorway pages to the Open Directory, and make sure that everything you do submit is relevant; you need to ask yourself if the page you are submitting would actually hold your attention if you went to it from the Open Directory listings.

You should remember that individual editors of the Open Directory will each have their own rules about spamming, and if you are unsure about how many sites a particular editor will accept you should email and ask; in most cases editors will be happy to give you assistance. The category editors are listed at the bottom of each category page.

Resubmission   You can safely resubmit if your site has not been listed within about six weeks. Before you do so, it's worth emailing the category editor to find out why your site was not accepted. If the category you submitted to does not have an editor, then you should email the editor of the category directly above the one that you chose to submit to. Following this, resubmit your site to the category you originally selected, and if this still does not work submit your site to the category above the one you chose previously. If you still don't have any luck, try emailing staff@dmoz.org; this will put your request in front of an actual staff member of the Open Directory.

If your site listings disappear   If you have only lost your listings for one editor, then you have probably only offended that editor and the rest of your listings will be OK. However, if all your site listings disappear it's very likely that you have violated the Open Directory's submission policies and been banned from the Directory altogether. You can email the Open Directory at staff@dmoz.org to appeal, but if you have been banned altogether it is unlikely that you will be reaccepted. The main things to look out for are:

- Affiliate lists. Do not submit your site if it is a list of products that link to an affiliate site such as Amazon; the Open Directory editors do not like this and you will not be accepted.
- Doorway pages. Do not try to submit doorway pages that simply redirect to another page on your site; you will be blacklisted for doing this. Some people also try to submit mirror sites to the Open Directory. These are sites that share the same content but have different URLs; the scam involves submitting each URL as an individual listing, and does not go down well at all with the editors.

Updating your listing   To update your listing, if this is necessary to reflect new website content, you should visit the category that your site is listed in and select the 'Update URL' link that is found at the top of the page. You're not really supposed to update your listing if you are merely not happy with it. The Open Directory states that you should only apply to update it if you need to:

- Replace an old URL with a new URL when it has changed
- Correct spelling and grammatical errors in the site's title and description
- Suggest a new title when the title on the site has changed
- Suggest a new description when the scope of the site has changed.

A form will appear to fill in that asks you to enter your URL, and then to edit the title and description of the site. You will also have to explain to the editor why you are updating your listing. Updates usually take a while to be acted upon, and if you are merely editing your listings to improve your ranking the editor will not be happy. Be careful when you are using this function, and only use it to update your listing when you really need to. As with resubmission, if your listing is not updated as requested, you should email the category editor; if that fails, email the staff at the Open Directory.

Special tips to get listed

As for Yahoo!, make sure your site is ready for submission. There should not be any broken links, and the content should be relevant and well presented. Remember, you are trying to impress the editor of a particular category. It also helps to add a link to the Open Directory to your website. If you want to get extra bonus points, link this back to a particular category; this will make the editor of that category more responsive to your submission. Editors of the Open Directory feel a sense of ownership over their particular categories as it is a volunteer-based service, so anything you can do to raise the profile of their category will impress them and make them more inclined to list your site.

Another tip is to become an editor yourself. You can do this be going to the category that you would like to edit, and clicking on the 'become an editor' link at the bottom of the page. This will bring up an application form. You will need to explain your expertise and interest in the subject, and whether you have a business interest in the category. It is unlikely you will be able to become an editor of a category that is directly related to your business, and it is also unlikely you will be able to edit the top level of a category; you should start at the bottom of the hierarchy and work your way up. The most important part of applying is to add two or three URLs of websites, including a title and description; you should take your time preparing this. If you have an interest in the performance of specific sites in a category, it is definitely worth becoming involved as an editor.

Useful links

Here are some useful links to help you find out more about the Open Directory:

- The Open Directory newsletter (http://dmoz.org/cgi-bin/newsletter/), which is primarily for editors of the Open Directory, but can also be viewed by the public. This will give you a good idea of how editors view the Open Directory, and what they will look for when deciding whether to accept sites.
- The Open Directory guidelines (http://dmoz.org/guidelines.html), which is again primarily for editors of the Open Directory, but will give you a good idea of the guidelines they are expected to follow. It outlines what is deemed as spam, the type of site editors like to accept, and how editors are selected or removed.
- The Open Directory feedback form (http://dmoz.org/cgi-bin/feedback.cgi?), which can be used to send feedback to Open Directory staff.

One of the best ways to start your SEO campaign is to get listed in the major directories. The main point here is that directory listings will make your site visible to many of the main spider engines as well as in the directories themselves.

Directory listings are reviewed and either accepted or rejected by human editors, and their content is organized into hierarchical categories. The major web directories looked at here are Yahoo! and The Open Directory Project. You should start with Yahoo!; a Yahoo! business category listing is essential for any serious business. The sign-up fee should not be a problem for most businesses, and represents great value for money when all is taken into consideration. Next, you should move on to the Open Directory, which is free, and will help your ranking in engines such as AOL Search, Google, HotBot, and Netscape. Remember that you can contact the Open Directory editors if you are having problems with getting your listing accepted.

As your submission will be reviewed and accepted or rejected by a human editor, the most important criteria for acceptance are the quality of your site, the category selected, and how well written your title and description are. Selection of the most appropriate category is very important and requires a fair amount of work. When submitting your site, submit your homepage URL through the particular directory's 'add URL' page. You can submit your site through using just the online form, but make sure you have all the necessary information at hand before you submit. Do a search on the directory for the keywords or phrases you would like to be found for, and see which categories return results. You then need to decide which is the most appropriate for your site. Check which other sites are in each category before deciding; if there are 100 sites in one and 20 in another you may be better off choosing the latter category, as your visibility will be higher. Most importantly, make sure the category is totally appropriate to your site. After you have chosen a category, submit your site.

You are presenting your site to another human, and therefore you should consider the process as the development of a relationship. Make sure you have read the submission guidelines outlined in this chapter, and be polite if you ever need to get in direct contact with an editor. Editors have the power to change your site title and description; if they decide to do this it will be for a good reason, but if you do not want it changed you must make sure that the copy is relevant and reflects your site's content accurately.

Write your site title first. If the directory specifies that the title must be your site name then you must comply, but where there is scope to go beyond this make sure you include your main keyword at the start of your title. Spend time writing your description, as it is very important – it is what a directory user sees when coming across your site in the directory. Make sure you keep within the specified word count for each directory, and that you weave your main keywords into the copy. Your description should be focused and read well, and not just be a list of keywords.

Chapter 5
Traffic and keyword tracking

How to research keywords for your website

Keywords are the heart and soul of SEO, if you choose the right words and phrases to promote and represent your website then your visitor will find you; if you choose the wrong words then you run the risk of leaving them confused and lost. When choosing keywords you have to strike a balance between those keywords that are highly competitive, that a lot of sites are using, and those that are not so competitive, but will drive less traffic to your site.

When deciding on a keyword, quantity of visitors should not necessarily be your top priority. Quality targeted traffic should be your goal, and you should be looking to optimize the pages on your site for the keywords that will bring the greatest number of prospects.

The first step in choosing keywords is to know your audience, to find out what terms people are using to search for your products or services. There are a number of tools for this which will be covered in more detail further into this chapter. The research you put in here will be invaluable to you. Do some searches to see what keywords your main competitor sites come up for; you may want to tap onto these. Look at the language that successful sites in your industry use to attract visitors – this is a great way to learn how you can effectively get your message across. Look at the log reports for your website and track the keywords used by visitors to your site; this will give you ideas on keywords that you might have missed out on and will show you how visitors are finding your site. Read online articles related to your industry, visit newsgroups and forums, and check out any related industry websites for research information.

Brainstorming is a great way to think of new keywords. There are tools out there that will do this for you, but it is also worth brainstorming yourself as these tools are just automated programs that do not have the wealth of information about your industry that you do. The first thing to do is to sit down and write down every word that you can think of that someone might use to track down your site. If your site sells running shoes then you might come up with the following as a start:

1 Shoes
2 Running shoes
3 Trainers.

These terms, however, are very general and you will find that web users can be very specific when they search. Though it is worth optimizing your site for general keywords, you will be up against much fiercer competition than if you concentrate on specific phrases and keywords, so it is worth going into much more depth on the keywords. Your list might look like the following:

- nike running shoes
- asics running shoes
- man running shoes
- best running shoes
- brook running shoes
- balance new running shoes
- adidas running shoes
- running shoes womens
- mizuno running shoes
- review running shoes
- running shoes trail
- nike running shoes womens
- discount running shoes, and so on . . .

The most important thing to bear in mind while you're brainstorming is that you should try to think of what *you* would look for when searching for your site; ask friends and colleagues as well and get their opinion. Once you have some strong major keywords you can branch out from there. A good rule of thumb is to come up with 40–50 keywords and phrases, and narrow down from there to about 20 of the most targeted. To help you decide which are the most effective keywords you should use some of the tools and packages that we're going to look at later in this chapter.

Keywords' page placement

Once you've brainstormed for keywords that will work for your site the next step is to actually position them. There are a lot of different places that keywords can go on your page, the more places you can place your keywords the better, but don't put them everywhere in a page as this is known as 'keyword stuffing' and can be seen as spam by search engines, which can potentially get you banned from their index.

You should only target 2–3 keywords for each page on your website. If, for example, you are building a travel website there is no way you can possibly cover the thousands of relevant keywords on your homepage alone, so you have to spread the keywords you have chosen throughout your site on relevant, targeted pages. Search engine spiders and robots are not intuitive and they will be looking for the strongest keywords on each page so they know to return that page when those keywords are searched for through their search engine. If your site is about 'landscape gardening' then you need to make sure this phrase appears regularly throughout the site copy and title tags, especially in the headers and at the start of paragraphs. The most important places to position your keywords are:

- Page titles
  The title of your page is the most important place to have your keywords, as it is generally given the most weight by search engines.
- Headlines
  Headlines have to be formatted using the <h1> to <h6> HTML tags, otherwise they won't be recognized by search engines. They are seen to carry more weight than the rest of the text in your site as they are usually used to identify a theme for a paragraph or to introduce a new section of content.
- Body copy
  The body copy of your site is the most obvious place a search engine spider will look for content. You have to work the keywords into the main body copy of the page, which is the copy that any user will see. If you cannot work the keywords into the main text then they should probably not be there.
- Links
  The links on the page are those words that are hyper-linked to other pages on your site. These are sometimes given more weighting than the rest of the words on your page.
- META tags
  Your META tags should contain your keywords. META tags are no magic solution though, and many search engines do not give them much weighting at all. Nonetheless it is worth putting any keywords that appear on a particular page into the META tags.
- ALT-texts
  This is the text that is used to describe images. You can see this text when you hover your mouse over an image. Make sure your ALT-text contains your keywords.

Page titles

The page title, as mentioned above, is the most important piece of information on each of your web pages for search engine optimization purposes. The words you use in the page title contain much more weight to search engines than any other content, and look like this in HTML code:

```
<title>Page title here</title>
```

Figure 5.1 *The title tag in a web page*

The page title can be found in the 'head' of an HTML page, and you should limit each of your page titles to about 60 characters. Google allows you 66 characters for your title and Yahoo! allows you 120, so if you need a long title use the main keywords in the first 66 to make it Google-friendly.

You should make sure that each of your pages has a unique page title, using the most important keywords on that page. The page title is also what users will see as the title that appears in the search results so it should also be a call to action for a user to visit your site. If you want your site, for example, to rank highly for the keywords 'landscape gardening london' then maybe a simple title like 'Landscape Gardening in London, Open 7 Days a Week' would be effective. Write a few different titles for each page on your site and then decide which one you think will be the most effective.

Bear in mind that your titles will also be used by website resource librarians, directory editors (such as the Open Directory), and other webmasters when they link to your website, so make them friendly. If you have simple, relevant titles that they can easily add to their pages then they will be more likely to do this and in turn link to your site. By writing relevant titles you will also receive more targeted traffic from these links.

META tags

META tags are keywords placed in the header of each of your website pages. META tags are hidden from web users, and are used by you to describe the content on your page. META tags are useful for search engines to better understand the content on your web pages, and it is highly recommended that you fill them in correctly. They are not a magic solution though, and you will not receive high rankings if you only fill in your META tags and nothing else.

Only keywords that appear in the page should appear in that page's META tags. There are lots of different types of META tags, but the only ones you will need to consider are the keywords tag and the description tag. The META tags are placed inside the header tag at the top of the HTML code just below the page title:

```
<head>
  <title>Page title here</title>
  <META NAME="DESCRIPTION" CONTENT="Put your description here.">
  <META NAME="KEYWORDS" CONTENT="Put your keywords here.">
</head>
```

META keywords

The keywords tag is often misused, we have seen many examples of site owners who stuff the tag full of keywords in the hope of getting a ranking for everything listed, even keywords that have nothing to do with the content on the Web page. It is because of this the many search engines do not give the META tag much weighting when indexing a web page as it is not a very reliable method. You should make sure each page on the site has its own unique set of META keywords, and you should never copy the same set of keywords for all your web pages, making sure the keywords you use are totally relevant to each particular page – a good rule of thumb is to only use words that are used in the body copy of the page. It isn't important to separate the keywords with commas as search engines will remove the commas before reading the keywords, but it can be useful to you as it will make it easier to read in the HTML code itself. Use the top 3-5 keywords for each page in that page's keywords, remember that the more keywords you use the less weight they will be given by the search engines.

META descriptions

The META description is used by some search engines to present a summary of the Web page along with the title and link to the page. Not all the search engines use META description, some will use the text from the body copy on your page and others will use a combination of the two, but you should make sure you have relevant META descriptions on all your web pages so that the search engines can read them if they need to. A META description is simply a description of the content on that page, so write a summary that is no longer than 150–200 characters long and include any keywords you have used on the page. Make sure the description is attractive and will entice users to click to check out your site.

Keywords in the URLs

There is a lot of debate over whether it matters if you include your keywords in your URLs. If you end up with a URL like www.running-shoes-london-discount.com, then this may look good for the search engines, but will be totally unfriendly to a site visitor. As a general rule, don't use hyphens if possible – they can prove very confusing. However if you can get a URL with keywords, such as www.sprite.net, that is easy to explain and remember then you should do so. The individual page names in your site can help boost your site ranking, so www.sprite.net/search.html could help boost ranking for the page if 'search' was one of the keywords on that page.

Keyword research tools

There are a number of keyword research tools on the Web that will help you identify the best keywords to target for your website. Here are a few of our favourites:

- Wordtracker – www.wordtracker.com. This is a great tool that will help you brainstorm for keywords, and then track their performance over all the major search engines. There is a small registration fee but it is well worth it. We use this tool regularly.
- Digital tracker keyword suggestion – http://www.digitalpoint.com/tools/suggestion. This is a great tool for tracking keywords. We use it regularly. It allows you to track your performance in Google for keywords you specify.
- Overture Keyword Selector Tool – http://inventory.overture.com/d/searchinventory/suggestion/. This shows how often a keyword was searched for in a month on Overture and all related searches for the entered keyword. An excellent tool for brainstorming.
- Google keyword tool – https://adwords.google.com/select/KeywordToolExternal. The Google keyword tool is a tool for generating keywords for your AdWords campaigns, but it is also a great brainstorming tool, and gives you an insight into what is being searched for on Google.

Copywriting for search engine optimization

How you present the body copy on each page in your site, and how the copy is phrased, including keyword placement, can make a huge impact not only on your site's search engine positioning, but also on its general success, as how you communicate information about your products or services is crucial in building site traffic. Here are some key points to bear in mind when writing web copy:

1 *Choose your keywords carefully*. Essentially you need to choose the most effective keywords for that page. If they do not fit comfortably into the rest of the text then they should not be on the page.

2 *Text length*. The optimum length for text on a web page is around 250 words. This will give you the opportunity to include your keywords, whilst also keeping your message relevant. 250 words will give site users the impression that the page has a good amount of content, therefore providing an element of security to them, and will also give the search engines plenty to index.

3 *Write smart*. Include each of your keywords or phrases 5–6 times each throughout the copy on a page. Don't stuff a page with keywords; if it becomes too crowded don't be afraid to cut some keywords out. Include keywords in the headlines and sub-headings of a page, as they

will receive more weighting from the search engines there, and include them in the links. Headlines on each page should be a call-to-action and should be around 50–75 characters each.

4 Remember when writing your web copy that you are writing for your site users rather than the search engine spider, and that good web copy is usually already search engine-friendly. It is important, however, to get to the point fast in your copy. When people read web pages they don't actually sit and read, they scan through, so you should use the 'inverted pyramid method', i.e. make your point first, then get through the supporting information second.

5 *Use the least amount of words for what you have to say.* Be concise – a web page of 2500 words is much less likely to be read than one of 250. It takes far more thought, planning and skill to make your point in fewer words.

6 *Write to a person, not a group.* Write conversationally and be enthusiastic. This will engage the reader and make you and your product appear more friendly and human.

7 *Don't talk down to your site users.* Be humble and your reader will feel more inclined to read what you have to say. Don't try to confuse your reader with jargon – you will look like you don't know what you are talking about.

8 *Spoon feed the information.* Try to present your information in the cleanest, most logical way possible.

Web traffic tracking and analysis

Many businesses build websites, invest in SEO and online marketing campaigns, but then devote no time or effort to analysing how well the site is performing. There are many easy-to-use, affordable tools to help you track website traffic, and you can even do it yourself using your site's log files. By tracking and analysing your website traffic you can do more than just check how many people are visiting your site; you can also track their behaviour through your website and evaluate the effectiveness of your online marketing efforts. Here are four reasons why you should be tracking your website traffic:

1 *Evaluation.* If you are spending a lot of time and money on pay-per-click keywords, and building reciprocal links, you need to know which ones are performing. By actively tracking your pages you will be able to see which are receiving hits, where the hits are coming from (including which search engines) and you'll be able to clearly identify areas for improvement.

2 *Knowledge.* Where is your traffic coming from? Why are you receiving that traffic? You need to know the answers to these questions.

3 *Site structure.* Tracking your traffic will let you see any defects your website has. Tracking software should allow you to see how many error pages are being generated when users visit a non-existent link, allowing you to catch any bad links that have slipped through your site's QA. Tracking software will also allow you to see what platform users are accessing your website from, and show you if there are any associated problems.

4 *User base.* Perhaps most importantly traffic tracking will allow you to understand your user base more effectively. You can track users as they move through your site, and see which pages are popular and which are getting no hits. Where users leave your site is also very important; identifying these 'exit pages' will allow you to work out why a user is leaving the site there.

Tracking terminology

You will encounter a wide range of terminology when monitoring traffic. Here is a breakdown of the main terms:

- *Visit.* These are all requests made to the site by a specific user in a period of time. A visit is over if a set period of time passes without any further accesses. You will be able to identify your users using cookies, their username or their IP address.
- *Hit.* A hit is a request for a file, not a web page. A visit may consist of a number of hits, including graphics, video and audio files, javascript files, and so on. Counting hits is different to counting page views, and many people give hit numbers when they should give page view numbers as the hit count will generally be much higher.
- *Page view.* This is the number of times an individual page is viewed as a whole entity.
- *Unique view.* A page view by a unique site visitor in a 24-hour period.
- *Referrer.* This is a page that links in to your site and is a great way to track who is linking to you (including search engines) and to see where your traffic is coming from.
- *User agent.* This is the software that is accessing your site. It can be used to describe a PHP script, a web browser or a search engine spider. You can track which search engine spiders have indexed your site by looking for their user agent, allowing you to see who has indexed you and how often you are indexed.

Ways to track your site traffic

Trackers. Tracking software can be used to count the traffic coming to your website. It will break visitor statistics down by date, time, browser type, pages viewed, and so on. There are a number of free tracker services available, but you will more often than not have to display their logo on your site as a button or graphic in exchange for the service. It is best to avoid these services unless you have no other means to execute tracking scripts on your server.

Using Your Internet Service Provider's (ISP) log files. Your ISP will keep log files which will record every single hit on your website. Analysing this data can be a perfect way for you to track where your site visitors are coming from, and what route they're taking through your site. It will also let you know which browser they are using and what pages they exit your site from. It is important you check with your hosting company that they offer access to the log files for your site before you sign up with them. The main types of log files are 'access', 'referrer', 'error' and 'agent'.

Access log

The access log will give you information on who has visited your site, which pages they have visited and the duration of time they spent on the site. This information is essential for you to keep tabs on whether your site is working for you.

Referrer log

The referrer log contains information about the source of the visitor to your website. If it was a search engine you will also be shown the keywords that were used to find your site. What follows is a list of the most common search engine robots that you can use to identify which search engines have visited and indexed your website. It contains the name of the search engine, what IP addresses they use and the name of their robot.

Often multiple IP addresses are used, in which case we just give a flavour of the names or numbers. Inktomi is a company that offers search engine technology and is used by a number of sites (e.g. www.snap.com and www.hotbot.com).

Wherever <nn> appears this indicates a number of different digits may be used.

Table 5.1

Search engine	Robot identifier	IP addresses
www.alexa.com	ia_archiver	green.alexa.com sarah.alexa.com
www.altavista.com	Scooter Mercator Scooter2_Mercator_3-1.0 roach.smo.av.com-1.0 Tv<nn>_Merc_resh_26_1_D-1.0	test-scooter.pa.alta-vista.net brillo.pa.alta-vista.net av-dev4.pa.alta-vista.net scooter.aveurope.co.uk bigip1-snat.sv.av.com mercator.pa-x.dec.com scooter.pa.alta-vista.net election2000crawl-complaints-to-admin.webresearch.pa-x.dec.com scooter.sv.av.com avfwclient.sv.av.com tv<nn>.sv.av.com
www.altavista.co.uk	AltaVista-Intranet jan.gelin@av.com	host-119.altavista.se
www.alltheweb.com	FAST-WebCrawler crawler@fast.no www.fast.no/faq/faqfastwebsearch/faqfastwebcrawler.html Wget RaBot Agent-admin/ webmaster@kisco.go.kr	209.67.247.154 ext-gw.trd.fast.no 202.30.94.34
www.entireweb.com	Speedy Spider	62.13.25.209

(Continued)

Table 5.1 (*Continued*)

Search engine	*Robot identifier*	*IP addresses*
www.excite.com	ArchitextSpider	Musical instrumentss are used in the name such as: viola.excite.com cello.excite.com piano.excite.com kazoo.excite.com ride.excite.com sabian.excite.com sax.excite.com bugle.excite.com snare.excite.com ziljian.excite.com bongos.excite.com maturana.excite.com mandolin.excite.com piccolo.excite.com kettle.excite.com ichiban.excite.com (and the rest of the band) more recently first names are being used like philip.excite.com peter.excite.com perdita.excite.com macduff.excite.com agouti.excite.com
(excite)	ArchitectSpider	crimpshrine.atext.com ichiban.atext.com
www.google.com	Googlebot googlebot@googlebot.com http://googlebot.com/	c<nn>.googlebot.com
(inktomi)	Slurp.so/1.0 slurp@inktomi.com	q2004.inktomisearch.com j5006.inktomisearch.com
(inktomi)	Slurp/2.0j slurp@inktomi.com www.inktomisearch.com	202.212.5.34 goo313.goo.ne.jp
(inktomi)	Slurp/2.0-KiteHourly slurp@inktomi.com; www.inktomi.com/slurp.html	y400.inktomi.com
(inktomi)	Slurp/2.0-OwlWeekly spider@aeneid.com www.inktomi.com/slurp.html	209.185.143.198

Table 5.1 (*Continued*)

Search engine	Robot identifier	IP addresses
(inktomi)	Slurp/3.0–AU slurp@inktomi.com	j6000.inktomi.com
www.infoseek.com	UltraSeek InfoSeek Sidewinder	cde2c923.infoseek.com cde2c91f.infoseek.com cca26215.infoseek.com
www.looksmart.com	MantraAgent	fjupiter.looksmart.com
www.lycos.com	Lycos_Spider_(T-Rex)	bos-spider<n>.bos.lycos.com 216.35.194.188
http://search.msn.com/	MSNBOT/0.1 http://search.msn.com/msnbot.htm)	131.107.163.47
www.northernlight.com	Gulliver	marvin.northernlight.com taz.northernlight.com
www.teoma.com	teoma_agent1 teoma_admin@hawkholdings.com	63.236.92.148
www.wisenut.com	ZyBorg (info@WISEnut.com)	–

A more in-depth list can be found on the Web at http://www.jafsoft.com/searchengines/ webbots.html, which is an excellent resource for user agents.

Error log

The error log is useful for you to track whether users are coming across errors when they visit your site, such as broken links. Usually the error log will contain the type of server, date and time of the visit, the error code generated and an explanation of the error and a path to the file that caused the error.

Agent log

The agent log provides you with information on which browser and operating system has visited your website.

Log files contain a huge amount of information about how your visitors are using your site and are an extremely important tool in site management.

Web traffic analysis software. These are tools that analyse your log files and create traffic reports that you can view over specific time periods. Depending on which software you use you will get different quality reports. You will generally get a free analyser installed on your hosting package, but you can also buy more advanced programs that will provide more management advice.

You should look out for the following features in a piece of web traffic analysis software:

- columnar and graphical format results, to help interpretation
- yearly, monthly, daily and hourly usage statistics
- the ability to display usage by site, URL, referrer, user agent (browser), search string, entry/exit page, username and country.

SEO software

It's not enough simply to optimize your website and hope for high traffic; you need to use tools and techniques to achieve success. A search optimization strategy is made up of three parts (Figure 5.2):

1 Subscription to commercial registrations
2 Page architecture and structure of your website
3 Links popularity.

Each one of these parts has a number of tools on the market that help to automate the processes, but before you can use these tools you need to have defined goals for your strategy. Even if the campaign just establishes name recognition, this is an admirable goal. Search engine marketing is no different from any other advertising or marketing campaign; all your goals have to be defined.

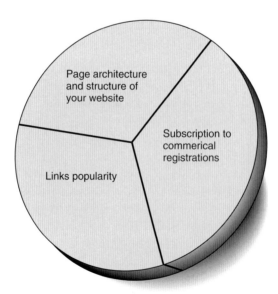

Figure 5.2 *The SEO pie chart*

Several types of data are needed to measure the success of the search engine marketing campaign, including:

- Search engine submission and ranking reports
- Click-through reports
- Monthly traffic reports, indicating unique visitors, search phrases with engines detail, entrance and exit pages
- Site administrative reports indicating number of users viewing
- Monthly sales data.

When you are working with a site that has a large number of new or changing pages, it would be ideal to have a tool that could do a deep submit to the various search engines, according to their different limits. You also need some page analysis tools, to help the service go beyond its submission roots. In an ideal world, your application would submit multiple pages from your site to the major crawler-based search engines and then measure the results. If a user tries to find you and you're listed, but not within the first 10–30 matches, the listing is almost worthless – no matter how many engines you submitted your site to. Ranking well on the major search engines is the ultimate goal. To help you to do this you need software tools, and some of these are described here.

Tools of the trade

Page generator
You need to create HTML 'doorway' pages based on keywords and details you enter about your business. This will give you a head start in reaching the top of the search list. These pages will also act as alternative entrances to your website, giving searchers a greater chance of finding you.

Submission tool
You must be able to submit any pages you choose to the most important search engines. Resubmitting can sometimes provide an extra bump up the charts, so the Submitter should be scheduled to resubmit regularly.

Reporter
This should be able to check your site's position in the major search engines. You must be able to find out how you rank on every keyword or phrase that is important to you, on all the major engines.

Scheduler
You must be able to activate the Reporter daily, weekly or monthly to check your website's positions automatically. You should be close enough to know immediately if your site stays

on top, falls in rank, or falls out of the index altogether. This allows you to release a new doorway page or re-optimize an existing one before sales start dropping. Submitting can also be automated by most schedulers on the market.

Traffic analyser

This tracks your visitors and where they came from automatically. It should be able to answer questions such as 'What keywords are people searching for to find my site?' or 'Which referring site sends me the most traffic?'

Identifying your best content

If you have a large site, you'll have the issue of not being able actively to submit all the pages you have within the submission limits of the major search engines. Search engines can and do crawl independently of what they receive via their Add URL pages. Submitting to Add URL pages is absolutely no guarantee that your pages will actually get listed. However, submission generally doesn't hurt, and can at least help to ensure that the search engines know about the pages you consider to be important. This is where good analysis tools can help you to understand which of your pages deserve priority in the submission stream. A good analysis chart will show you at a glance the 'index values' for each of your pages. You can think of this as a content quality rating, and you should be able to examine the location, frequency and uniqueness of the terms on the page.

There are a number of doorway page-checking services that will analyse your existing content to see if it can be improved. The problem with all of these services is that there are no actual rules for them to follow. One checker may say that a page is great, while another reports serious problems. You may, for example, find that your checker is counting words and thinks that there are too many in your title tag, although there are no particular limits published by the search engines regarding words or characters in a title tag. You should write a title of about 5–13 words in length, which uses some of your key terms and entices people to visit your site, but at the same time isn't misleading as to your site's content. If the checker queries this, you need to make a qualified decision – either to overlook this result or to try another checker.

If a checker does like your META keywords tag, then it has probably found that you do have the correct tag and that it is formatted correctly. Unfortunately, that is as accurate as the process gets. The rules are very few, and any enhancements on them are usually unique to a particular checker. The checker tries to guess what words you're trying to feature in your META tag by looking for phrases between commas in the META keywords tag. Unfortunately, commas are not required and can be detrimental to search engine ranking. As a result the checker gets confused, thinking, for instance, that you're trying to feature 'search optimization and checkers'. As it also can't find that phrase in the body copy, it reports that there are not enough keyword matches, which can result in a lower search engine ranking.

META tag checkers

META tag checking tools are less ambitious than page checking tools, and are much more widespread. They essentially look to see if you have a title, a META description tag and a META keywords tag. They also check to see that these are formatted correctly and, finally, that the lengths don't exceed general standards. For the record, most search engines that support the two major META tags allow a description of 200–250 characters and a keywords element of 1000 characters. Character length checking software will tell you if your tags use too many words. You need to be able to limit these word counts, as there are no rules and you can only base your decisions on experience. There are certainly no official rules regarding how many words META tags can have, although working to a count of 1000 characters appears to give the most flexibility across all the search engines.

Keyword density analysers

These are tools that tell you how frequently a term is being used in relation to other words in your documents. Imagine, for example, you have a website with 50 or 80 existing pages. You need software that can import all the files at once for analysis. You can then enter a search phrase, for the 'whole phrase', and you'll quickly be able to see which of your pages already use that search phrase with some frequency. These pages are the pages that you'll want to optimize for that phrase. Ensure that you use the search phrase as part of your page title and within your META tags. If you find that none of your pages actually use the search phrases you want to be found for, start reworking your body text to include these terms. A good density analyser can see the top three keywords or search phrases that each of your pages appears targeted toward, and by revising your page copy you can push up the values of particular words. Just use the page analyser again after making changes, to see how the scores have been changed.

It would be helpful to be able to choose what information you want to have displayed for each page – such as the page title and META tags. This information is usually available in other ways, but not in a unified table that can be downloaded. You should be able to tag pages that have been optimized in case you want to see only the pages in your site that are NOT optimized. The ability to sort by URL could also help if you want to find a variety of pages quickly, instead of having to locate them individually.

Rules for a perfect SEO strategy

People frequently ask questions about what 'rules' should be followed to construct the perfect page for each crawler-based search engine. How many times should a phrase appear on a page for top ranking? How often should a term be repeated in a META tag? How are spam penalties administered? The truth is that these statistics are not available but, from constantly search optimizing sites, analysing results and preparing strategies for the next approach, it is possible to gain an idea of what achieves results. There are always exceptions to perfect page formulas.

In this chapter we are trying to help you to identify the tools that plug into your site's natural traffic. After all, if you do not have an audience for your website, nothing you do in the long run will work. We are not suggesting that you go out and try to build perfect pages with these tools, quite the opposite – we want you to do everything possible to tap into your 'natural' traffic. So if you have already done the work on your content and site architecture, then the tools described here will be of great help.

If you choose to use automated submission software, try to do so responsibly by scheduling your Reporter missions, not over-submitting your URLs, avoiding the creation of hundreds of doorway pages, and not running Reporter on Google or any other anti-querying software. In fact, using any type of software that runs automatic queries on Google is against their terms of service, and so you run the risk of your IP address and/or site being banned. Remember that if you bombard the search engines, it is NOT going to help you achieve high rankings. Also, consider the fact that this book presents the concepts and approach of search engine marketing. As a discipline it is continually evolving, so never assume you know everything – this discipline can only be mastered through a continual culture of learning. Start each campaign by analysing the previous one, and in this way you will evolve the next solution as a step forward in your eStrategy. It is only when you have made hundreds of these steps that you will have achieved something significant.

Software exposed

Automated software has always had its fan club, and although management information software that both analyses and manages your campaigns can be very good, some submission software can have a devastating effect on your results. These autosubmit tools that claim to submit your website to 'thousands of search engines' turn out to be failures at attracting visitors, but excel at getting you thousands of pieces of unsolicited email. For $100 or more, they claim to be able to advertise to 100 000 or more engines. Most of these engines or directories are specialist industry engines – which is great if you are a restaurateur searching on a catering engine for new furniture, but not so good if you're not. The top 15 search engines will produce 95 per cent of the traffic for your site, so that's where you should be investing your money. In reality there aren't thousands of relevant search engines, and the majority of web surfers around the world use only a handful of portals for all their searches. Nearly three-quarters of all search-engine referrals come from the top four services – Yahoo!, Google, MSN and AOL Search.

So what about the other 'thousands' of search engines that autosubmission tools promote? These are mainly a way of collecting email addresses from naive owners of new websites. These 'hot' addresses are then sold as prime prospects to spammers, and can receive two to three thousand unsolicited emails. The 'hundreds of thousands' of search engines don't in fact exist, and instead many submission programs count entries they submit to 'free-for-all' (FFA) listings. These unedited sites accept anyone who submits a listing, but attract no visitors. Being listed in FFA sites may actually damage your ranking – if your site is new and you submit to a free-for-all engine, and then Google finds a thousand free-for-all links, it'll hurt you.

Experience has shown that most submission tools aren't necessary to get a website into the major search engines. Optimizing a site so it contains relevant search terms is a better use of your time than trying to get into 100 000 places. To research appropriate keywords you can visit Wordtracker, which offers a free trial service (see http://wordtracker.com/). Pick three or four words that you want people to associate with your site, and then make sure these words appear where search engines look for them.

Search engine submission software

The list of tools available can be broken up in to eight areas:

1 *Deep submission tools*. These tools are designed to submit many pages from your site to crawler-based search engines. They may also have other capabilities, such as page analysis features, but on the whole their main focus is on deep submission.

Position Pro – www.positionpro.com
eLuminator – www.inceptor.com
Web Position Gold – www.webpositiongold.com
Priority Submit – www.prioritysubmit.com
Search Mechanics – www.searchmechanics.com

2 *Multisubmission tools*. Multisubmission tools are designed to submit your website to hundreds of crawler-based search engines and human-powered directories at the same time. These tools should be reserved for targeting the many minor search engines that aren't worth the time required to do a manual submit. Free-for-all sites are likely to end up sending you a lot of spam, so use a temporary email address or one different from your main address for submission purposes. Most marketers prefer manual submission, and think that it is more effective.

Self Promotion – www.selfpromotion.com
Addweb – www.cyberspacehq.com
Dynamic Submission 2000 – www.submission2000.com
Jim Tools – www.jimtools.com
Submit Wolf Pro – www.trellian.com
VSE Befound – vse-online.com

3 *Position checking/tracking tools*. With these tools you can see how your pages are ranked on different search engines. A better way to measure search engine performance is through log analysis, which shows you the way in which people have come to your website. Position checking tools can place a burden on search engines, which is one reason why Northern Light blocks them. Google also may block some usage.

Agent Web Ranking – www.aadsoft.com
Be On Top – www.trellian.com

Rocket Rank – www.rocketrank.com

Submit It – www.submitit.com

Search Engine Power Pack – www.netmechanic.com/powerpack

Site Snare – www.sitesnare.com

Top Dog Pro – www.topdogsoftware.biz

Search Engine Commando – www.searchenginecommando.com

Web Ranking Reports – www.webrankingreports.com

Web Rank – www.webrank.com

4 *Page analysers/'perfect page' tools*. These are tools designed to help you produce the 'perfect page' for crawler-based services. Unfortunately, there is no guarantee that these perfect pages will actually rank well.

BruceClay.com SEOToolset – www.bruceclay.com

Position Weaver – www.positionweaver.com

Azooq – www.azooq.com

Search Engine Optimizer – www.se-optimizer.com

Search Mechanics – www.searchmechanics.com

5 *Keyword density analysers*. Many 'perfect page' tools provide keyword density analysis. These tools tell you how frequently a term is being used in relation to other words in your documents. Achieving the 'perfect' keyword density is no guarantee of ranking success.

Keyword Density Analyser – www.grsoftware.net

KeywordDensity.com – www.keyworddensity.com

Page Sneaker – www.sonicposition.com

Word Counter – www.wordcounter.com

6 *META tag checkers*. These tools are designed primarily to determine whether your META tag coding is correct. There are no official rules for META tags that the search engines follow; each search engine has its own set of unreleased filters to watch for excess repetition.

Idesignbusiness META Tag Generator – www.idesignbusiness.com/META_tag_generator.htm

Advanced META Tag Generator – miscellaneous.javascriptsource.com/advanced-META-tag-generator.html

HitBox Doctor – http://resources.hitbox.com/cgi-bin/page.cgi?tools/doc

Metty – http://www.clickfire.com/freeware/metty/

Search Engine Power Pack – www.netmechanic.com/powerpack/

Trellian MetaEditor – www.trellian.com

Sprite MetaBuilder – www.sprite.net/MetaBuilder

7 *Bidding managers*. These tools are designed to help you research and optimize paid listings with services like Google AdWords.

Bid Rank – www.bidrank.com

Go Toast – www.gotoast.com

PPC Bid Tracker – www.ppcbidtacker.com

Compare Your Clicks – www.compareyourclicks.com

PPC Bid Cap Calculator – paypermaster.com/bidcalc.html

8 *Link and support software.* Useful if you want to create Yahoo!-like listings of websites, or categorize information within your own site.

Hyperseek – www.hyperseek.com/

Links – www.gossamer-threads.com/scripts/links/

Bookmark Us! Script – http://javascript.internet.com/page-details/bookmark-us.html

See what people are searching for

- AltaVista Real Searches, at http://www.altavista.com/sites/search/real_searches
- Ask Jeeves Peek Through The Keyhole, at http://www.askjeeves.com/docs/peek/
- Espotting Keyword Generator, at http://www.espotting.com/advertisers/register01.asp
- Galaxy StarGazer, at http://www.galaxy.com/info/voyeur.html
- Google Zeitgeist, at http://www.google.com/press/zeitgeist.html
- Kanoodle Search Spy, at http://www.kanoodle.com/spy/
- MetaCrawler MetaSpy, at http://www.metaspy.com/
- Wordtracker, at http://www.wordtracker.com/
- Yahoo! Buzz Index, at http://buzz.yahoo.com/

Chapter 6
The mobile Internet

The wireless revolution

In the last five years we have seen the IT sector move its focus away from personal computing to mobile/wireless communications. Mobile phones have been gaining in popularity, and encroaching into the realms of PDAs and laptop computers. However, it's not just the popularity of mobile phones that has been so interesting to the marketer, but also the explosion of multimedia services. We have entered a new era – the 'all mobile' era in which mobile phones do it all. Many who read this book will have seen it in the Internet explosion, and if you are lucky enough to be as old as me then you will have seen it in the desktop publishing era. Marketing has changed. Let's look back a few years and try to define the foundations of the mobile era.

Mobile phones have become much more than entertainment handsets. Consumers already expect a high-end electronics experience from their state-of-the-art digital cameras, camcorders and game consoles. They are beginning to expect that same experience on their mobile phones, with a broad range of compelling, interactive content. Current 3G handsets now feature high-resolution colour displays, integrated video cameras, audio and video content streaming, Internet access at broadband speeds, location-based services, and multi-user 3D gaming. These rich computing environments will encourage and facilitate the development of business applications for mobile phones. We are finally seeing the convergence of the PDA, the mobile computer and a telephone in a single device. High-speed data transmission with UMTS/3G is widely available in most countries around the world. This has made mobile services more user-friendly, and mobile browsing more practical. The sheer power to transmit more information in a shorter timeframe means that connecting to any remote device is practical.

Mobile browsing is showing the strongest potential for growth in mobile services, as voice has become a commodity and SMS traffic levels are reaching an upper limit. Thirteen per cent of mobile subscribers reported accessing news and information via a mobile browser in the previous month. A marked gender difference characterized mobile browsing, with 17 per cent of men subscribers and 9 per cent of women subscribers using their mobile phones to access news and other information. Browsing activity was driven by a need for context-sensitive information. Over half of all browsers sought weather information (57 per cent), and more than 40 per cent of browsers accessed maps and directions (41 per cent), sports scores and sports news (44 per cent), national news (44 per cent), and movie and entertainment listings (40 per cent). When it comes to news and information on your mobile phone, subscriber propensity to consume has to do with who foots the bill, according to m:metrics. Mobile browsing is ushering in an era of 'always on, always with you'.

SMS is no longer the only way to bill mobile services. The arrival in the mobile world of other, more traditional, billing methods is shaking up revenue sharing. To make it as easy and quick as possible to pay for content, Bango.com, one of our WAP partners, determines the best payment option and presents this first. This decision is based on your country, your network operator and the amount of money you want to spend. The mobile phone provides people with a novel way of satisfying their need to communicate, to stand out from their peers and to stay informed. It is important to remember from the outset that the mobile phone did not create this need; rather, it has always been here.

Mobiles really took off in 1996, becoming fashion accessories for all. Although pre-pay vouchers were still around the corner, the cost of monthly subscriptions was finally within most people's grasp. The phones were bulky, there was no SMS, and reception was poor. For schoolchildren (who wouldn't be able to afford a mobile phone for another year or so), a new range of flashy transparent pagers was all the rage. The growth in the number of mobile phones in use has brought with it some significant changes, not only on a technological level but also in terms of the impact on society. The involvement of the mobile phone in the basics of everyday life has been a much more gradual process. Anyone who is interested in how mobile phone use has developed and grown will look to the Japanese model, which provides a useful case study. Not only has NTT DoCoMo had inconceivable commercial success in Japan with its i-mode brand, but the mobile phone has also reached the point where it is now a presence across all sections of Japanese society.

The Japanese model

In Japan, the mobile phone has been integrated into social and cultural life. Three reasons are given for this phenomenal growth in mobile phone usage in Japan: the mobile phone is personal, portable and pedestrian.

The mobile phone is personal

When your mobile phone is switched on, your cellular network provider knows exactly where you are in the world to within 100 metres or so. At any one time, your phone is usually able to communicate with more than one of the aerial arrays provided by your phone network. They're 10 or 20 kilometres apart (less in cities), and it's usually within range of at least three of them. Therefore, by comparing the signal strengths and time lags for the signals at each station, your network can triangulate your position and work out where you are. This is true whenever your phone is switched on, whether you're using it or not, because every so often it sends out a check signal to make sure everything is working as it should be.

The mobile as a personal statement; your phone reveals a great deal about who you are. This desire for individuality can also be seen in the straps and accessories which people in Japan use to decorate their handsets, and the clip-on fascias that are used to customize the external appearance of handsets all over the world. Users want to customize their handset as a way of injecting their personality into a characterless piece of technology. Whole businesses have grown around this personalization, and have been a key driver of mobile web access, both in Japan and elsewhere, with ring tone and wallpaper downloads proving to be the most popular sites on the mobile web (see Figures 6.1 and 6.2). Our own experience of building an MMS distribution system to send out wallpapers with fashion statements has helped the UK market to perceive the mobile phone as a fashion accessory. The Japanese term for the mobile phone – keitai – means 'something you carry with you'. People's mobile phones say a lot about their online social lives that they can carry with them wherever they go. The mobile has become a proxy for the information and social connections that are always at hand. People want to be connected and online any time, anywhere – and mobile phones provide this.

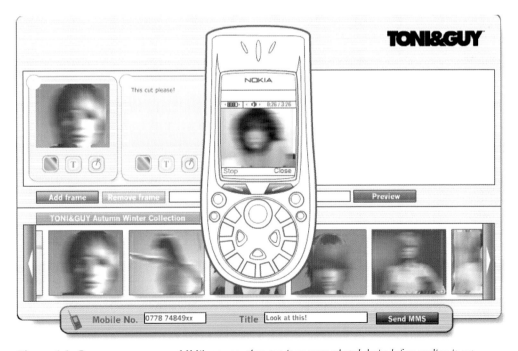

Figure 6.1 *Once you compose your MMS, you can then test it on your selected device before sending it out*

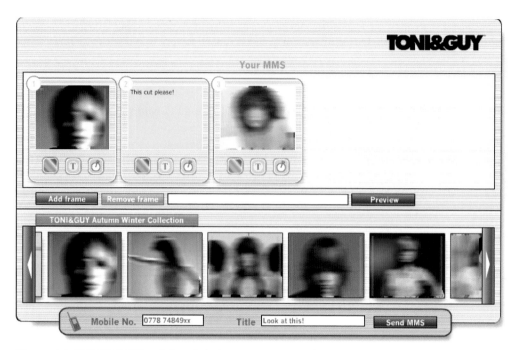

Figure 6.2 *TONI&GUY hair fashion for both MMS messaging and wallpaper distribution*

The mobile phone is portable

The mobile industry is no longer just the delivery of voice on a cellular phone. The introduction of data services, multimedia content and advertising means that many different types of companies are becoming involved with mobile phones. Media companies such as Reuters and Bloomberg now offer their business information through mobile phones. Entertainment companies like Disney sell cartoon characters and advertise via mobiles. It would be more accurate to think of the mobile phone as a device that provides what has been called 'always on, always with you' connectivity, of which voice is just one component.

Among young people in Japan, for instance, it has been observed that the mobile phone is not so much a phone as an email machine; for their counterparts in Europe and elsewhere, SMS text messaging plays a similar role. For young people used to surfing and communicating online with email, instant messaging and the Web, the mobile phone is the most important everyday tool that they have. Mobile phones are intimately tied to an individual, to an extent that colleagues and friends would never answer a mobile phone that belongs to someone else – even a spouse. In Japan, even a spouse looking at someone else's handset uninvited is socially unacceptable behaviour. When you call a mobile phone, you have a pretty good idea who will be on the other end of the line. Japanese teenagers much prefer to call their friends on their mobiles, as it allows them to avoid talking to a parent. It also provides young people with a real sense of freedom. In North Africa, pre-paid mobile phones have been credited for providing greater independence for young women.

The mobile phone is pedestrian

The mobile phone is pedestrian, both in that it is used while on the move and in that it has become a mundane, everyday item. Mobile phones provide a short-term engagement that has been compared to a coffee or a cigarette break as a kind of 'refreshment'. It is now illegal to use a hand-held mobile phone when you're driving, even when you're stationary at traffic lights or in a queue of traffic in most countries. Usage includes making or receiving calls or pictures, text messaging, and accessing the Internet. You must always pull over to a safe location prior to using the phone – risk using a hand-held mobile phone when driving and you risk a fine. You can also be prosecuted for using a hands-free mobile phone if you fail to have proper control of your vehicle.

Inbetween time

You can use a mobile phone to play a game while travelling on the bus to work, to listen to the radio while standing in the queue at the supermarket, or to catch up on the latest news headlines when you've got time on your hands. You have your mobile phone with you all the time, and you can use it to fill the downtime between your other activities. Camera phone users still prefer to use a traditional camera or a higher quality digital camera for what they consider to be their important photos, and camera phones are used instead to capture fleeting and mundane moments of everyday life.

Specifically universal

Carriers don't have a really strong track record of selling mobile marketing services. They're yet to provide 3G users with a compelling reason to use video calling, and selling MMS as 'like SMS, but a picture' didn't work out too well. MMS is finally starting to see some momentum as a content platform and delivery device, but many carriers still don't have much of an idea on how to sell users on P2P MMS.

In Japan, however, there are many specifics of the Japanese context that have led to such widespread acceptance and adoption of mobile phones. Cultural differences between continents or even between neighbouring countries – to say nothing of legal restrictions and other rules and regulations – can lead to variations in mobile usage and habits and the effective provision and marketing of mobile services. The desire to communicate more easily and have more timely access to information is universal. Many of the observations made regarding mobile phone use in Japan apply equally to mobile markets all over the world.

Location, location, location

Analysts are already predicting that location-based services will play an important part in the development of the mobile Internet. One of the most obvious technologies behind LBS is positioning, with the most widely recognized system being the Global Positioning System (GPS). Location-based services answer three questions:

1 Where am I?
2 What's around me?
3 How do I get to where I want to go?

They determine the location of the user by using one of several technologies for determining position, then use the location and other information to provide personalized applications and services. Traffic advisories, navigation help (including maps and directions) and roadside assistance are natural location-based services. Other services can combine present location with information about personal preferences to help users find food, lodging and entertainment to fit their tastes and pocketbooks. The fact that mobile phones are used on the move means that any information delivered to a phone can be rendered more useful if it is tailored to the user's location. If you search for a pizza restaurant on a mobile Internet search engine, for instance, you want the results to be sorted based on how near they are to wherever you happen to be.

Recent research

The gender gap

A piece of research we recently did for a client in the entertainment industry brought out some interesting results. For us, probably the most interesting revelation was that there is no gender gap when it comes to mobile game play. With the voice service penetration levelling out, mobile service providers are looking for new ways to generate revenue. Mobile content providers utilize successful Internet content in mobile phones to generate revenues. Creative mobile content will help earn big bucks for mobile content providers. There is a rapid expansion in mobile content market, with a sharp increase in 2.5G and 3G handset adoptions. The global mobile entertainment market will reach €18.6 billion in 2006 and will soar to €45 billion by 2009, says a new report from market analysts Juniper Research.

Some of the least focused mobile content is mobile blogging, mobile books and mobile search. In fact, these particular content areas have tremendous potential to compete with other major content areas by the end of the decade. Mobile books have the ability to attract people of all age groups and both sexes. First launched in Japan, mobile books have been a success – full-length novels, short stories and comic books can be read. Cellphone novels remain a niche market compared with ring tones, music downloads and video games, says Yoshiteru Yamaguchi, Executive Director of NTT DoCoMo.

Regarding mobile games, 31 per cent of female subscribers and 34 per cent of male subscribers report having played in the previous two months. What is interesting here is that men are 65 per cent more likely to download a game than are women. The main reason for this disparity is that too many of the titles available for sale are action/adventure and sports games – genres that are more likely to appeal to men. Ring tones aren't just for teens. A teenager's penchant for reckless spending, helped along by advertising from ring tone providers, has turned the ring tone market over the last five years into a major earner. However, a crackdown of sorts in 2005 began with a code of conduct. In addition, the availability of MP3 from the major record labels is leading to a decline in the traditional ring tone market.

Text messaging

Text messaging has wide appeal and can lead to behavioural addictions and increased security risks, according to a renowned psychiatric clinic in Britain which has reported a huge rise in 'technology addictions'. Citing text messaging is an example of such a behavioural addiction; the clinic has noted that some patients spend up to seven hours a day in Internet chat rooms or SMS texting.

Over half – 70 per cent – of subscribers aged 25–34 years had sent or received text messages in the previous month, while 40 per cent of those aged 35–44 communicated via text. Among younger subscribers texting is ubiquitous, with 85 per cent of those age 18–24 sending and receiving text messages. Of those aged over 65 years, 20 per cent use text messaging. Relative to its size, T-Mobile is the market leader in text messaging, with more than half of its subscribers using the service.

Photo messaging

Photo messaging is still a fledgling service. More than 60 per cent of subscribers who took a picture with their camera phone had also sent a photo message to another phone or email address in the previous month. The fact that people aren't just taking pictures but are starting to send them as well indicates that operator enthusiasm for the service may be well-founded. While the overall penetration of photo messaging is still low, at 10 per cent, Sprint has taken an early lead with 12 per cent of its subscribers sending a photo to another mobile subscriber.

We have been involved in MMS delivery for a number of years, with our most successful campaign for retailing java applications being the sending of MMS to previous subscribers with sound, promoting the game 'Pub Fun Duck Shoot'. From the 10 000 distributed MMSs we had a take-up rate of 5 per cent, which resulted in 500 downloads within the first 24 hours of issuing the MMS. Our experience shows that you can expect response to be near immediate, with traffic still coming in within 24 hours.

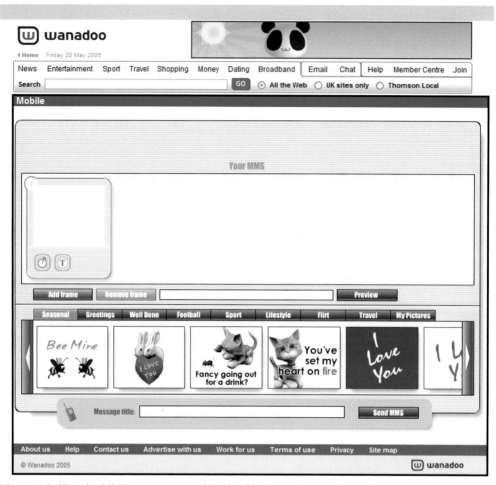

Figure 6.3 *Wanadoo MMS composer, run and developed by Sprite Interactive Limited*

Table 6.1 shows the European mobile subscriber consumption of content and applications in May 2005. When it comes to news and information on your mobile phone, subscriber propensity to consume has to do with who foots the bill. Those with corporate accounts or accounts that are otherwise subsidized by their employer are significantly more likely to use the browser on their handset to access that kind of data, compared with subscribers who are personally responsible for their bill.

Our own analysis shows that consumers want their 3G mobile phones to receive travel alerts, redeem coupons and pay for car parking tickets, i.e. to have simple, straightforward functionality both now and in the future. However, voice calls and SMS messaging are clearly currently the main functions of a mobile device. Ironically, media content (such as watching videos or listening to music) was absent from our 'top 10' list. When we asked what the most interesting future

Table 6.1 *European mobile subscriber consumption of content and applications in May 2005*

Content/application	Percentage of subscribers (%)
Sent or received text	40
Received text message alert	9
Sent photo message	11
Used mobile messenger	9
Used mobile email	18
Downloaded mobile game	5
Downloaded ring tone	16
Downloaded graphic	7
Accessed news via browser	15

function would be, many respondents were looking forward to using their phones to help speed up and simplify various financial transactions.

Today's top 10 mobile functions:

1 Voice
2 SMS
3 Alert subscriptions
4 Calculator
5 Taking pictures
6 Mobile gaming
7 Using operator portals
8 Mobile search
9 Surfing WAP sites
10 Alert subscriptions.

Tomorrow's top 10 wish list:

1 Travel alerts
2 Parking meter payment
3 Special offers and general marketing communications
4 Season tickets
5 Credit/debit cards
6 Flight check-in
7 Vending machine payment
8 Retail checkout

9 Loyalty cards

10 Mobile coupon redemption.

Understanding the wireless world

In the rest of this chapter we will look at the different types of companies that make up and profit from the wireless world. We'll then take a look at the different technologies and systems in place in the wireless world, in order to give you the basic understanding to make the most of the rest of this book. There are several types of companies that operate in the wireless world, and the number is growing as the industry expands. All these companies are important parts of the overall structure, and all of them generate revenue from it; they range from the behemoth network operators down to the ring tone and content aggregators. As the mobile industry has now turned from a specialized technology market to a mass consumer market, practically any company can enter the wireless world; the question that needs to be asked is – how can a company best profit from the range of services on offer?

The main players in the wireless world

1 *Phone users*. These are the end-users who use all the services, whether they are aware of it or not. They are the 'grass roots' of the wireless world.

2 *Network operators*. Network operators are the 'overlords' of the wireless world; without network operators there would be no networks. Each country has a number of competing network operators (see Appendix A). The main network operators in the UK are Vodafone, Orange, T-Mobile, O2, and 3. Operators route messages, bill phone users and collect revenue from them. There is some crossover with fixed landline operators in some countries, but generally they are separate entities.

3 *Access providers*. These are go-betweens for companies and mobile networks. They offer companies a window to the wireless network and let them take advantage of the technologies on offer (GPRS, SMS, WAP, etc.). An access provider will manage commercial and technological relationships with network operators and will try to guarantee a quality ('always-on') service.

4 *Platform providers*. Platform providers are similar to access providers, except that they go one step further to provide a software-based platform to enable the launch of a mobile-based service. They handle the whole process, from user experience through to network billing and customer support, and because of this they need to work closely with and have an in-depth knowledge of the other service providers in the wireless world.

5 *Content and application developers*. With the advent of rich media browsing on mobile phones, content developers became an essential part of the wireless world – and an important extra revenue stream both for themselves and for the rest of the industry. Sprite Interactive is one of the top content providers in the UK, and this company, like a number of other content providers, will produce topical and entertaining content for mobiles, either to specification or as part of their own in-house catalogue. Examples of mobile content include news streams, ring tones, logos, Java games, videos, Java applications, and so on.

6 *Content aggregators and publishers*. These are the companies that sell the content developed by content and application developers directly to the phone users. There can be some crossover

between content aggregators and content developers, but generally the two areas are separate. Content aggregators generally advertise products in magazines and newspapers, from their own web portal and on the television. Examples of large content aggregators are redsuitcase.com (Figure 6.4) and Mob.tv.

Figure 6.4 *The redsuitcase website – www.redsuitcase.com*

7 *Corporate companies.* This group includes all kinds of companies who have an interest in the wireless world as a means of communicating with their customers, employees and suppliers, and generating revenue.

8 *Marketing and media agencies.* These agencies are involved in the wireless world on a strictly consultancy level, advising companies on how best to penetrate the wireless world.

9 *Mobile consultants.* There is usually some crossover here with access or platform providers. Mobile consultants advise companies on how best to define and implement their wireless strategy. As briefly mentioned above, there is a large amount of crossover in the industry between the different types of players. A number of content developers also run sites to sell their content, so can also be defined as content aggregators, and many of the platform and access providers are also aggregators. Each company needs the others in order to best profit from the wireless world. As well as asking how can they profit from the wireless world, companies also need to ask how much revenue they are going to make once the idea has filtered its way down to and then through all the other companies above them. It is also worth noting that below network operator level there is now a large number of companies offering very similar services, so to get the most from access and platform providers it's best to consider a number of different options. Some of the best and most imaginative mobile content is coming out of smaller, independent development houses.

Mobile virtual network operators

A mobile virtual network operator (MVNO) is a mobile operator that does not own its own spectrum and usually does not have its own network infrastructure. Instead, MVNOs have business arrangements with traditional mobile operators to buy minutes of use (MOU) for sale to their own customers. Many are familiar with resellers of telecom services such as long distance, local exchange and mobile network services. MVNOs are similar, but they will usually add value – such as brand appeal, distribution channels and other benefits – to the resale of mobile services. An example of a UK-based MVNO that has done this is Virgin Mobile, which provides SMS messaging for as little as 3p per text. Successful MVNOs are those that have positioned their operations so that customers do not distinguish any significant differences in service or network performance, yet offer some special affinity to their customers. Well-diversified independent MVNOs can offer a product mix that traditional mobile operators cannot match – for example supermarket MVNOs could offer a package of shopping rewards and benefits. MVNOs have full control over the SIM card, branding, marketing, billing and customer care operations.

Business issues

The major benefit to traditional mobile operators cooperating with MVNOs is to broaden the customer base at a zero cost of acquisition. It is likely that traditional operators will continue to embrace MVNOs as a means of deriving revenue to offset the enormous cost of building new networks. As more MNVOs expand in the marketplace, they are likely first to target pre-paid customers as a means of low-cost market entry themselves. MVNOs are a means of encouraging competition, which ultimately leads to greater choice and lower prices.

Wireless technologies

Now we have covered in brief the main players in the wireless world, the majority of the rest of this chapter will be spent looking at the main different technologies in the wireless world. The wireless industry is one based on advanced technology, so before embarking on a wireless campaign or strategy you should arm yourself with the necessary knowledge to be able to understand and take advantage of this technology. The areas that will be covered are WAP and the mobile Internet, messaging (SMS/MMS), i-mode, application environments (Java, Flash, Symbian), and 2G and 3G networks. A number of these areas are covered in much more detail later in the book; this chapter aims to give you the basic understanding of them to begin your journey into the wireless world.

WAP and the mobile Internet

WAP stands for Wireless Application Protocol, and it is the standard by which mobiles and some PDAs access the Internet; for example, if you are told to access a WAP site from your mobile, you are accessing a mobile Internet site. WAP is used to deliver information to mobiles and as a gateway to download content, so it is a very important part of the wireless world. The most recent version of WAP is WAP 2.0, which is a step up from the fairly basic WAP 1.0. It allows the user to download rich content and to have content 'pushed' through to them, and lets developers create pages that are much closer to standard websites in look and feel. Building an effective WAP site is covered in much more detail in Chapter 8.

Messaging

Without doubt, one of the main areas of growth in the wireless world over the past four or five years has been in messaging. To give you an idea of the vast numbers of messages sent, on New Year's Eve 2004 alone in the UK 111 million SMS messages were sent!

There are four main messaging technologies:

1 SMS
2 Smart messaging (from Nokia)
3 EMS (Enhanced Messaging System)
4 MMS.

SMS was the first of these technologies to emerge, and it started life as a straightforward person-to-person messaging service which succeeded because it was simple to grasp, and support for it was so widespread. SMS lets you send and receive messages made up of text and numbers to and from mobile phones (and specially equipped landlines). Nokia created an extension to SMS, called smart messaging, that is available on more recent Nokia handsets. This form of messaging can be used for over the air (OTA) phone configuration and updates, picture messaging, logos, and so on. The value of smart messaging is that messages can be sent over the standard SMS infrastructure and therefore operators do not need to upgrade their infrastructure. EMS emerged between SMS and MMS, and allows the sending of relatively simple media and extended text messages. MMS is a rich version of SMS; it has been accepted as standard by the 3GPP (the mobile standards authority), and it enables the sending of sounds, pictures and video to and between handsets. MMS messages take the form of short presentations, and the use of MMS as a business tool is wide and varied; for example in animated business cards, greeting cards, cartoons and maps.

What is SMS?

The first SMS message was sent in December 1992 from a PC to a mobile phone on the Vodafone network. SMS is currently one of the most widely used wireless technologies, and its usage amongst phone users remains very high. It accounts for around 60–80 per cent of average revenue per user (ARPU) and, though its percentage of total ARPU is decreasing due to the emergence of other communication technologies, its usage will remain steady. In the top 20 European countries over 200 billion SMS messages are sent each month, but the usage of SMS goes far beyond peer-to-peer communication; it is a great business tool for interacting with end-users, and it provides a convenient and widely accepted way of billing the user.

How an SMS message is sent

SMS messages are generally no more than 140–160 characters in length, and contain no images or graphics. When a message is sent it is received by a short message service center (SMSC), which must then get it to the appropriate mobile device. To do this, the SMSC sends an SMS request to the home location register (HLR) to find the roaming customer. Once the HLR receives the request, it will respond to the SMSC with the subscriber's status: (1) inactive or active; and (2) where the subscriber is roaming. If the response is 'inactive', then the SMSC will hold onto the message for a period of time. When the subscriber accesses their device, the HLR sends an SMS notification to the SMSC, and the SMSC will attempt delivery. The SMSC transfers the message, in a short message delivery point-to-point format, to the serving system. The system pages the device and, if it responds, the message gets delivered. The SMSC receives verification that the message has been received by the end-user, then categorizes the message as 'sent' and will not attempt to send it again.

An SMS message is made up of two parts. The first is the header, which is the message protocol information, and includes the sender's address, type of coding and message validity. The second consists of the data – that is, the body of the message with the information to be transmitted. An SMS can be interpreted with three types of encoding: 7-bit, which is the code for the Latin alphabet; 8-bit, which is the code for data; and 16-bit, which is used for Greek and Arabic alphabets (the number of characters for 16-bit is limited to 70).

There are two types of SMS transmissions: mobile originated (MO) and mobile terminated (MT). MO messages are messages sent from a mobile phone; these can be sent to another mobile, a computer or a landline. MT messages are messages sent by the network to a mobile phone. To enable the identification of corporate servers by the networks specific numbers can be used; these are called shortcodes.

Benefits of SMS as a marketing tool

What would get your attention – a printed letter telling you when the installer is coming to connect your broadband, or a text message the day before, reminding you not to go out? The business use of SMS is wide and varied, and it provides a unique intimate link with your customer base. Advantages of text messaging as a communication tool include the following:

1 *Texting is reliable.* Text messaging is generally reliable – you're more likely to get a message twice than not receive it at all. Also, as you can tell when a message has been received, you can automatically resend if it hasn't arrived within an acceptable time.
2 *Texting is quick and easy.* Text messages are ideal for getting information to employees who are rarely at their desks, or for sending out information to thousands of customers at the press of a button. Texting has become such a part of everyday life that 'txtspeak' dictionaries have emerged, with characters and words developed specifically to speed up the texting and communication process.
3 *Texting is cheap.* It is generally cheaper to send out text messages than to communicate by phone or direct mail. The pricing model for SMS as a whole is simple; the end-user will pay a fixed rate for each message, and intense competition in the market has helped keep costs low.
4 *Texting is discreet and confidential.* Incoming messages are discreet and will not interrupt the person you are communicating with to the same extent as a phone call. It can be easier to text than to talk, and it does guarantee an extra level of privacy.

What is MMS?

The multimedia messaging service (MMS) adds images, text, audio clips and, ultimately, video clips to SMS (short message service/text messaging). Although SMS and MMS are both messaging technologies there is a dramatic difference between the two of them as far as content goes, with the average size of an MMS message being much larger than that of an SMS message. At the heart of MMS technology is the synchronizes multimedia integration language (SMIL) application, which allows the creation and transmission of 'presentations' over a mobile phone. These presentations take the form of miniature slide shows, much like a scaled-down version of Powerpoint. SMIL lets the user define what each slide contains, the timing for each slide, and the order in which the slides appear. SMIL data is not necessary and is not supported by certain handsets, but without the SMIL code MMS data is displayed as successive content that the user must scroll through.

Unlike SMS messages, which are sent through GSM, MMS messages are sent through WAP. This means that additional network infrastructure has had to be developed. The MMS Centre (MMSC) is the key point of an MMS network. When a message is sent, WAP carries the message between the MMSC and the mobile phone. When an MMS message is composed and sent to another phone, it is transmitted from the sender's handset via WAP to the sender's operator's MMSC. This operator then sends it to the MMSC of the operator of the recipient's handset; the recipient's operator then sends the recipient notification that there is an MMS and, once the recipient opens the notification, the MMS is sent through to their handset from their operator's MMSC.

This works in the same way if a subscriber wants to download an animated logo or wallpaper; once the content provider has received the subscriber's request, the provider will send an MMS to the subscriber's operator's MMSC. This operator then sends the subscriber notification, and they can then download the MMS in the same way as before. The beauty of MMS is that it provides a complete development and billing environment. Sprite Interactive has worked extensively with MMS since its launch, developing the MMS composer application for Freeserve (Wanadoo) (Figure 6.3).

MMS is significant because:

1 It is a natural evolution from text messaging, which already has a large user base, especially in Europe and Asia
2 It has support from key operators and industry players
3 MMS messages can be sent to and from email
4 Richer applications can be developed using MMS than with SMS.

Unlike SMS communication, MMS communication is not necessarily discreet, i.e. rich media lends itself to being 'flaunted' rather than remaining discreetly in the background. This trend is already noticeable with richer media such as ring tones. A popular example of MMS in action is photo messaging (using an inbuilt camera to take a photograph and then sending that photograph as a message or an email). Other examples of where the technology has been used include:

- weather reports with images
- stock quotations with diagrams
- slideshows of football goals
- animated business cards or maps
- video messages with the use of 3G networks.

MMS has not proved to be as successful as many people in the industry predicted when it was launched, and its use today is mainly for photo messaging; there are several reasons for this. First, there is an education and ease-of-use issue. MMS is not as simple to use as SMS and, as a communications tool, is more on a par with email; it is simply easier to send an email than it is to send an MMS, and it is easier to send an SMS to communicate with someone than it is to send an MMS. With SMS a user can be sent an address to download images or videos onto their mobile; it is easier to follow this kind of message than to receive the same content by MMS, which may also have size restrictions. Moreover, many phones do not come set up for MMS, and phone users may need to call their operator to find out settings, and then have to enter these into their phone manually. This may deter many phone users who do not want to change settings on their phone. Finally, and probably most importantly, is the issue of price. MMS messages are at least twice as expensive as SMS messages, and sometimes more; this is clearly off-putting to phone users.

i-mode

i-mode is NTT DoCoMo's mobile Internet access system, widely popular in Japan. The 'i' in 'i-mode' stands for information. i-mode is also a whole multibillion-dollar ecosystem, and is part of Japan's social and economic infrastructure. Approximately 30 per cent of Japan's population uses i-mode about ten times or more a day, and the system allows them to send email, to book train tickets and to perform other Internet-style activities. There are over 42 million i-mode subscribers in Japan out of a total mobile market of around 70 million, which is a considerable share. i-mode started in Europe (Netherlands, Germany, Belgium, France, Spain, Greece and Italy) in April 2002, and expanded to Taiwan and Australia during 2004.

What is the difference between i-mode and WAP? Both i-mode and WAP are complex systems. There are several important differences in the way i-mode and WAP-based services are presently implemented, marketed and priced. i-mode uses cHTML, which is a subset of HTML and is relatively easier to learn for website developers than WAP's mark-up language 'wml'. Another difference is that at present in Japan i-mode is 'always on', while WAP systems in Europe operate on a dial-up basis. Another major difference is that at present an i-mode user is charged for the amount of information downloaded plus various premium service charges, while WAP services are charged by connection time.

The success of i-mode

There is no single reason why i-mode has been so successful; its success is due, to a large extent, to the fact that NTT-DoCoMo made it easy for developers to develop i-mode websites. In Japan, home PCs are not as widespread as in Europe and the USA, so Japanese people tend to use their i-mode handsets more for Internet access than do Europeans or Americans. A low street price to Japanese consumers for i-mode-enabled handsets means that there is a low entrance threshold; this, combined with the Japanese population's general love of gadgets, has caused the market to become flooded with i-mode-enabled handsets. The i-mode system is also relatively inexpensive to use, being 'always on'. Moreover, the billing system that i-mode uses (micro-billing) makes it easy for subscribers to pay for value-added premium sites, and is attractive for site owners wanting to sell information to users. The i-mode system has been effectively marketed in Japan as a fashionable accessory, which has definitely helped, and the use of cHTML for site development has led to an explosion of content, as ordinary consumers have been able to develop content. The presentation of content has also helped i-mode to grow, as it is so easy to get to grips with, and the AOL-type menu list of partner sites gives users access to a list of selected content on partner sites that are included in the micro-billing system and can sell content and services.

Business applications for i-mode

There are many business applications for i-mode. Both content and services can be sold on i-mode; for example, airlines sell air tickets via i-mode, media companies sell cartoon images via i-mode, securities houses sell shares and investments via i-mode, and Japanese government lottery tickets are sold via i-mode. The subscriber can have a virtually private network on i-mode. Many companies use i-mode for customer relationship management (CRM). Since about one-third of Japan's population uses i-mode practically every day, i-mode allows companies to engage in dialogue or other interactions with a large part of Japan's population.

Application environments

There are currently three main application development environments for mobile phones: J2ME, Symbian and Flash Lite. We'll look at a very brief overview of the environments here.

J2ME is the environment with by far the most widespread handset support. The majority of games and applications on sale today have been developed in J2ME; it is a versatile environment, and as handsets get more powerful so does Java support. Symbian content is restricted to Symbian handsets, for example high-specification Nokias, Sony Ericssons, and so on. Symbian applications tend to be much richer than J2ME, with enhanced features and graphics, but are generally priced higher. Flash Lite is the newest application environment, but could make the biggest impact of the three once handset support is widespread enough. Flash Lite opens up the Flash environment to mobile developers, which will lead to advanced user interface development, widespread sound and graphic support, and universal network connectivity, so developers can create dynamic applications which obtain data from existing web services or download different portions of an application based on what the user is doing on their handset.

Mobile generations

What are 1G, 2G, 2.5G, 3G and 4G?

Technically, generations are defined as follows:

- 1G networks (NMT, C-Nets, AMPS, TACS) are considered to be the first analogue cellular systems, which started in the early 1980s. There were radio-telephone systems even before that.
- 2G networks (GSM, cdmaOne, DAMPS) are the first digital cellular systems, which were launched in the early 1990s.
- 2.5G networks (GPRS, CDMA2000 1X) are the enhanced versions of 2G networks with data rates of up to about 144 kbps.

- 3G networks (UMTS FDD and TDD, CDMA2000 1X EVDO, CDMA3000 3X, TD-SCDMA, Arib WCDMA, EDGE, IMT-2000 DECT) are the latest cellular networks, which have data rates of 384 kbps and more.
- 4G is mainly a marketing buzzword at the moment. Some basic 4G research is being done, but no frequencies have been allocated. The 'fourth generation' could be ready for implementation around 2012.

What is so important about 3G?

Today's 3G networks provide high-speed, high-bandwidth support to bandwidth-hungry applications such as full motion videos, video calling and full Internet access. With 3G you can watch music videos, chat with your friends via video calling, send video messages and even watch mobile TV. 3G roll-out has so far been quite slow, but expect to see 3G-enabled applications and content becoming widespread across mobile networks and service providers.

Why have a WAP search engine?

First, using an ordinary search engine through a wireless device may not be possible or inconvenient. WAP search engines should be designed for low-bandwidth and small screen viewing. More importantly, an ordinary search engine is going to direct you to normal web pages, which again aren't designed for hand-held devices. A WAP search engine will direct you to WAP pages, all of which are specifically meant for your device.

The so-called mobile Internet is seen as the next big battleground for web giants such as Google and eBay. According to Yahoo! chief Terry Semel, while a billion people around the world have PCs, around three billion have mobile phones.

Google WebSearch on your phone or mobile device can search through 8 billion pages. While on the go, you can use the Web to find ingredients for a recipe, answer a trivia question to prove that you're right or find facts on your favourite sports team. To access a WAP search engine:

1 Access the mobile Web browser on your phone or mobile device.
2 Type www.google.com in the URL field (if you get an error message, type www.google.com/xhtml*).
3 Type your search query.
4 Highlight the 'Google Search' button and press 'Enter'.
5 Ten search results will appear on the page. You can scroll down to the bottom of the page; select the 'Next' link to view the next ten results.
6 Once you have selected a link, Google will reformat the selected web page to fit your phone screen as in Figure 6.5.

Figure 6.5 *Lifestyle WAP pages*

Chapter 7

Page design and page architecture

Placement tips and page architecture

A search request on a search engine turns up thousands or even millions of matching web pages. Most users never visit the pages beyond the ten 'most relevant' matches on the top page, so there is intense competition to be in the top ten. It's rare for users to visit the following pages of matches; being listed at eleven or beyond means that most people will miss your site. Some esoteric products or product names are more likely to be in the top ten; however, sometimes a large community in other industries shares the most ambiguous product labelling. This creates a problem not only for the search user but also for the search engines, which have to create millions of indexed pages to cater for this.

Keyword density is an important part of this labelling process because search engines use this information to categorize a site's theme, and to determine which terms the site is relevant to. The perfect keyword density will help achieve higher search engine positions. Keyword density needs to be balanced correctly (too low and you will not get the optimum benefit, too high and your page might get flagged for 'keyword spamming').

An interesting case study is a client of Sprite Interactive, EMB, an actuarial company that creates its own software and has a product called prisEMB. The last three characters happen to be EMB's name. Most people who know the product name will almost certainly know of the website; however, people who do not know the correct spelling of the product are going to have a problem. The following section will look at some solutions to this problem.

Site architecture can definitely impact your results with search engines. Most search engines don't know anything beyond two directory levels, but they'll index 40–50 files in those directories alphabetically. So you must place your most important pages at the first or second directory level, breaking them up into 50 files per directory. Be sure to name your files and directories with your keywords, and don't use the underscore to separate keywords – use hyphens instead.

Entry pages

These pages are sometimes known as landing pages, and are the pages that bring traffic to the site. Once you have decided what entry pages you need, you should optimize them and then submit each of these pages to the search engines. Treat these as stand-alone pages, just like your homepage. When visitors land on one of your entry pages, will they know where they are? Who you are? What the page is about? Include full navigation on all entry pages, and make it obvious what the page and site is about. Don't assume that visitors will find the index page first.

If users don't quickly see what they are looking for, they'll leave your site frustrated and may never return to your site. Here are some pointers for making sure that doesn't happen:

- Link to the page on your site that provides the most useful and accurate information about the product or service in your ad.
- Ensure that your landing page is relevant to your keywords and your ad text.
- Try to provide information without requiring users to register. Or, provide a preview of what users will get by registering.

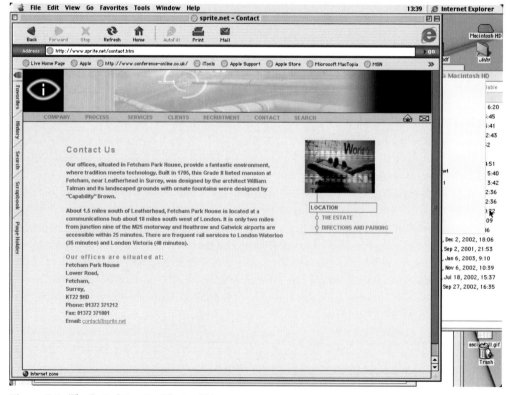

Figure 7.1 *The Sprite Interactive 'Contact Us' page*

- In general, build pages that provide substantial and useful information to the end-user.
- You should have unique content (which should not be similar or nearly identical in appearance to another site).

If searchers land on your 'Contact Us' page, for example, and all they see is your address and an input form, that doesn't tell them anything about what you're offering. You should always build global navigation into your site and treat all pages as potential landing pages. Figure 7.1 illustrates this point.

To help reinforce the relevance of the topic, name all your images after keywords, as image searches will pick these up. All your rich media and PDFs should also be named after your keywords.

- Avoid hidden text or hidden links.
- Don't employ cloaking or sneaky redirects.
- Don't send automated queries to search engines.
- Don't load pages with irrelevant words.
- Don't create multiple pages, subdomains, or domains with substantially duplicated content.
- Avoid 'doorway' pages created just for search engines, or other 'cookie cutter' approaches.
- Provide unique and relevant content that gives users a reason to visit your site first.

Site map

It is always worth having a site map on your website. This can be a very important entry page. Correctly built site maps can fuel searches, especially if they have links to every single page that your visitors care about. Submit your index page and your site map. Put your site map at the root level, and name it after your keywords. Use global navigation on the site map. Add all your website descriptions of the company or services at the top of the page or in the left column before the links, and use keywords in your links as well. Avoid using graphics; keep to text and this page will work wonders for you on all search engines. Keep the site maps as simple as possible. Our preferred option is to keep site maps to text only. Here are a few more tips:

- Provide an easy path for users to navigate around your site
- Avoid excessive use of pop-ups, pop-unders, and other obtrusive elements throughout your site
- Avoid altering users' browser behaviour or settings (such as back button functionality, browser window size).

Good site architecture is when:

- The title of the page is relevant to its content
- The site has a consistent global navigation scheme
- Page layout is consistent and is based on a template
- Directories are set up in a structured manner consistent with the navigation.

Help your target audiences

Each website has two target audiences: the primary audience is the end-user, while the secondary audience consists of the directory editors and search engine spiders. Your goal in search engine optimization is to receive regular traffic over time from both the search engines and the directories. Search engines do three things: they index text, follow links, and measure popularity. Of these, the measure of popularity is the factor most influenced by end-users.

Visible text

Search engines see text, so if you have to perform any kind of action to view text then almost certainly the search engine will not be able to see it. ALT text is not visible, so it's not as important to the search engines as visible text. However, you must include your keyword phrase in your ALT text. ALT tags can be used as text in logos, image maps, navigation elements, Flash movies, and photos. ALT text in a clear gif is considered spamming. You should always put width and height on image maps so the browser knows the size of the graphic; by doing this you are speeding up the process of having some content appear quickly on screen in particular text. The graphics will then follow.

Cascading style sheets

Cascading style sheets (CSS) are used to control web page design parameters, such as margins, font/typeface, link appearance, colours, and placement. CSS massively decrease download time, but style sheets themselves have no effect on the search engines. You should always make use of a robots exclusion file on sections of your site that the search engines have no interest in, such as your style sheets, CGI-BIN, and any pages under construction, to keep them from getting indexed. All search engines support this protocol – after all, the last thing you want is to drive traffic to your site and then present searchers with an incomplete landing page. There is always a period when you have kicked off your search optimization strategy but not quite finished the site build, and this is when these anomalies occur. The best thing you can do is present those pages that are finished and block the pages that are still work in progress.

META tags

The most valuable feature offered by META tags is the ability to control web pages for both searching and administration. META tags will help keep your pages more up to date, make them easier to find, and even stop them from becoming framed, but they have never been a guaranteed way to gain a top ranking on crawler-based search engines. META tags can also help you provide keywords and descriptions on pages that for various reasons lack text – maybe because of image maps, large images, splash pages and frames pages. They might also boost your page's relevancy.

Simply including a META tag is not a guarantee that your page will suddenly leap to the top of every search engine listing. They are useful tools, but not a magic solution. They can be used to identify the creator of a page, its HTML specs, the keywords and description of the page, and the refresh parameter. Statistics show that only about 21 per cent of web pages use keyword and description META tags. If your competitor is using them and you aren't, they may have an advantage over you. META tags are something that visitors to your website are usually not aware of, but it was probably your META tags that enabled them to find you in the first place.

There are several META tags, but the description and keywords tags are the most important for search engine indexing. The description tag presents a description of the page in place of the summary the search engine creates, and the keywords tag provides keywords for the search engine to relate with your page.

Metadata as currently structured, is open to spam and deception, and most search engines give META tags very little weight.

Well-tagged pages might not help you rank well in search engines, but once visitors find your site, they may then search its pages, and the more structured data you can provide to the site search tool, the more likely it is that your visitor will find the exact pages they're looking for. Summary descriptions are always an aid to navigation; they're just time-consuming to write. Pages that contain hard-working content merit good description tags.

In context, search engines do not take META tags too seriously. They must come up with clever methods of ranking content, and weeding out the bad stuff, which is an impossible job. In spite of its stellar reputation, we can see that Google's index has its share of link farm spam, keyword spam, and so on. Google doesn't completely ignore META tags. They may give a very low weight to keyword tags – we'll never know how much. More importantly, the index will grab a description META tag as a 'fall-through' if a site's homepage doesn't contain much, if any, usable text, nor any ALT tags on images.

For all website owners who just want to get on with the business of producing great content or selling great products, I hope you'll someday feel less compelled to bother with those illusive keywords and description META tags. Search engines can't put too much emphasis on ranking methods that are too wide open to spam. If the engines don't pay much attention to META tags, they might be a waste of your time but, if you are in a competitive industry and you are looking for every advantage, read on to find out how to manage META tags.

Placement of META tags
META tags should always be placed at the head of the HTML document between <HEAD> tags and before the <BODY> tag. This is very important with framed pages, as missing out the tags on these pages loses them to the search engine. If you only use META tags on the frameset pages, you'll miss a large number of potential hits. The problem with frames is the inability of most search engines to understand whether a page is a content page or a navigation page. Figure 7.2 is a screen grab of an HTML META tag in source mode. The example shows a title tag, then a META description tag, then a META keywords tag.

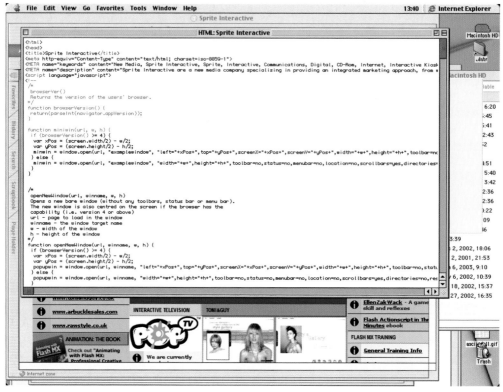

Figure 7.2 *HTML META tag in source mode*

The title tag

The HTML title tag isn't really a META tag, but it's worth discussing in relation to them. Whatever text you place in the title tag (between the <TITLE> and </TITLE> shown in Figure 7.2) will appear in the reverse arrow of a user's browser when he or she is viewing the Web page. If you look at the reverse arrow in your browser, you should see that same text being used, similar to the screen grab in Figure 7.3.

Some browsers will supplement whatever you put in the title tag by adding their own name, as you can see Microsoft's Internet Explorer doing in Figure 7.3. The title tag is also used as the words to describe your page when someone adds it to their 'Favourites' or 'Bookmarks' lists.

The title tag is crucial for search engines. The text you use in the title tag is one of the most important factors in how a search engine may decide to rank your web page. In addition, all major crawlers will use the text of your title tag as the text for the title of your page in your listings. For example, Figure 7.4 shows how Google lists the Sprite web pages. You can see that the text 'Sprite Interactive' is used as the hyperlinked title to the Sprite homepage as listed in Google's results.

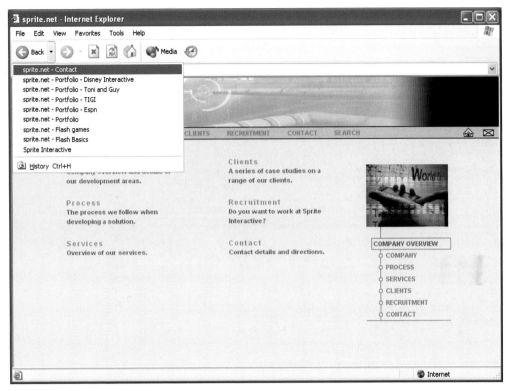

Figure 7.3 *An example of the reverse arrow showing site titles*

Think about the key terms you'd like your page to be found for in crawler-based search engines, then incorporate those terms into your title tag in a short, descriptive fashion. That text will be used as your title in those engines, as well as in bookmarks and in browser reverse bars.

The META description tag

The META description tag allows you to influence the description of your page in the crawlers that support the tag. In Figure 7.2 you can see a small description file. Google ignores the META description tag and instead will automatically generate its own description for this page. Others may support it partially. You can see in Figure 7.4 that the first portion of the page's description comes from the META description tag, and the remaining portion is drawn from the body copy of the page itself. However, not all search engines work like Google.

It is worth using the META description tag for your pages, because it gives you some degree of control with various crawlers. An easy way to use the tag is to take the first sentence or two of body copy from your web page and use that for the META description content.

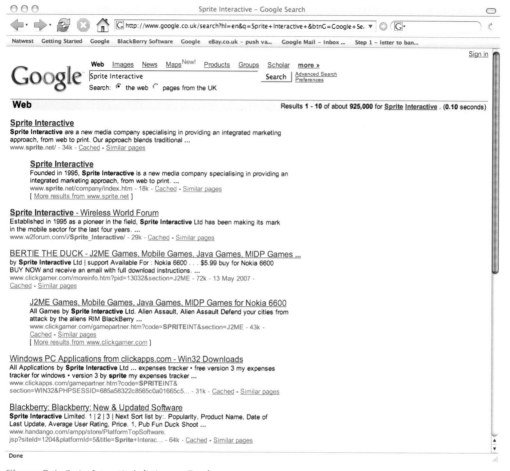

Figure 7.4 *Sprite Interactive's listing on Google*

The META keywords tag

The META keywords tag allows you to provide additional text for crawler-based search engines to index along with your body copy. Generally, up to 1000 characters may be indexed. On the few crawlers that support it, it can be useful as a way of reinforcing the terms you think a page is important for. The text in the META keywords tag works in conjunction with the text in your body copy.

The META keywords tag is also sometimes useful as a way to help your pages rank for synonyms or unusual words that don't appear on the page itself. For instance, let's say you have a page all about the 'pre-press' design but you never actually mention the word 'origination' on this page. By having the word in your META keywords tag, you may help increase the odds of ranking if someone searches for 'pre-press and origination'. Of course, the highest way of increasing the odds is by having the word 'origination' in the title and body copy of the page itself.

Avoid repeating a particular word too often in a META keywords tag, as this could actually harm your page's chances of ranking well. For clarity, separate keywords and multi-keyword phrases by commas. You do not have to use commas in the tag. By leaving out commas or spaces, there is more room for words. Here is how the team at Sprite Interactive writes META tags:

```
<META name=''keywords'' content=''keyword1, keyword2, keyword3''>
```

That's 29 characters, including spaces, between the quotes after *content=*. But sometimes you might need the additional space, so you can leave out the commas, like this:

```
<META name=''keywords'' content=''keyword1 keyword2 keyword3''>
```

With the commas removed, the content portion of the tag is only 27 characters. If you have a lot of keywords, these small differences add up and become worthwhile.

An alternative method is to use commas but to leave out the spaces:

```
<META name=''keywords'' content=''keyword1,keyword2,keyword3''>
```

This is still 27 characters and is perfectly acceptable as it still retains the commas. The official specs say only that elements should be separated by commas. Most search engines say you don't need commas, so don't use them if you want to squeeze in every last keyword that you find in your thesaurus.

Quite a few search optimization companies don't bother with commas. This is in order to increase the chance of matching a string of words or a phrase that someone may enter. If your web page is about search optimization, having the keyword *optimization* in your META tag is not suddenly going to make it come up when people search for *Search*. In contrast, adding some extra words like *service* or *consulting*, if they don't appear on the page already, may help you to appear when someone searches for *optimization service* or *search consulting*.

The META tag should always reflect the keywords that are on the page already, especially those that are unique. A few synonyms may be added, but overall the tag should be kept tightly focused.

How big can the tags be?

There is no common size for either the keyword or the description META tags. Commonly, search engines accept about 1000 characters for the keywords tag and 200 characters for the description tag. They can be longer, and going over the limit does not mean that your tag will be thrown out; it just means that the search engines will not use the excess material beyond their own respective limits.

When search engines warn against repetition, they generally mean spamming attempts such as this:

```
<META name=''keywords'' content=''Search Optimization, Search
Optimization, Search Optimization, Search Optimization, Search
Optimization, Search Optimization, Search Optimization''>
```

There's no good reason for the words *Search Optimization* to appear so many times. In contrast, the tag below is not a spamming attempt:

```
<META name=''keywords'' content='' Search Optimization, Search
consulting, Search services, Searching, Surf Searching''>
```

The word *Search* is repeated so many times in order to preserve phrases, the objective being that the words should appear in the tags exactly as someone might enter them into a search box.

As a note of warning, the repetition may still be too much for some search engines, which may downgrade a page the more often a word is repeated in a tag. Some pages can do perfectly well with multiple repetitions of a word, but it makes sense to repeat as little as possible. None of the search engines have published standards or specifications on this. Most search engines will see phrases as phrases, so if you think searchers are going to search for a particular string of words, include phrases in your keywords tag. However, always make sure that each page within your website has tags that match its content. Only a page that deals with eMarketing promotions should include that phrase in its tag. Never 'overload' your tags. The major search engines do not expect the title tag to come first, or the META tags to appear in any particular position. There are many reasons why a page may not rank well, and changing the order of your tags alone will not result in any improvement. Stick with what works for you.

META robots tag

Crawlers will try to index all your web pages, and to follow links from one page to another. This tag lets you specify that a page should not be indexed by a search engine. Simply add the opt-out text between your head tags on each of the pages you don't want indexed. Most major search engines support the META robots tag. However, the robots.txt convention of blocking indexing is more efficient, as you don't have to manage the opting out on a page level. If you do use a robots.txt file to block indexing, there is no need also to use META robots tags. The robots.txt standard is a text file placed in the root server's HTML directory. If, for example, we did not want the entire Sprite.net site to be indexed, we would make a file that would be found under the URL http://www.sprite.net/robots.txt. An engine respecting the standard would ask for the file before trying to index any page within the site. To exclude the entire site, the file would say:

```
User-agent: *
Disallow: /
```

The *user-agent* portion lets you specify engines or browsers; more than likely you will want to specify all the engines and browsers, and the * is specifying everything. The *disallow portion* is where you specify directories or file names. In the example above, the * is used to protect everything within the site. You can also be more specific and block particular directories or pages:

```
User-agent: *
Disallow: /Search/
Disallow: /contactUs/
Disallow: /portfolio/
Disallow: /clients/disney.htm
```

Now the engines respecting the standard will not index anything in the site with the addresses:

http://www.sprite.net/Search/
http:/www.sprite.net/contactUs/
http:/www.sprite.net/portfolio/

This page is also blocked:

http://www.sprite.net/clients/disney.htm

Because the robots.txt file must go in the server's root directory, many of those using free web space will not be able to use it.

Security and robots.txt

Not every search engine respects the robots.txt convention, although all the major ones do. Other web users may take advantage of the file. All they have to do is enter the address to your robots.txt file, and they can then read the contents in their web browser. This may contain data that is off limits to other users. If you don't want the robots.txt file to be a roadmap to sensitive areas on your server, keep those sensitive areas off the Web or password-protect them.

Other META tags

There are many other META tags; those listed here are just some of the more useful ones.

META tags have two attributes:

```
<META HTTP-EQUIV=''name'' CONTENT=''content''>
```

and

```
<META NAME=''name'' CONTENT=''content''>
```

HTTP-EQUIV

META HTTP-EQUIV tags are the equivalent of HTTP headers. HTTP headers are how your web browser requests a document from a web server. When you click on a link, the Web server receives your browser's request via HTTP. The web server has to make sure that the page you've requested is there, and then it generates an HTTP response. That response is called the 'http header block'. The header tells the Web browser information about displaying the document. META HTTP-EQUIV tags usually control or direct the actions of web browsers, and are used to refine the information that is provided by the actual headers. They are tags that are designed to work with web browsers as normal headers. Some web servers may translate META HTTP-EQUIV tags into actual HTTP so that web browsers see them as normal headers; others, such as Apache and CERN httpd, use a separate text file that contains META-data.

Name

META tags with a NAME attribute are used for META types that do not correspond to normal HTTP headers. For example:

1 *Expires.*

```
<META HTTP-EQUIV=''expires'' CONTENT=''Thur, 20 Jan 2003 08:11:57
GMT''>
```

This means that that document will expire on Thursday, 20 January 2003 08:11:57 GMT. Web robots delete expired documents from a search engine, or, in some cases, schedule a revisit.

2 *Content-Type.*

```
<META HTTP-EQUIV=''Content-Type'' CONTENT=''text/html;
charset=ISO-2022-JP''>
```

The HTTP content type may be extended to give the character set. It is recommended that you always use this tag, even with the previously default charset ISO-8859–1. Failure to do so can cause display problems where the document uses UTF-8 punctuation characters but is displayed in ISO or ASCII charsets.

3 *Content-Script-Type.*

```
<META HTTP-EQUIV=''Content-Script-Type'' CONTENT=''text/javascript''>
```

This specifies the default scripting language in a document (see MIMETYPES for applicable values).

4 *Content-Style-Type.*

```
<META HTTP-EQUIV=''Content-Style-Type'' CONTENT=''text/css''>
```

This specifies the default style sheet language for a document.

5 *Content-Language.*

```
<META HTTP-EQUIV=''Content-Language'' CONTENT=''en-GB''>
```

This may be used to declare the natural language of the document. It is used by robots to categorize by language.

6 *Refresh.*

```
<META HTTP-EQUIV=''Refresh''
CONTENT=''3;URL=http://www.sprite.net/contact.html''>
```

This specifies a delay in seconds before the browser automatically reloads the document, which can result in the loading of an alternative URL.

7 *Window-target.*

```
<META HTTP-EQUIV=''Window-target'' CONTENT=''_top''>
```

This specifies the named window of the current page, and can be used to stop a page appearing in somebody else's frameset, i.e. it prevents another site from hijacking your pages.

8 *Ext-cache.*

```
<META HTTP-EQUIV=''Ext-cache'' CONTENT=''name=/jobs/path/index.db;
instructions=Help pages''>
```

This defines the name of an alternate cache to Netscape Navigator.

9 *Vary.*

```
<META HTTP-EQUIV=''Vary'' CONTENT=''Content-language''>
```

This implies that if a header Accept-Language is sent, an alternative form may be selected.

10 *Robots.*

```
<META NAME=''ROBOTS'' CONTENT=''NOINDEX,FOLLOW''>
```

This stops robots indexing on a per page basis, but will allow it to follow links from this page. Robots include:

NOINDEX – this prevents indexing

NOFOLLOW – this stops the crawler from following the links on this page

NOIMAGEINDEX – this stops images on the page from being indexed, but allows all the text to be indexed

NOIMAGECLICK – this stops direct links to the images; instead there will only be a link to the page

NOARCHIVE – this stops Google from caching pages.

11 *Description*. For example:

```
<META NAME=''description'' CONTENT='' Sprite Interactive is a new
media company specializing in providing an integrated marketing
approach, from web to print. Our approach blends traditional design
experience with new media development, our service is focused on
consultancy, digital marketing and promotions, search optimization,
online games and e-magazines.''>
```

This gives a short description of your site, and is used by search engines to describe your web page. It is particularly important if your page has very little text, is a frameset, or has extensive scripts at the top.

12 *Keywords*.

```
<META NAME=''keywords'' CONTENT='' New Media, Sprite Interactive,
Sprite, Interactive, Communications, Digital, CD-Rom, Internet,
Interactive Kiosks, Intranet, Extranet, Screen Saver, Cross Media,
Cross Media Solutions, Internet, Brochures, Corporate Literature,
Presentations, Interactive Presentations, Search Optimization,
Digital Marketing, Online Promotions, Consultancy, Games,
E-magazines, Games Library, Print Media, Fetcham Park, Integrated
Marketing, Design, Web Design, Information Architecture,
Copywriting, Multimedia, CD Business Cards, Technology, WAP,
Integrated Magazines''>
```

These are keywords used by search engines to index your document, in addition to words from the title and document body. Typically, keywords are synonyms and alternates of title words. Sprite has built a META tag builder which it is freely available from http://www.sprite.net/MetaBuilder.

This form allows you to create very complicated META tags using much more than the keywords and description tags, if you wish. Sprite will be credited with a commented credit line in the tag. Figure 7.5 shows you the interface for this.

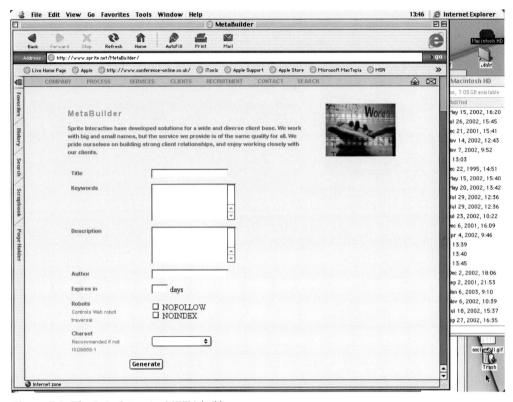

Figure 7.5 *The Sprite Interactive META builder*

The law

There are several legal issues concerning the use of tags on your website. There have so far been five key legal suits that focused on sites that utilized someone else's keywords within their META tags. The largest of these suits brought a settlement of $3 million.

Usually, the misuse of META tags becomes an issue because people believe that you are using their investment in their brand by 'hijacking' their traffic. This happens when your website comes up when someone searches for your competitor or a big brand name. So far, most defendants have lost on this issue. You need to ask yourself if there is a legitimate reason for using someone else's brand name, or whether you are trying to deceive users. Using a competitor's term in your tags is no guarantee that you'll do well, especially if your competitor's site has been properly optimized.

Within a competitive environment, the temptation to spam people is great. You do this by repeating a brand name over and over with the intention that you get past the filters and make it to the top of the rankings, but it's hard to prove to a judge that this tactic is not deceptive or misleading.

Is it ever legitimate?

There may sometimes be a case for the right to use brand names or a competitor's terms in your META tags. For example, a book retailer might argue that people looking for 'Cinderella' are doing a generic search for anything on Cinderella, and thus the retailer needs to include the term 'Disney' to ensure that his site is properly indexed, so he can draw the traffic to the Disney section of his site. Furthermore, the retailer might want to create a page comparing Disney's Cinderella to another publisher's version. He has every right to use the word Cinderella on that page. Furthermore, he would have every right to use the word Cinderella in his META tags in order to classify the page properly. The key to all of this is not to overuse a term in a META tag. The issue is whether a company is being deceptive and trying to fool people into coming to a site that appears to be something else.

What if someone uses your own trademark?

A company that tags its own pages properly should have a higher ranking for its trademarked terms, mainly because they have many, many pages relevant to those terms, which are reinforced by the META tagging, the URL and the title of the page. Tagging your own pages will make you so dominant that the people attempting to hijack your traffic will not be ranked. This is a great way of solving the problem without resorting to expensive legal action. If you do decide to use trademarks in your tags, you might consider using the following guidelines in order to limit potential problems. The guidelines can help site owners to avoid problems or defend themselves should someone suggest that they are infringing trademarks. They are not legal guidelines.

1 Use a brand name in the META keywords tag only if you mention it on the page
2 Avoid repeating the brand name more than once
3 Brand names should only be used in the title tag when they are a prominent feature of the page's content.

META tag lawsuits

The five key lawsuits that have focused on the use of someone else's keywords with a site's META tags are described briefly here.

1 The first known case dealing with the issue of misleading META tags was the Oppedahl & Larson action. The defendants had no clear reason for using the name of Oppedahl & Larson, which is a law firm that has dealt in domain name disputes. It was believed that the defendants hoped to capture traffic that would gain them domain name registration fees or website hosting clients. The court banned them through a permanent injunction from using the name without authorization. Oppedahl & Larson's complaint can be read on http://www.patents.com/ac/
2 On 27 August 1997, Insituform sued National Envirotech for using its name in its META tags. It was alleged that some slogans and images from Insituform were also used. META tags were central to the case, as the words only appeared in the META tags and not on the screen. The judge decided that the only plausible reason for these registered trademarks to be in the META

tags was to misdirect people to the National Envirotech website. National Envirotech removed the disputed material. The parties reached a settlement, but the judge also issued a permanent injunction. You can read more about this case on http://www.cll.com/keyword.htm

3 In Playboy *vs* AsiaFocus and Internet Promotions – Civ. No. C-97–3204 (N.D. Cal., Sept. 8, 1997), Playboy sued two adult website operators who spammed their pages with the word Playboy and Playmate hundreds of times in the site names, the domain names and in their slogans. This helped them rise to the top of some search engine results for a search on 'Playboy'. The San Francisco federal judge issued a preliminary injunction against the operators, deciding that trademark infringement and false representation could be proven.

4 In Playboy *vs* Terri Welles – Civ. No. C-97–3204 (N.D. Cal., Sept. 8, 1997), a judge refused to grant an injunction against Terri Welles, Playboy's 1981 Playmate of the Year, to prevent her from using terms such as 'Playmate' and 'Playboy' on her web pages and within her META tags. He gave the reason that Welles had a legitimate reason to use them in order to describe herself, and to catalogue her website properly with search engines. The judge also noted that Welles was not using the terms in an attempt to mislead users into believing they were at a Playboy site. You can read more on this and the Appeal in Welles Case at http://caselaw.lp.findlaw.com/data2/circs/9th/0055009p.pdf (US Court of Appeals, For the Ninth Circuit, Feb. 1, 2002), and on Terri Welles' counterclaim case at http://www.terriwelles.com/legal/counterclaim.html

5 In Brookfield Communications Inc. *vs* West Coast Entertainment Corp, West Coast won the first time round after using Brookfield's 'MovieBuff' trademark in its META tags. However, this was reversed on appeal and the case was sent back with a grant of preliminary injunction. The appeal found that the use of the trademark in the META tag created 'initial interest confusion', because users visited the West Coast site first. You can learn more about this case if you do a VerdictSearch for Brookfield Communications Inc. *vs* West Coast Entertainment Corp on http://www.lawnewsnetwork.com

JavaScript

Most search engines weight the text that appears at the top of your pages more heavily than that which appears further down. They assume that the first paragraph of the article tells you all the main points. Using JavaScript at the top of your documents may impact your pages' relevancy, as some search engines may put the biggest priority on scripting code rather than on your opening paragraphs.

Using a META description tag can help to solve the listing issue, but won't keep the JavaScript from still being indexed and possibly degrading relevancy. If you surround the code with a comment tag, this should stop most engines from seeing the code. What is supposed to happen is that nothing between <!– and –> is indexed by a search engine that ignores comments. However, remember that code strings can contain the > character ?. You may use .js files, which are 'external' files that contain your JavaScript code. You call to them from within your page, and the JavaScript code is then only loaded by browsers that understand JavaScript. Since most search engines don't read JavaScript, you start to tackle a key stumbling block of most search engines.

Make your site useful

You can spend a large amount of time trying to get good search engine rankings and lots of visitors. However, when visitors arrive at the site they may still find a poorly designed, badly written website with content that bears no relevance to either the keywords or the title tag. Success is not about how many page views you get but about how many sales you get, and it is amazing how many people miss this simple concept. Making your pages 'people-friendly' is as important as making them search engine-friendly. It is much easier to triple your sales effectiveness and conversions to your site than to double your traffic.

Use keyphrases, not keywords

It is difficult if not impossible to get high rankings based on keywords. Instead, you need to consider using keyphrases. The way to do this is ask yourself what users trying to find the site would type in when searching. Make a list of these phrases, and test them out on the search engines. See if you can find your type or product or services. Think about variations on the keyphrases and write them down. Two great resources for finding out which keyphrases are the most effective are the Overture.com Search Suggestions Page, and WordTracker. On Overture's search suggestion page, type in a very general keyphrase (like 'New Media') and it will tell you all of the more specific keyphrases that relate to that keyphrase, and how many hits they get. This is a great way of finding out what your keyphrases actually are.

The art of the <TITLE> tag

So many websites have titles that are good for people but abysmal for the search engines. This is a big mistake. A title like 'Alex Michael – Animating in Flash 8' is a disaster! The golden rule is that the most important keyphrases should be in the <TITLE> tag. So what you do is look at your keyphrases, make a list of all the important words, and create a title tag that uses the top one or two. Also, keep in mind that browsers only display the first few words of a title tag (whatever fits into the title bar of the window). So while the first sentence of your title tag should be 'human readable', the rest can be just a list of keyphrases.

There is some debate as to whether a very long title tag is a good thing or a bad thing when it comes to search engines. Some people are concerned that a very long title tag might result in the search engines deciding the page is a 'spam page'. Our advice is to keep the title between 15 and 20 words. However, you might want to try longer title tags on some of your pages, just to see what happens! So Alex Michael might have a title that looks like this:

```
<TITLE> Alex Michael – Animating in Flash 8, Storyboarding,
Games</TITLE>
```

The reason for this is that the three most important places to have keyphrases and phrases are in your title tag, your META tags, and your first paragraph. You want them to all contain the same important words, as this increases your keyphrase density and improves your rankings.

The first paragraph

The first paragraph of your page should expand upon everything in your title and META tags. You need to have all the keyphrases in it. However, since this is going to be read by people, it needs to be written with them in mind. This is where you introduce yourself to your guests, so you want to make a good impression. Try to put this first paragraph as close to the <BODY> tag as possible. Avoid putting graphics or other HTML in front of your first paragraph as much as you can. Also, use the <H1> or <H2> tag to emphasize your opening sentence.

Do not put up spam pages or anything that looks like spam! Keyphrases should not appear too many times, because that might make the search engines think your page is a spam page trying to rank highly for a particular phrase. So, how much is too much? This varies from search engine to search engine. Google likes pages with less than thirteen repeats of a keyphrase, for example. The best advice is to try to keep the number of repeats of important phrases down to ten or less in all instances – in the title, META tags, and the text of the page.

The major search engines are actively penalizing/banning sites that employ the following techniques:

- Machine generated pages
- Pages that contain hidden text and hidden links
- Large volumes of text pages
- Link farming and link spamming; all free-for-all (FFA) links
- Cloaking – a practice in which the search engine and the end-user do not view the same page
- Sites with numerous unnecessary host names
- Excessive cross-linking of sites to inflate a site's apparent popularity artificially – affiliate spam.

On 4 February 2006, car maker BMW's German websites were kicked out of the Google index. BMW.de at this time had a PageRank of 0. Previously this site had the number 1 PageRank. BMW's international site is marketed differently now and has the number 1 PageRank.

The reason for the ban is likely to have been because the BMW websites were caught employing a technique used by search engine optimizers using doorway pages. A doorway page is stuffed full of keywords that the site feels a need to be optimized for; however, as opposed to real pages, this doorway is only displayed to the Googlebot. Human visitors will be immediately redirected to another page upon visit. And that's exactly what happened at BMW.de, as reported.

Whilst BMW removed the pages almost immediately after the news broke (having had them live for almost 2 years), it was too late. German BMW is now suffering what is known as the 'Google death penalty' – a ban from almost any imaginable top search result, and a degrading of the PageRank to the lowest possible value.

Consequently, a search for gebrauchtwagen bmw, which had a page at BMW.de as a top result, now shows AutoScout24.de as a top result. A search for BMW.de using Google's site operator doesn't yield any results, either.

How many pages exactly are affected by this is hard to tell, but a search on Yahoo! for BMW.de returns 41 500 pages – including cached copies of many of the keyword-stuffed doorway pages, like bmw.de/bmw-kauf.html, which now return a 'file not found' message. Most of the pages can still be accessed from Yahoo!'s cache, while others – like a doorway page stuffed with the phrase 'BMW review' – are missing from Yahoo!'s cache, but can still be accessed at Archive.org if you disable JavaScript.

This penalty is a good example of what can happen to sites going against the Google webmaster guidelines – no matter how big or important one might deem the site. Google writes:

> If an SEO creates deceptive or misleading content on your behalf, such as doorway pages or 'throwaway' domains, your site could be removed entirely from Google's index.

Google's guidelines go back to a single philosophy: webmasters should optimize for humans, not machines, because Google doesn't like to be cheated.

The importance of domain names

Make sure your domain name reflects your service or product. This is the best investment you'll ever make. There are three major reasons for getting your own domain name:

1 Some search engines won't list you unless you do
2 People are more likely to buy if you have your own domain name. What looks better to you – 'http://www.alex.com/' or 'http://members.aol.com/alex123/'?
3 You can change your web hosting service without messing up all of your search engine listings.

There is no benefit in having a long domain name. A domain name with lots of keywords in it (e.g. seo-url-promotion-website-Designsite-alex.com) will not get a higher ranking in the search engines. *None* of the major search engines will significantly boost your rankings based on keywords in your URL, so the added benefit of keywords in the URL is insignificant. Don't waste your money. Go for a short, memorable domain name, either one word or two words combined, or with an i, e, i- or e- prefix.

Avoid search engine tricks

Some 'experts' advise trying to trick search engines by, for example, putting keyphrases in comments or putting them in text that is the same colour as your background, and so on. Do not try this, as most of these methods don't work and if they do they may stop working at any minute, as the search engines are constantly trying to detect them. You should help search engines by making it as easy as possible for them to get a good idea of what your page is about. That way, as search engines get better and better at rating the contents of sites, your rankings will improve over time with no effort from you.

Check your HTML

Almost all websites have HTML errors – even those that appear to display nicely on your browser. Browsers are very tolerant of errors, but it's a good idea to make sure your HTML is as perfect as possible because this increases the chance that your website will display the way you want it to on as many browsers as possible.

Have HTML links

Often, web designers only create image map links from the homepage to inside pages. A search engine that can't follow these links won't be able to get 'inside' the site, and unfortunately the most descriptive and relevant pages are often within inside pages rather than the homepage. To solve this problem, all you need do is add some HTML hyperlinks to the homepage that lead to major inside pages or sections of your website. Put them at the bottom of the page, and search engines will find them and follow them.

A site map page with text links to everything in your website will help the search engines to locate pages within your website. You must do a good job of linking internally between your pages. If you naturally point to different pages from within your site, you increase the odds that search engines will follow the links and find more of your website.

Frames can be a big problem, as some of the major search engines cannot follow frame links. Make sure there is an alternative means by which they can enter and index your site, either through META tags or smart design.

Search engines and dynamic pages

Crawler-based search engines have problems indexing web pages that are delivered via database programs, as this makes the site virtually invisible to them. This is because the page is dynamically delivered. An additional problem is that many dynamic delivery mechanisms make use of the ? symbol. Most search engines will not read past the ? in that URL; it acts as a stop sign to them and kills the indexing for that site. Other symbols that are often used include &, %, +, $ and reference to the CGI bin directory.

If your database program uses these, then you need to look at alternative ways of naming your content. Many major websites may not have a single page listed, because none of the search engines can crawl them. It's worth the time to see if your dynamic delivery problem has any easy solutions. There are workarounds that will let you create search engine-friendly URLs and still take advantage of a dynamically generated site; look for these. One site made this simple change and gained over 600 visitors a day from a particular search engine, simply because its content could now be listed. The following suggestions may help:

1 *Active Server Pages (ASP)*. These pages usually end in .asp. They are delivered by Microsoft's server software, and most of the major search engines will index these pages. Just avoid using the ? symbol.

2 *Apache*. Apache has a special 'rewrite' module that will allow you to translate URLs containing symbols. It is not compiled into the software by default, but many hosting companies add it anyway. You can find more about this by visiting http://www.apache.org/docs/mod/mod_rewrite.html

3 *Cold Fusion*. These files end in .cfm. Normally the database will use a ? symbol to retrieve pages, but there are workarounds to this that will make your pages accessible. Cold Fusion can be reconfigured to use URLs without the troublesome symbols. To learn more, visit the Cold Fusion site at www.ColdFusion.com.

4 *Direct submit/paid inclusion*. Directly submitting specific dynamic URLs to AltaVista increases the chance that they will be picked up by that search engine. Also, Google began increased finding of dynamic URLs as part of its normal crawls toward the end of 2000. Several search engines offer 'paid inclusion' programs where, for a fee, you are guaranteed to have the pages you want listed. These programs can usually handle dynamic URLs with no problem. The downside, of course, is that you have to pay.

5 *Server Side Includes* (SSI). The major search engines have no problems indexing pages that are built in part with SSI content. Search engines generally don't mind how your files end – in other words, even if your pages don't end in .html or .htm they'll probably still get indexed, assuming you've solved the ? symbol problem. However, Northern Light is rather picky. It will index any page ending in these extensions: .html .htm .shtml .stm .asp .phtml .cfm .php3 .php .jsp .jhtml .asc .text .txt., but it will not index pages ending in .cgi. However, there may be a problem if the pages use the cgi-bin path in their URLs.

6 *The ultimate solution: static pages*. If the database is simply used as a page creation tool, you can use it to create static pages – especially for sections of your site that don't change often. Alternatively, consider creating a mirror of your dynamic content in static pages that the search engines can spider, and then linking these pages to content within your database. These pages are known as 'landing pages'. You need to create mirror pages on your server that search engines can crawl. E-commerce sites, where information about prices and product availability can be stripped out of the databases and mirrored as non-dynamic pages, provide good examples of the use of landing pages. It is quite possible for a user, having landed on your pages, to be diverted to any part of your database.

In conclusion

Search engines see the Web in the same way as someone using a very old browser might. They do not read image maps, and they may not read frames. So anticipate these problems, or a search engine may not index any of your web pages.

Of all the META tags you may come across, the META description and META keywords tags are probably the most important. However, remember to make sure your pages have visible text. Give the spiders a link architecture to help them find visible text. Use the Robots Exclusion Protocol to exclude information that you do not want to be visible to search crawlers, and keep the most important pages in the top-level directory on your server.

Content needs to be relevant to users who are searching. Make sure the page architecture helps that search, and that the landing page has a clear navigation system.

If you have a legitimate reason to use trademarked terms in your META tags, then you can certainly do so. However, you may be facing a suit regardless of the correctness of your action. If you push the keywords terms to extremes, such as by spamming, you will probably not get onto most of the search engines.

To find quality links manually, search for websites that have the same theme as your own. When requesting a link, be sure to highlight what your site has to offer their visitors and why they should link to it. A compelling case will increase your chance of success. Link quality simply means how well positioned the pages are that link to you. If you are linked to by a spammy link farm, you get a penalty; conversely, if you are linked to by a directory like Yahoo! or Dmoz you get a boost. What about the hundreds of free directories? Yes, they all help. Take a few days and submit your site *manually* to every directory that will take it. There may be local directories, and regional directories can often supply plenty of incoming links. Every relevant link helps.

Chapter 8

Building an effective WAP site

WAP and the mobile Internet

The Wireless Application Protocol (WAP) is an open specification that enables mobile users to access and interact with information and services. WAP was developed by the WAP Forum, an industry group set up in 1997, which has now been consolidated into the Open Mobile Alliance (OMA).

The Open Mobile Alliance

The OMA was formed in June 2002 by nearly 200 companies, including mobile operators, device manufacturers, and content and service providers. The OMA aims to represent the whole mobile value chain, and consolidate into one organization all specification activities in the mobile world. The OMA has a number of goals:

1 To deliver high quality, open technical specifications based upon market requirements that drive modularity, extensibility and consistency amongst enablers to reduce industry implementation efforts.
2 To ensure that OMA service enabler specifications provide interoperability across different devices, geographies, service providers, operators and networks, to facilitate interoperability of the resulting product implementations.
3 To be the catalyst for the consolidation of standards activity within the mobile data service industry; working in conjunction with other existing standards organizations and the industry to improve interoperability and decrease operational costs for all involved.
4 To provide value and benefits to members in OMA from all parts of the value chain, including content and service providers, information technology providers, mobile operators and wireless vendors, such that they elect actively to participate in the organization.

(Source: The OMA website − http://www.openmobilealliance.org/about_OMA/index.html).

WAP works in a similar way to the Internet − users can view WAP sites from many different companies and individuals with a range of content. A lot of things available on the Internet are also available on WAP. Phones are slower, smaller and have less memory than PCs, so WAP was designed to maximize the experience of Internet applications within the restricted environment of the mobile phone.

WAP is a communications protocol and application environment and can be built on any operating system, including PalmOS, EPOC, Windows CE, FLEXOS, OS/9 and JavaOS. Products that support WAP include digital wireless devices such as mobile phones, pagers, two-way radios, smart phones and communicators. WAP is designed to work with most wireless networks, such as CDPD, CDMA, GSM, PDC, PHS, TDMA, FLEX, ReFLEX, iDEN, TETRA, DECT, DataTAC and Mobitex.

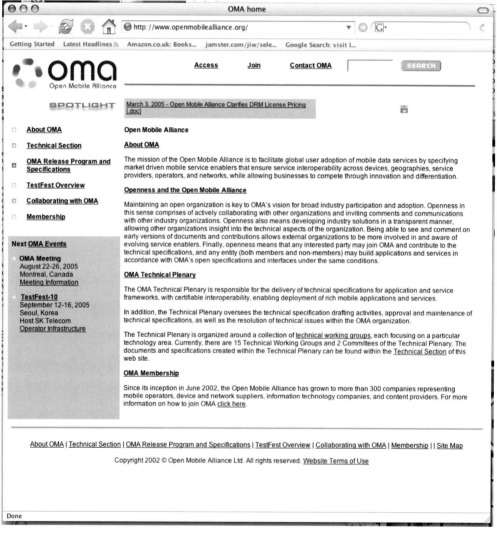

Figure 8.1 *The OMA website – www.openmobilealliance.org*

The WAP system

A WAP enabled system consists of:

1 a WAP gateway
2 an HTTP web server
3 a WAP device.

The WAP gateway is a mediator between a WAP device and an HTTP or HTTPS server; it routes requests from the WAP device to the server. When the HTTP server receives a request from the WAP gateway, it sends this information to the device using a wireless network. The WAP device in turn sends requests to the WAP gateway, which translates WAP requests to web requests, allowing the WAP client to submit requests to the Web server. After receiving the response from the server, the WAP gateway translates web responses into WAP responses or a format understood by the WAP client, and sends it to the WAP device.

WAP can be used for lots of different applications, including:

- email
- shopping
- news reports
- travel information
- checking share prices
- checking weather
- entertainment news and views
- horoscopes
- to download or to play online games
- sports reports
- chat rooms.

For companies or individuals wishing to monetize their content in the mobile space, launching a WAP site or mobile browsing service is essential. Mobile browsing provides a stand-alone medium on which companies can promote their services, and WAP sites provide a great opportunity to market and sell content and services to a massive audience. Many companies are building their mobile Internet sites, but are realizing that it's not as simple as creating a mobile version of a website.

Mobile Internet pages are designed to be viewed on the small screens of a phone, so they generally don't have lots of graphics or colours. The basic operation is quite similar to that of simple web pages – users view a page, and on the page there generally are a number of links to other pages (Figure 8.2). Users select the link they want to follow by scrolling to it and clicking a button on their handset.

Figure 8.2 *The WapJam WAP site*

Mobile Internet design guidelines

Mobile Internet sites are not as easy to use or develop as their computer-oriented website cousins, owing to the smaller screens, text input via a keypad, and many different user situations. Severe design mistakes continue to be made in mobile Internet site development; we have seen this a number of times and have put together a set of guidelines for site development that will make sure your mobile Internet site will be accessible and usable.

An unusable site will prevent users from being able to perform even the most simple of tasks. Sites need to be rational and contain relevant content that is easy to browse through. One of the most important areas to consider with mobile Internet site development, as with website development, is information architecture.

A well-designed 'information architecture' will enable users to find information quickly and in a rational, well thought-out way; it is the key to having a usable site. Before building your site, take the time to sit down and plan it out – where the links will be, what areas the site will contain, which areas contain what content, and so on. This may seem obvious, but it will give you the structure to be able to build your site in a logical way. The information architecture provides the skeleton to build the rest of the site on, and even the most simple of sites needs thinking out before you start designing and building it.

Websites generally aid the user with some kind of navigation bar, which will provide links to the key areas in the site as well as back to the homepage. Backwards navigation is another area you will need to consider carefully when developing a WAP site, as users frequently want to return to the page they have just visited.

PDA navigation

When designing a mobile Internet site for a PDA or small computer such as a Pocket PC or Palm, the device's browser will usually have a built in back button like a desktop browser. There are a couple of main rules of thumb to be considered when developing a site for a PDA; these are only general, but will help you develop a user-friendly site.

1 Avoid navigation bars, as these will take up too much real estate on the screen. Instead, you should use information in a 'tree' format to identify where the user is in the site – for example, Home > Games> Action.
2 Avoid the use of 'back' links, as users will have to find them and they will take up valuable space on the screen. As mentioned before, the device's browser will usually have a back button and you can prompt the user to go back using the navigation system outlined in point (1) above.

Top tips for WAP

WAP is a flexible medium and, like all media, works best when the content is tailored specifically to it and takes advantage of its many attributes. Here are some general tips for creating a user-friendly, efficient WAP site; they are by no means set in stone, as each project will be unique, but they provide a set of rules for creating a solid site, whatever the brief.

Splash screens

Splash screens should be avoided as a general rule. If you are only developing a site for a high-speed audience (3G) then you can include a screen, as the download time will be that much less, but on slower networks splash screens add a lot of time to the experience because users have to download a large image before they can begin browsing your site. This will associate your brand with time wasting, and it is also possible that large images will cause problems on lower-specification handsets.

Figure 8.3 *The Voltimum WAP site on a PDA and computer*

Think about your navigation

Strong information architecture is the key to a strong site, whether a website or a WAP site. Ensure the user can go 'back' from every page, as not all handsets have back buttons. It is a sure way to lose customers if they cannot get to where they want to go, or they get lost whilst navigating around your site. They should be able to return to the main homepage with one click from wherever they are in the site. One great way of keeping your users on track is to give each of the links in the site a number; this makes it easier for users to recognize the link the further they go into the site, and it differentiates between links. Make sure each link is on a separate line, and develop your navigation with the user in mind at all times.

Check and test your site

This is obvious, but is one of the most overlooked areas of site development. It does not take long to check your site for broken links, but time and time again we see commercial sites that have dead links. This is even more of a turn-off for users in the unfamiliar mobile Internet environment than it is in the Web environment, and will present a negative, lazy image of your brand. You also need to test your site on a variety of handsets on a variety of networks. An emulator is not enough; whether for Java applications and games or WAP sites, you should always test it on all the handsets you think will be viewing the site, and on all the networks the site will be available to, as you will undoubtedly find problems. The interaction of a mobile device, a WAP gateway and the mobile Internet site is not predictable, and testing will save you a lot of grief later on down the line. You can also test your site using the various desktop browsers on your PC (Figure 8.4). However, this method should never be used as an alternative to a real handset.

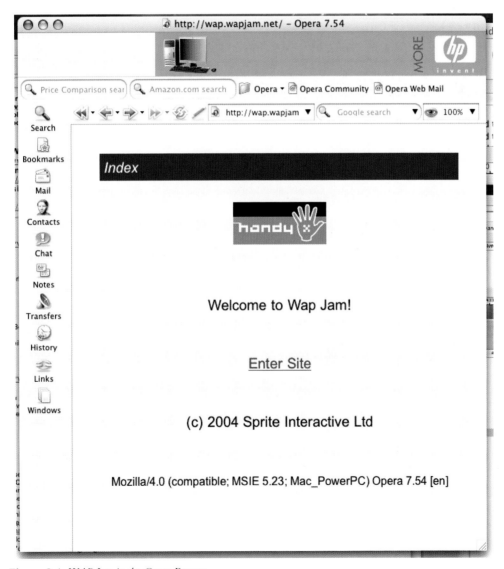

Figure 8.4 *WAP Jam in the Opera Browser*

Easy access

Make it easy for the user to type your site URL – for example, wap.wapjam.net. Too often we come across a company with a long URL that would be hard enough for a user to type on a computer keyboard, let alone a phone handset. Ideally the URL should be the same as your web URL, which is possible by using a script to detect which type of browser is looking at your site. Alternatively you could use the 'WAP' prefix, so www.wapjam.net becomes wap.wapjam.net, and so on.

Images

Be careful with image use. Many images will render differently on different handsets, or not even render at all, as some older handsets have size restrictions on the images they can display. Well-used images such as icons and headers can add a lot to the user experience, enhancing a boring text-only site (see Figure 8.5). The trick here is to test what you are developing

Figure 8.5 *Good use of images on the Sprite lifestyle WAP page for Orange*

on a number of different handsets and be aware of the limitations of the phones you are developing for.

User input

Make sure that the user doesn't have to enter any unnecessary information or fill in long forms. Text input on a handset is hard at the best of times, and you should bear this in mind. Very few phones on the market have any kind of keyboard device, and most of the phones you will be developing your site for will have unique input buttons. To get around this offer drop-down menus and lists wherever possible, and when text entry is totally necessary use a search mechanism where the user types in letters and gets a list of options back. Forms should be pre-populated with the most common information in order to save on user input, allowing the user to modify it afterwards.

Communicate

You should always let the user know what is happening. On a mobile Internet site, things take a lot longer than they do on a website. You may have a number of screens for a user to go through to enter information; if so, tell them. If something is going to take a long time to load or download, tell the site users; they may close the connection to the site if they think it has frozen up while something is actually happening in the background. Site users are generally happier if they know what is going on or what is expected of them, so guide them through whatever processes on the site they need to complete – you could, for example, let them know where they are on a step-by-step basis by saying 'step 1 of 3' on the first page of a three-page form.

Logging in

Make sure users don't need to log in or register right up until the point when they have to complete a transaction. This will encourage them to explore your site and give them a reason for entering their details; they will know what is coming. If users have to register or log in before they can even look at your site, then this can be an immediate put-off. If you can, you should allow for auto log in; this will depend on whether the user's phone is set up to accept cookies – many new handsets are.

Make sure your site is appropriate

Making sure you have a relevant site that actually works as a mobile Internet site is essential.

If your website consists of pages and pages of text, this will not be ideal for a WAP site. Rather than developing a cut-down version of your website, try to see where your WAP site can provide added value. Make sure the content on the site is totally relevant and of use to the phone user; you need to work within the limits of the technology to provide the best possible service.

The XHTML Basic

The XHTML Basic document type includes the minimal set of modules required to be an XHTML host language document type, and in addition it includes images, forms, basic tables, and object support. It is designed for web clients that do not support the full set of XHTML features; for example, web clients such as mobile phones, PDAs, pagers, and set-top boxes. The document type is rich enough for content authoring. Google currently supports the XHTML mobile profile (WAP 2.0), WML (WAP 1.2), and cHTML (iMode).

The motivation for XHTML Basic is to provide an XHTML document type that can be shared across communities and that is rich enough to be used for simple content authoring. You can add Google Mobile Search to your site – Google Web Search and Image Search configured for mobile devices. By adding Google Search to your mobile website, you can enable mobile users to find whatever they're looking for.

Google adds new sites to the mobile web index every time their crawler crawls the Web. To let Google know about your mobile site, as well as when you make changes, simply submit a mobile sitemap. Use of the Google Sitemaps program is absolutely free.

To help ensure our mobile crawlers can crawl and index your site:

- use well-formed markup
- use the right DOCTYPE and Content-Type for the markup language you are using
- validate your markup.

You can find more information about mobile web best practices at:

Mobile web best practices 1.0 (W3C draft guidelines) http://www.w3.org/TR/mobile-bp/

W3C mobile best practices working group http://www.w3.org/2005/MWI/BPWG/

If your site serves content in mobile markup languages you can make sure that your site will serve this content to Google's mobile crawl by requesting headers from Google's mobile crawl. Google always uses the HTTP 'Accept' header to explicitly tell your site that it should return documents with mobile content types, if available, rather than standard HTML. If your site respects this standard, it will return mobile content correctly to our mobile crawl.

In some cases, Accept headers are ambiguous so make sure you have got it right. For example, text/HTML is the content type for both cHTML, which is appropriate for certain types of mobile devices, and HTML, which is generally intended for desktop computers. Google's mobile crawl does its best to appear to be a mobile device, so if your site tries to detect mobile devices in other ways in a case like this, it will probably work for Google's mobile crawl as well.

Background and requirements for XHTML

Mobile devices are targeted for particular use of format and graphics. They support the features they need for the functions they are designed to fulfil. The common features found in these document types include:

- Basic text (including headings, paragraphs, and lists)
- Hyperlinks and links to related documents
- Basic forms
- Basic tables
- Images
- Meta information.

This set of HTML features has been the starting point for the design of XHTML Basic. Since many content developers are familiar with these HTML features, they comprise a useful host language that may be combined with markup modules from other languages according to the methods described in 'XHTML Modularization' [XHTMLMOD]. XHTML Basic may be extended with a custom module to support richer markup semantics in specific environments.

Wireless Mark-up Language

Wireless Mark-up Language (WML) is a markup language designed for displaying content on WAP devices. It is part of the WAP application environment, and is the equivalent of HTML for the Web. WML is based on XML, and is derived from xHTML (the XML version of HTML). There are, however, many differences between WML and HTML. One of the main ones is that WML has a different mechanism for linking between pages, which are called 'cards'. WML browsers are a lot less flexible than HTML browsers, and many are currently not tolerant of page errors. WML browsers also enforce the requirement of matching closing tags. The browsers in WAP devices read the WML of a 'card' and interpret it to produce the page that users see on their handset. They get around the limited functionality of WAP devices, such as limited processing power and limited memory.

WML uses the 'card' system, with pages organized into 'decks'. Each page or 'card' is the basic unit of navigation and the user interface. A 'deck' is the equivalent of a web page, and a 'card' is a portion of that page that can be seen on the screen at any one time. The user can only view one card at a time, but WML browsers read the whole deck from the server to minimize interaction with the server, which would create lag. Such lag would make your site appear to be slow. When developing for WML you will need to always be aware of the limitations and

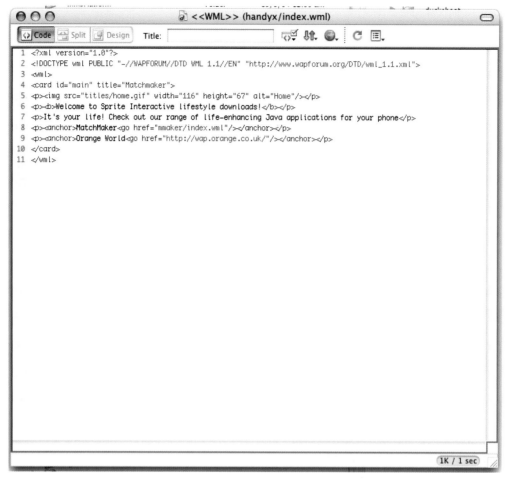

```
1  <?xml version="1.0"?>
2  <!DOCTYPE wml PUBLIC "-//WAPFORUM//DTD WML 1.1//EN" "http://www.wapforum.org/DTD/wml_1.1.xml">
3  <wml>
4  <card id="main" title="Matchmaker">
5  <p><img src="titles/home.gif" width="116" height="67" alt="Home"/></p>
6  <p><b>Welcome to Sprite Interactive lifestyle downloads!</b></p>
7  <p>It's your life! Check out our range of life-enhancing Java applications for your phone</p>
8  <p><anchor>MatchMaker<go href="mmaker/index.wml"/></anchor></p>
9  <p><anchor>Orange World<go href="http://wap.orange.co.uk/"/></anchor></p>
10 </card>
11 </wml>
```

Figure 8.6 *Example WML code*

issues related to screen boundaries when writing code for cards. Figure 8.6 provides an example of WML code.

WAP site developer tips

We have put together a number of more technical tips for WAP site developers, to help you best take advantage of the technology.

Soft keys

Keep right and left soft key labels short, as some handsets only display the first few characters. This goes for developing any application that uses the soft keys. It is worth replicating soft keys (Figure 8.7) with a link on the page as well, as on some handsets soft keys are not intuitive.

Figure 8.7 *Phone 'soft keys'*

`<go>` tags

When linking to a card that has already been visited don't use the `<go>` tag, as it will reload the card and extend the history stack, which can cause problems with devices with limited memory. You should use the `<prev>` and `<exit>` commands instead to retrieve the page from the history stack.

Dial through

You should use the `<wtai://wp/mc>` command to allow users to dial a number directly simply by clicking on the link. This is not supported by all handsets, but makes life much easier for users. You should also think about how you display numbers on pages. Some phones that do not support the above function have the ability to 'capture' numbers written on pages to enable the user to dial them or save them. Be careful not to format numbers with digits (such as brackets), and list each number on a page in as simple a format as possible.

Format attributes

There are problems with format tags, which allow you to constrain the user to a particular set of letters or numbers when filling in a form. On some devices the implementation of this feature is less than friendly, requiring users manually to enter digits such as colons and full stops in the middle of date or time fields, but with no prompt, and refusing to accept the entry until they get it right. For numerical entries you should constrain the entry to numbers or allow for free text entry, and point out in the text on the page how the user should be formatting their entry.

The <prev> action

Make sure you include this on every page of your site, otherwise some handsets will simply not be able to navigate backwards. You should also put it on the first page of your site, otherwise you could trap the user into your site. This may seem like a good idea, but is hardly going to endear you to a potential customer!

Disabling caching

The instructions to disable caching vary for each handset, so you need to be aware of this when developing. If you are presenting timely information (such as up-to-the-minute travel information) that you don't want to be cacheable, then you should think about displaying the time at the top of the page with a brief explanation of the caching system and a 'refresh' link to prompt the user to refresh the page for the latest information.

Deck size

Make sure you don't exceed around 1 kilobyte per deck for optimum performance. This size restriction will change in years to come as faster networks and handsets become more widespread, but currently you will need to provide an optimum service for a wide range of networks and handsets, so sticking to a lower size will get around device limitations.

Style tags and tables

Many of the most popular handsets do not support style tags or tables, so make sure you know the limitations of what you are developing for. Style tags and tables are really not necessary on a WAP site unless you are going to use sophisticated browser detection to ensure that the correct formatting is applied to the correct handset. As more advanced handsets become more widespread, you will be able to integrate style tags and tables into your WAP site.

Top WAP sites

There are many WAP sites out there of varying quality, but we've chosen a few of the best for you to check out as great examples of innovative, well thought-out WAP design:

- mobile.google.com – search and access Google's online information on your mobile
- wap.Samsungmobile.com – Samsung's mobile downloads site, with constantly updated downloads presented in a clear way to the user
- wap.wapjam.net – Sprite's WAP site with simple user interface and navigation allowing users to get to and download content in a friendly, well thought-out manner
- Wap.sonyericsson.com – a slick, stylish WAP site
- www.bbc.co.uk/mobile – information from the BBC
- uk.mobile.yahoo.com – Yahoo! services, including Yahoo!mail and Yahoo! news direct to your phone; this is a great example of a site that has a lot of fresh information
- www.amazon.co.uk/mobile
- pocketdoctor.co.uk – medical information on your handset; the lack of images is made up for by the rich information on offer
- wap.beachwizard.com – surf information on any beach in Europe
- mobile.nationalrail.co.uk – national rail timetables
- Mobileload, at wap.mobileload.com – a great selection of games and entertainment.

The long-term future of WAP

WAP today is still tied to a web-based mindset in many people's minds, which leads them to see it as just a technology – a means, that gives mobiles access to the Internet. However, WAP is much more than just a way to access the Internet, and features many new network protocols that can enable a new and completely different kind of content network than that of the standard Internet.

WAP technology today exists in a very primitive form compared to how it will evolve; it defines a workable alternative to the Web for content delivery of all sorts, and as handsets grow in power we should see a convergence between Web and WAP into a single standard. Owing to the flexibility of WAP it can be easily adapted, and we should see some exciting uses of the technology as it is developed into the future.

Chapter 9

Pay per click

Pay per click, or PPC, is an advertising technique used on websites, advertising networks, and search engines. Pay-per-click advertisements are usually text ads placed near search results; when a site visitor clicks on the advertisement, the advertiser is charged a small amount. There are many variants to the pay-per-click model, the most notable include pay for placement and pay for ranking. Pay per click is also sometimes known as cost per click (CPC). Depending on the search engine, minimum prices per click start at US$0.01 to US$0.50. These prices can reach up to GBP£17+ per click for services such as unsecured personal loans. Very popular search terms can cost much more on popular engines. This advertising model may be open to abuse through click fraud, although recently Google and other search engines have implemented automated systems to guard against this.

The advertiser bids on 'keywords' that they believe their target market would type in the search bar when they are looking for their type of product or service. For example, if an advertiser sells mobile games, they would bid on the keyword 'mobile games', hoping a user would type those words in the search bar. This results in a viewing of both your ad and others ads. The user then clicks on your ad, which results in loading up your page in the browser. These ads are called 'sponsored links' or 'sponsored ads' and appear next to and sometimes above the natural or organic results on the page. The advertiser pays only when the user clicks on the ad.

While many companies exist in this space, Google AdWords and Yahoo! Search Marketing, which was formerly Overture, are the largest network operators as of 2007. Even MSN has launched its own PPC services MSN adCenter – http://advertising.microsoft.com/home/home. Depending on the search engine, minimum prices per click start at US$0.01 (up to US$0.50). Very popular search terms can cost much more on popular engines.

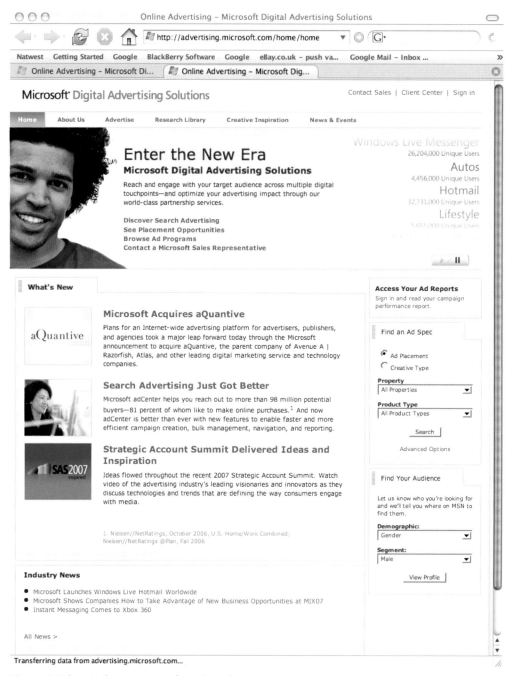

Figure 9.1 *http://advertising.microsoft.com/home/home*

Ad service functionality

The typical common functionality of ad services to track and manage campaigns includes:

- Targeting ads to different users, or content
- Uploading creative, including display advertisements and rich media
- Reporting impressions, clicks, post-click activities, and interaction metrics
- Trafficking ads according to differing business rules
- Optimizing and running a number of ad campaigns based on results.

Advanced functionality services like Google AdWords also include:

- Frequency capping creative so users only see messages a limited number of times
- Ordering creative so users see messages in a specific order
- Targeting users based on their previous online behaviour
- Excluding competitive creative so users do not see competitors' ads directly next to one another
- Displaying creatives so an advertiser can own 100 per cent of the inventory on a page.

Keywords and pay-per-click terms

Keywords are at the heart of achieving high search engine rankings. Search engine spiders look for the keywords in several places on a web page to determine what the site is about and index it accordingly. There is a limited amount of high-traffic, high-ranking keywords. Sometimes consultants disregard this fact entirely and build their entire business around letting their customers pick their own keywords and optimizing the customer websites for those keywords.

The trouble with inexperienced users picking their own keywords is that unless the user is well informed and has the correct software, newsletter, or tool to pick high-ranking keywords, most likely they will choose low-ranking, low-traffic keywords.

Google's Keyword Tool generator has a stats tool that includes search performance and seasonal trends. You can start your search by entering your own keyword phrases or a specific URL.

When a customer comes to an SEO company with a handful of low-ranking keywords they want their advertising optimized for, this makes it 100 times easier for the consultant to make good on its guarantee of improving click-throughs. It is easy to show high-ranking results to their customers after optimization, leading to initial customer satisfaction. Especially when the customer sees a graphic display showing them that five of their keywords are ranked number one, 17 are in the top 10, and 42 are in the top 20 on some of the searches. The customer can do a search on these search engines and verify these results.

The problem with this method is that most likely, these 48 top 20 URLs only collectively gain a few click-throughs a month, whereas one well-chosen, high-ranking, high-traffic keyword that a page is optimized for may gain thousands of clicks per month. Without information on what the high-ranking keywords are, the customer's banners will be optimized but will not gain the traffic they are seeking.

The Keyword Tool in Google allows you to build extensive, relevant keyword lists from one simple interface, generate keyword lists, review traffic estimations for existing and new keywords, and add your keywords directly into your ad groups from the same page. You can combine the relevant keywords you get with one another or with your existing keywords to make them more specific. Or, use the Negative Keywords tab to see negative keywords that might work for your ad group.

How to research keywords

The keywords you use in your advertising should be the start for keywords for your website. It's important to communicate on your website using the terminology that your visitors use. If you use the right terminology and phrases, they will find you. If you're using the wrong terminology, then you're leaving your visitor a bit confused and very put off using your site. You want your advertising to drive lots of traffic to your website. But quantity should never be your first objective; quality traffic should be what you're looking for. Find the keyword phrases related to your industry that your target market is searching for and measure them against your keyword.

Figure 9.2 *Keyword for Google AdWords campaign*

What do people search for?

You can search for keywords in three ways: use keywords you enter, your existing high click-through rate keywords, or any web page URL for your search. You can also expand your keyword search even further to include pages linked to from the original URL. Test the phrase in the search engines you're going to optimize for. For instance, our own keyword research showed that 'conversion data' is a phrase people are using in the search engines; however, if you search on Google using this exact phrase, you will see that people are actually looking for money conversion, religious conversion, weights and metric conversion, etc. – not sites about converting site visitors to buyers. This is why you need to look for the real reason why people are searching. In our case 'conversion data' might be worth testing on PPC for a short period of time, but it's not worth optimizing our organic pages for that phrase.

Targeted keywords and phrases

The next step is keyword measurement and experimentation. We decided to optimize for 'mobile java games' because this phrase showed that there should be reasonable traffic levels, good intent, and a high number of conversions from this phrase. We found that 22.50 per cent of people using that search term end up making a purchase of a java game from our website: www.handyx.net

When a person enters these keywords into a search engine, and your pages appear, you should be speaking their language. Your entire website is a resource about what they're looking for.

A number of tools exist for keyword selection, for us the most notable is Google's keyword selector. You first need to identify keyword phrases that you think fit well, then simply measure the results. After you play around with the results for a while you might start seeing significantly better results forecasts. You are only trying to do one thing and that is selecting the keywords immediately relevant to what your audience is looking for. Never forget it's quality you are looking for not quantity measure, and test those phrases so that you have the best chance of converting your search engine visitors into customers, clients, or subscribers.

To improve the conversion rate of your website, identify the keywords people are using associated to your industry, make sure that the search results from the keywords you select are relevant to your industry, and then optimize your site for those phrases. Finally, measure and test those phrases so that you have the best chance of converting your search engine visitors.

Brainstorm techniques

To 'brainstorm' something means that you're going to dedicate every part of your thought resources to a particular situation or problem. Brainstorming as part of the keyword researching process is important because it helps you come up with keywords and phrases to use in your content and site structure that are not so apparent, and which might in the long run prove big converters for a very low rate.

The keyword research process can be broken down into the following phases:

- Phase 1 – brainstorming, creating the list and checking it twice
- Phase 2 – finding a good keyword research tool
- Phase 3 – finalizing your list
- Phase 4 – planning your strategy
- Phase 5 – executing and then going to phase 1.

The first step of this process is to sit down and write every single imaginable word that someone might use in a search engine to find your site. For example, if you are constructing a site on mobile java games, you might come up with the following:

- Games
- Java Games
- Mobile Games
- Mobile Java.

However, not every person who is looking for 'Mobile Java' will come up with these particular terms. Therefore, you need to brainstorm for any and all keywords and phrases that people might use, such as:

- Arcade Games
- Mobile Arcade
- Games on phones
- Cell phone Games
- Mobile fun
- RPG Games
- Mobile Chess
- Shoot'em up games
- Desert War Java
- Java Phones.

The important thing to remember in brainstorming is that you should try to think of what you would look for, and stem out from there. The more specific you can get, the better. A good rule of thumb would be to come up with 40–50 keywords and phrases, and then narrow them down to the top 20 absolute most effective. How do I know which keywords and phrases will be effective? In other words, which key phrases will bring more searchers to your site and give them a better user experience?

The trick is to target the keyphrases that are most relevant for your site, not merely choosing the words that are the most searched for in terms of traffic. Instead, choose a couple of key phrases for each page in your site that are 'niche' phrases that have less competition.

There are a few other notable keyword tools that are worth checking out as they have been created especially for this purpose; my two favourites are Digital Tracker and Overture. Both of these sites will be able to tell you how many times in a given time period that particular key phrase was searched for.

For example, there are a lot of people that search for the word 'calorie', but probably not too many people that search for the phrase 'calorie counter'. If you have a site that is all about calorie counting, you're providing a service to those searchers who are looking for information on these kinds of products by targeting that particular phrase; plus, you're going to get more focused visitors that are already looking for what you're offering. It's a win–win situation.

Test the phrase in the search engines you're going to optimize for. For example, our own keyword research showed that 'conversion website' is a phrase people are using in the search engines; however, if you search on Google using this exact phrase, you will see that people are in fact looking for money conversion, religious conversion, weights and metric conversion. So these results are not about converting site visitors to buyers.

You need to look for the real reason why people are searching. In our case 'conversion website' might be worth testing on PPC, but it's not worth optimizing our organic pages for that phrase.

To do this yourself, identify keyword phrases that you think fit well with your marketing strategy, and then measure the result. It's about selecting the keywords immediately relevant to what your audience is looking for. The following is a list of some keyword selector tools that we have used over the years, achieving a notable level of success.

1 *Overture Keyword Selector tool:* Overture's Keyword Selector tool shows you how many searches have been conducted over the last month for a particular phrase and lists alternative search terms you may have forgotten about. Overture lumps singular and plural word forms into one phrase which has caused problems for us.

2 *Wordtracker:* Wordtracker is a paid-use tool that lets you look up popular keyword phrases to determine their activity and popularity among competitors. Their Top 1000 report lists the most frequently searched for terms, while their Competition Search option provides valuable information to determine the competitiveness of each phrase. This is very useful for figuring out how difficult it will be to rank for a given term; it sometimes highlights hidden phrases that have low competition rates, but high relevancy.

3 *Trellian Keyword Discovery tool:* This is a fee-based tool where users can ascertain the market share value for a given search term, see how many users search for it daily, identify common spellings and misspellings, and discover which terms are impacted by seasonal trends – very useful for PPC.

Figure 9.3 *Wordtracker website*

4 *Google AdWords Keyword tool:* Google's Keyword PPC tool doesn't provide actual search numbers for keywords. Instead, it displays a coloured bar, giving users only an approximation. Still, it may be useful.

5 *Google Suggest:* Google Suggest is a great way to find synonyms and related word suggestions that may help you expand your original list (Thesaurus.com); again, another way to locate synonyms you may have forgotten.

Figure 9.4 *Google Suggest is a great way to find synonyms*

Ad targeting and optimization

Automated and semi-automated means of optimizing bid prices, placement, targeting, or other characteristics, are just one aspect of ad serving technology. Significant methods include:

- Behavioural targeting – using a profile of prior behaviour on the part of the viewer to determine which ad to show during a given visit. For example, targeting car ads on a portal to a viewer that was known to have visited the automotive section of a general media site.
- Contextual targeting – inferring the optimum ad placement from information contained on the page where the ad is being served. For example, placing mountain bike ads automatically on a page with a mountain biking article.
- Creative optimization – using experimental or predictive methods to explore the optimum creative for a given ad placement and exploiting that determination in further impressions.

Categories

PPC engines can be categorized in 'Keyword', 'Product', and 'Service' engines. However, a number of companies may fall in two or more categories. More models are continually being developed. Currently, pay-per-click programs do not generate any revenue from site traffic to sites using these programs. Only when visitors click on banner advertisements or pop-ups is revenue generated.

Keyword PPCs

As of 2007, notable PPC Keyword search engines include: Google AdWords, Yahoo! Search Marketing (formerly Overture Services), Microsoft adCenter, LookSmart, Miva (formerly Find-What), Ask (formerly Ask Jeeves), 7Search, Kanoodle, and Baidu.

Product PPCs

These engines are also called 'Product comparison' engines or 'Price comparison' engines. 'Product' engines let advertisers provide 'feeds' of their product databases and when users search for a product, the links to the different advertisers for that particular product appear, giving more prominence to advertisers who pay more, but letting the user sort by price to see the lowest priced product and then click on it to buy.

Some of the noteworthy PPC Product search engines are: BizRate.com, Shopzilla.com, NexTag, PriceGrabber.com, and Shopping.com.

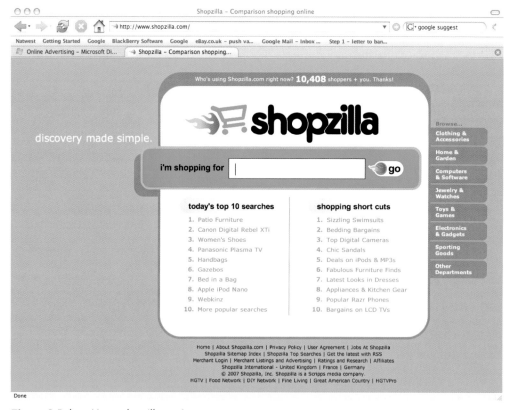

Figure 9.5 *http://www.shopzilla.com/*

Service PPCs

Some Product PPCs have expanded into the service space while other service engines operate in specific verticals. Service engines let advertisers provide feeds of their service databases and when users search for a service, offering links to advertisers for that particular service appear, giving

Figure 9.6 *http://www.tripadvisor.com/*

prominence to advertisers who pay more, but letting users sort their results by price or other methods.

Examples of PPC Services search engines include NexTag, Pricethat SideStep, and TripAdvisor.

Pay per call

Similar to pay per click, pay per call is a business model for ad listings in search engines and directories that allows publishers to charge local advertisers on a per-call basis for each lead (call) they generate. The term 'pay per call' is sometimes confused with 'click to call'. Click to call, along with call tracking, is a technology that enables the 'pay-per-call' business model – a type of online advertising that mixes search functionality and on-the-phone interaction resulting in an appealing marketing opportunity for businesses, especially local businesses without a website.

From the consumer standpoint, it's much easier to call a local business than rely on email to ask details about pricing, programs and product availability. When your pipes are leaking, and you need to locate a plumber – fast – people will be searching for phone numbers, not relying on email.

Pay per call is not just restricted to local advertisers. Many of the pay-per-call search engines allow advertisers with a national presence to create ads with local telephone numbers. According to the Kelsey Group, the pay-per-call market is expected to reach US$3.7 billion by 2010.

Pay per action

(Pay-Per-Action on Google) Pay per action involves increasing your advertising reach while paying only for actions that you define. First, you create an ad and define the action that you want a user to perform when they visit your site, such as signing up for your newsletter or purchasing a product. Then you'll set the amount that you're willing to pay when this action is completed. Finally, you'll install a conversion tracking code on your website so that you can verify when an action has been completed.

Once you've completed these steps, publishers in the Google content network can choose to place your ads on their website. You'll only pay when a user clicks on your ad, visits your site, and completes your desired action.

Pay-per-action ads complement current campaigns by providing a new pricing model that extends your reach and allows you to pay only when a defined action is completed on your site.

Activity cost per time unit analysis

Activity cost per time unit analysis computes the cost per time unit for each activity in a simulated process. You can use this analysis to answer the question 'how much is this costing us per day?' for each activity in a process. Activities that have the highest costs per unit of time are often the best candidates for streamlining or even eliminating from a process. An example of one way you could use this analysis is to determine the cost per day of running a plant, to help decide whether to keep the plant open or to close it.

CTR – click-through rate

Click-through rate, or CTR, is a way of measuring the success of an online advertising campaign. A CTR is obtained by dividing the number of users who clicked on an ad on a web page by the number of times the ad was delivered (impressions). For example, if your banner ad was delivered 100 times (impressions delivered) and one person clicked on it (clicks recorded), then the resulting CTR would be 1 per cent.

Figure 9.7 *Examples of banners/buttons with a varied format for testing*

Banner ad click-through rates have fallen over time, often measuring significantly less than 1 per cent. By selecting an appropriate advertising site with high affinity (e.g. a movie magazine for a movie advertisement), the same banner can achieve a substantially higher click-through rate. Personalized ads, unusual formats, and more obtrusive ads typically have higher click-through rates than standard banner ads.

CTR is most commonly defined as number of clicks divided by number of impressions, and generally not in terms of number of persons who clicked. This is an important difference because if one person clicks 10 times on the same advertisement instead of once, then the CTR would increase in the earlier definition but would stay the same in terms of later definition.

CPM – cost per mille

CPM, or cost per mille or, less commonly, cost per thousand (CPT). In Latin mille means thousand, therefore, CPM means cost per thousand. CPM is a commonly used measurement in advertising. Radio, television, newspaper, magazine and online advertising can be purchased on the basis of what it costs to show the ad to one thousand viewers (CPM). It is used in marketing as a benchmark to calculate the relative cost of an advertising campaign or an ad message in a given medium. Rather than an absolute cost, CPM estimates the cost per 1000 views of the ad.

An example of calculating the CPM:

1 Total cost for running the ad is $15 000.
2 The total audience is 2 400 000 people.
3 The CPM is computed as CPM = $15 000/(2 400 000/1000) = $0.625.

CPT – cost per thousand

The term CPM, cost per mille is more commonly used – see above.

eCPM – effective cost per mille

Effective cost per mille, or eCPM, is a phrase often used in online advertising and online marketing circles. It means the cost of every 1000 ad impressions shown.

CPM is considered the optimal form of selling online advertising from the publisher's point of view, as a publisher gets paid every time an ad is shown.

eCPM is used to determine the effectiveness of a publisher's inventory being sold via a CPA, CPC, or CPT basis. The eCPM tells the publisher what they would have received if they sold the advertising inventory on a CPM basis (instead of a CPA, CPC, or CPT basis).

eCPA – effective cost per action

Effective cost per action is a phrase often used in online advertising and online marketing circles.

CPA is considered the optimal form of buying online advertising from the advertiser's point of view, as they only pay for an advert when an action has occurred. An action can be a product being purchased, or a form being filled, etc. The desired action to be performed is determined by the advertiser.

eCPA is used to measure the effectiveness of advertising; it tells the advertiser what they would have paid if they purchased the advertising inventory on a CPA basis, instead of a CPC, CPM, or CPT basis.

CPI – cost per impression

The cost per impression, or CPI, is often measured using the CPM (cost per mille) metric and is a phrase often used in online advertising and marketing related to web traffic. It is used for measuring the worth and cost of a specific eMarketing campaign. This technique is applied with web banners, text links, email spam, and opt-in email advertising, although opt-in email advertising is more commonly charged on a cost per action (CPA) basis.

This type of advertising arrangement closely resembles Television and Print Advertising Methods for speculating the cost of an advertisement. Often, industry agreed approximates are used. With television the Nielsen Ratings are used and print is based on the circulation a publication has.

For online advertising, the numbers of views can be a lot more precise. When a user requests a web page, the originating server creates a log entry. Also, a third-party tracker can be placed in the Web page to verify how many accesses that page had.

CPM and/or flat rate advertising deals are preferred by the publisher or webmaster because they will get paid regardless of any action taken.

For advertisers a performance-based system is preferred. There are two methods for paying for performance:

1 CPA – cost per action/acquisition, and
2 CPC – cost per click-through.

Today, it is very common for large publishers to charge for most of their advertising inventory on a CPM or cost per time (CPT) basis.

The CPA can be determined by different factors, depending where the online advertising inventory is being purchased.

CPC – cost per click

Cost per click (CPC) is an advertising technique used on websites, advertising networks, and search engines.

Keyword bucketing

Keyword bucketing is a tactical execution of a pay per click (PPC) strategy. Its purpose is to create highly targeted text ad on the search engines to increase click-through rate (CTR) and return on advertising spend (ROAS), which is the amount of revenue generated per unit of currency spent on a given advertising method.

Keyword bucketing involves categorizing all your keywords into similar 'buckets'. Once that is done, a specific ad is written for each keyword bucket.

Measuring effectiveness

There are three standard ways to measure the effectiveness of your online advertising spend:

- Return on Advertising Spend (ROAS)
- Conversion Rate
- Return on Investment (ROI)

Return On Advertising Spend (ROAS) tells you how much revenue you generated per pound spent on a given advertising vehicle.

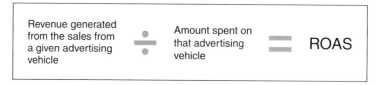

Conversion Rate determines how many visits to your site 'convert' to a sale or 'action'.

Return on Investment (ROI) tells you how much profit you generated per pound spent on a given advertising vehicle.

| Profit generated from the sales from a given advertising vehicle | ÷ | Amount spent on that advertising vehicle | = | ROI |

Chapter 10
Pay-per-click strategies

Most people reading this book will probably be embarking on an SEO strategy for the first time, or looking at reconsidering their current strategy. Like all projects, the first stages are the honeymoon stages. People want to meet you, they have plenty of ideas to share with you and, most importantly, they are open to working with you. There's potential for change and people reflect on your ideas to make those changes. Enjoy this stage, as things get tough from here on.

Welcome to the in-house SEO life cycle, which looks like an upside down bell curve. Over time, things can improve as you figure out how to navigate through the personalities, politics, and red tape of your organization, and things start to get implemented. But things can also get very difficult, especially if you made a few big promises. People do not have the patience to wait for good news, and maybe you skipped the bit that told everybody it would take six months before they could see anything tangible. Whatever good news you might have promised at the beginning of the project, it will start to come back and haunt you.

Life in-house is wonderful in the honeymoon period, and then it gets progressively worse as the novelty wears off; for example, you might have to pay a lot of attention to internal detail. Sometimes it is just impossible to implement something internally, but every day expects the results to come in at the agreed time. It starts getting frustrating. You begin to face more opposition. Communication seems off and you're starting to wonder what happened. SEO changes will become difficult to schedule and IT doesn't seem as interested in SEO. Once you finally get changes prioritized and scheduled, you plead that they won't get cut to make time for other enhancements. After three to six months, you'll begin to feel that the honeymoon has ended and reality has set in. This is the challenge of getting SEO stuff done.

Take this knowledge about the in-house life cycle and run with it by using it very wisely. During this phase, you have the key people's attention. This is the time to network and build relationships. Once the honeymoon ends, you may find it difficult to get these people's time and attention. If you leverage your honeymoon to its fullest potential, there will be fewer big issues to deal with, allowing you to choose your battles more wisely.

Management wants data and, in our experience, if you can give a snapshot of where you are in a campaign you're halfway there. But if things are not fully setup or have not gone to plan, or have just gone downright wrong, then this will reflect badly on you. Don't waste all of this interest and priority on the easy stuff – you may be better served by having IT focus on the big stuff and leave page copy, page title and meta data changes to much later in the in-house SEO life cycle.

Getting the right pay-per-click partner in place and starting to generate reports is probably the most satisfying way to account for trends later in the life cycle. If there is one piece of advice I can recommend to anybody embarking on a new strategy, it is use Google AdWords.

Google AdWords pay-per-click strategies

AdWords gives you 24/7 access to detailed performance reports that help you track the effectiveness of your ad campaigns. You can expect a prompt response to your email questions, typically within one business day. Google AdWords account is fully customizable for any advertiser, with no monthly minimum spending limit or time commitment, and only a minimal fee to set up your account. The snapshot features in Google AdWords allow you to get a quick overview of the account without going into to much detail. All the cost estimations tools are available as well as the recently launched Google Analytics. Web Analytics is the measurement, collection, analysis and reporting of Internet data for the purposes of understanding and optimizing web usage.

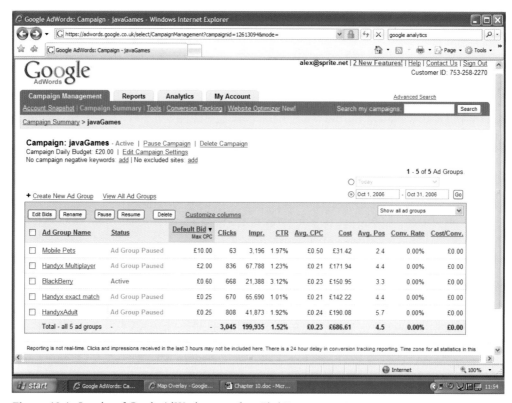

Figure 10.1 *Snapshot of Google AdWords account for a BlackBerry content site*

Web Analytics

Site performance measurement looks at how successfully the site is able to service visitors and customers. It involves aspects of the site such as the speed of page delivery, site availability and the responsiveness of transactional processes. Site technical performance can help explain visitor behaviour on the site and provides the context for marketing and site strategy.

Google Analytics allows this kind of analysis. These reports will tell you which screen resolutions, connection speeds, and browser platforms you should optimize your site for. For high-traffic sites you might also need to consider data such as page download times and site availability; you will probably need to subscribe to a performance management service such as Keynote or Gomez. One advantage of these types of services is that they also allow you to benchmark your performance against a range of other sites or your competitors.

On 9 May 2007, Google Analytics launched its much awaited new design of its free web analytics service with some major interface changes increasing discoverability and accessibility. But the biggest change is its simplification of all aspects of data analysis, which includes presentation. You can learn which online marketing initiatives are cost-effective and see how visitors actually interact with your site.

Google Analytics features the following:

ECommerce reporting

This reporting feature is probably the most effective for anybody retailing products from their site. It plugs in in all aspects of sales, allowing you to go through the full life cycle of a transaction. Even without an eCommerce website, you can monetize or add value to your website by using this feature in advanced website analysis. A sale is an obvious goal, but PDF downloads, registration, brochure requests or viewing a specific page can also be considered goals. This report provides an overview of eCommerce activity on your site.

Total revenue

Revenue is determined by the number of purchases and the average purchase value. Some important steps you can take to maximize revenue are:

1 Traffic Sources reports: purchase targeted advertising and write effective ads.
2 Content reports: make sure your landing pages show the information, services, or products that you promise in your ads.
3 Goals reports: simplify your conversion funnels so that fewer would-be customers abandon the checkout process.

Conversion Rate

This report shows the rate at which visits to your site result in purchases. Tracking conversion rates over time is an effective way of determining whether your marketing and website are becoming more or less efficient at turning visitors into customers. Note that conversion rates are most useful as company-specific benchmarks against which to assess marketing and site effectiveness because conversion rates vary considerably across businesses. In Analytics, the Conversion Rate indicates the percentage of visitors that convert on at least one of the goals you have defined for that profile. This rate, shown in the Conversion Rate report and in the Goal Conversion tab of the Visitors and Traffic Sources reports, is different to the AdWords Conversion Rate you see in your AdWords account. In AdWords, the Conversion Rate refers to the percentage of clicks that end in an AdWords conversion, defined by the AdWords Conversion Tracking code.

Average order value

Tracking changes to the average order value over time is important to many eCommerce sites, who monitor this metric to see if cross-promotions are working. This is an important metric that appears in many executive and shareholder reports for retail companies.

Product overview

This report shows the number of items sold, the total revenue, the average price, and the average order quantity for each product you sell online. Click any SKU to drill down and view detail.

Product SKUs

This report shows the number of items for each SKU sold, the total revenue, the average price, and the average order quantity for each product you sell online.

Categories

For eCommerce sites, understanding which products are selling online is crucial for generating relevant content, promotions and advertisements. This report shows the number of items sold, the total revenue, the average price, and the average order quantity for each product you sell online.

Transactions

This report is a list of all transactions on your site, and is useful for auditing your transactions.

Visits to purchase

Understanding your sales cycle is important to the overall success of your site. This report helps you understand how many visits it takes to convert your visitors into customers and the kind of content you need to create in order to reach your prospects.

Time to purchase

Understanding your sales cycle is imperative to the overall achievement of your site. This report helps you realize how long it takes to convert your visitors into customers and, by extension, the kind of content you need to create in order to reach new sales.

Figure 10.2 *Main screen with a simplified data analysis of bb.handyx.net*

Improved user interface

This is a much improved user interface with leading-edge web 2.0/AJA technology. Focusing on data-driven and not menu-driven navigation, Google Analytics offers a user-friendly interface that intuitively provides options, information and customization.

Site Overlay

Google Analytics displays your website pages superimposed with click and conversion data for each link. Site Overlay doesn't require any downloads or other plug-ins to run. It allows you to easily see which links lead to conversions, just by browsing your site. You can intuitively browse your website directly on your links and immediately see the popularity and effectiveness of each link on every page of your site. These powerful and graphic reports display the effectiveness of your site design in a visual method and, as you see from Figure 10.3, they are instantly understandable.

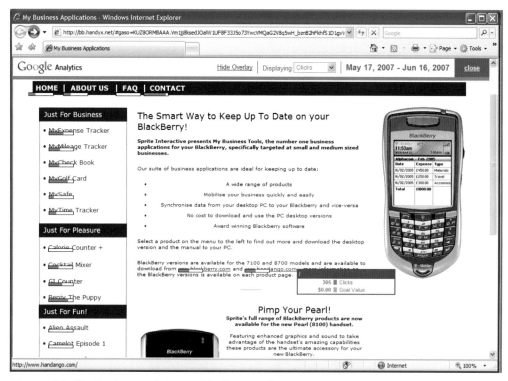

Figure 10.3 *Site Overlay – vastly improved for dynamic websites*

GeoTargeting

This allows you to discover at a glance where your best customers are located – drill down through four levels of geography to city level. GeoTargeting maps, reports, and cross-segmentation allow

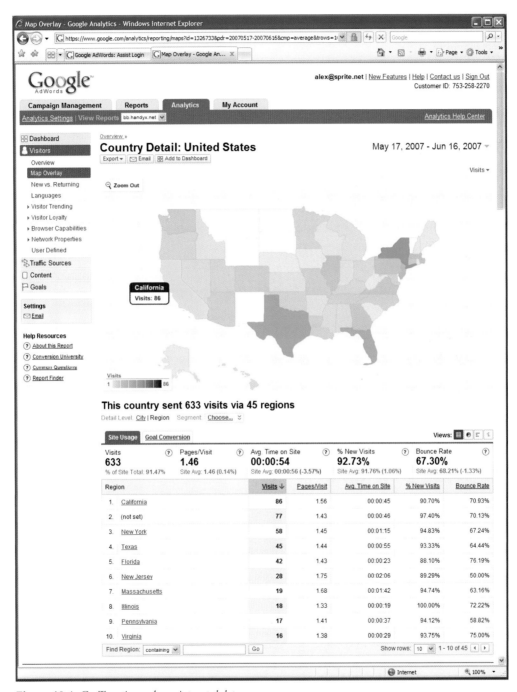

Figure 10.4 *GeoTargeting – clearer integrated data*

you to find out where your visitors come from, and which markets have the greatest profit potential. Compare date ranges to see the impact on traffic to your site. If you are seeing unusually high visitor volume then this tool allows you to explore and analyse this market opportunity. This can minimize wasted PPC spend by better targeting your ads to the more successful regions. The visualizing of the source of your traffic can really allow you to increase efficiencies and seize opportunities. You can also find out your visitors' connection speed and which markets are the most lucrative. You can compare conversion metrics and visitor value for just about any other geographic location.

Scheduled email exporting

You can schedule and automatically send recurring emails using this feature within Google Analytics. Schedule reports can be emailed to various recipients in multiple formats. Schedule or send ad-hoc personalized report emails that contain totally customized information you want to share.

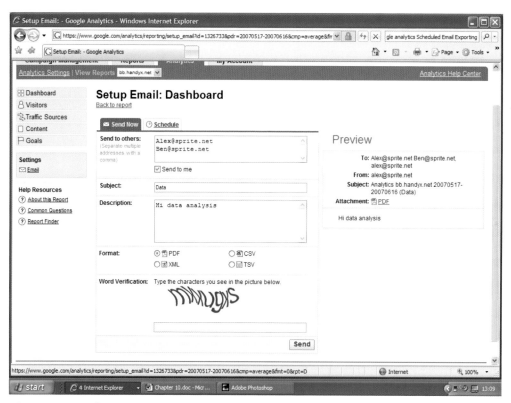

Figure 10.5 Email reporting

Improved advanced visitor segmentation

Define your own custom segments or dive into over 13 predefined segments such as geographic location and new *vs* returning visitors. Compare visitor behaviour, conversion metrics, and trends for individuals or groups of visitors. Since you often can't control which pages people enter your site through, you want to make sure if they don't find what they're looking for on the first page they hit, they know how to get to the information they want. This feature is one of the few ways you can track the navigational quality of your site. It is both a design and copy issue, since you can always write hyperlinks into copy that lead to related topics in other site areas. Being able to analyse the behaviour of your customer base helps you focus on some of these creative issues within your site.

Figure 10.6 *Visitor segmentation chart looking at new* vs *returning visitors*

The segmentation tool allows you to identify the common problem of returning visitors using the homepage as the primary entry page. Start your measurement efforts there, then move on to other important top 10 entry pages, tweaking the message on each to minimize 'percent single page access' visits on each page. On most sites, 85–95 per cent of the traffic is coming in through the top 10 entry pages. This tool allows you to see this problem graphically.

Funnel visualization

A 'funnel' is a series of pages through which a visitor must pass before reaching the conversion goal. The name comes from a graph of visitors who reach each page – the first page counts the most visitors, and each successive page shows less visitors as they drop off before reaching the final goal.

This is probably the most useful feature to help eliminate bottlenecks in your checkout and conversion processes in order to reduce abandonment. You can create custom configured funnels to pinpoint where visitors leave your funnels and find out where they go. Visitors are usually excited about what you're offering – they speed through the first few steps in the conversion process, and then exit your site. It's mysterious, but it doesn't have to be. The funnel visualization feature shows you all the bottlenecks in your processes – attributable to such factors as confusing content or maze-like navigation – so you can eliminate or work around them and start funnelling visitors through the steps you want them to take, all the way through to conversion.

The purpose of tracking these pages is to see how efficiently your pages direct visitors to their goal. If any of the funnel pages are overly complicated, or not designed to be user-friendly, then you will see significant drop off and lower conversion rates.

Trend reporting

Sometimes, it's not enough to know how well your site or ads performed this week. You need to know how this week compares to last week – or how this month's Fridays compare to all the Fridays last month. Are conversions 'up' or 'down'? And, if so, by how many percentage points? This trend reporting feature is a very convenient way to compare metrics across months, days, weeks, or any two date ranges. Google Analytics shows you a simple diagram for whether you are 'up' or 'down' for each metric.

Interactive trend reporting is built into Google Analytics reports, which means that you can tell where you stand on any metric but, best of all, it uses data to support your AdWords campaigns.

Google Analytics maximizes the effectiveness of interactive marketing. Even the smallest frustration or uncertainty can waylay customers. The wide variety of PDAs (Personal Digital Assistants) makes it challenging to attract customers from the start. Once an application seeker lands on a website, they must complete purchasing information online. If the application process seems too lengthy or complex, or requests for technical information are made too soon, then customers may abandon their efforts. It can be very difficult to pinpoint the reasons customers don't complete a purchase of an application.

We applied Google Analytics to maximize the effectiveness of interactive marketing campaigns and fine-tune the www.handyx.net site to acquire and keep online customers. We needed to run a number of campaigns and to keep a pulse on which keywords and campaigns were most effective, and determine what types of customers were purchasing the different types of applications, as well as track abandonment rates for each page. We had to continually fine-tune site design and application processes as and when we detected any kind of trend in order to boost conversion rates.

The basis of the analytics was a new Google AdWords campaign employing hundreds of keywords to drive traffic to the application site. We determined that search-based advertising is more effective in driving traffic and garnering leads than banner advertising or other online marketing efforts. Full tracking integration with Google Analytics took less than one week, and has enabled us to track customers from initial ad responses through to completed purchases.

End-to-end tracking

By integrating Google Analytics, we have a closed-loop view of our online marketing efforts. We can see where completed purchases originated, even down to knowing which keyword a customer searched on to land on the site. This level of detail is extremely powerful in shaping ongoing advertising campaigns and acquiring the most desirable customers. We use Google Analytics to determine where and when customers leave each page. From the beginning, we were successful at driving traffic to the site – but abandonment rates were high. We turned to the funnel reports in Google Analytics to determine abandonment rates on specific pages or at certain stages of the application process.

Google Analytics also gauges which AdWords/keywords deliver the best results, as well as providing information on cost per click on the handyx website. We concentrated search keyword buys on the most effective family of keywords and fine-tuned the copy in both search-based and banner ads to focus on the most return-intensive creative. We adjusted landing pages, depending on which keyword users clicked on. We also revised the copy throughout the site, primarily on the landing pages, to better communicate goals for each page. After the adjustments, the average bounce rate on the top five entry pages decreased 22 per cent, and the conversion rate for the landing pages focused on search keyword buys increased more than 28 per cent.

In conclusion, evaluating online initiatives is not just about analysing website traffic, but about understanding the 'why' and the 'what for'. As you use Google Analytics, remember to take advantage of other data sources – sources that help you put your visitor and customer at the centre of your thinking.

Appendix A

W3C Mobile Web Best Practices

Mobile Web Best Practices 1.0

Basic Guidelines

W3C Proposed Recommendation 2 November 2006

This version:
> http://www.w3.org/TR/2006/PR-mobile-bp-20061102/

Latest version:
> http://www.w3.org/TR/mobile-bp/

Previous version:
> http://www.w3.org/TR/2006/CR-mobile-bp-20060627/

Editors:
> Jo Rabin, mTLD Mobile Top Level Domain (dotMobi)
> Charles McCathieNevile, Opera Software [Early Drafts]

Abstract

This document specifies Best Practices for delivering Web content to mobile devices. The principal objective is to improve the user experience of the Web when accessed from such devices.

The recommendations refer to delivered content and not to the processes by which it is created, nor to the devices or user agents to which it is delivered.

It is primarily directed at creators, maintainers and operators of Web sites. Readers of this document are expected to be familiar with the creation of Web sites, and to have a general familiarity with the technologies involved, such as Web servers and HTTP. Readers are not expected to have a background in mobile-specific technologies.

1 Introduction

1.1 Purpose of the Document

This document sets out a series of recommendations designed to improve the user experience of the Web on mobile devices.

The recommendations are offered to creators, maintainers and operators of Web sites and are intended as the basis for assessing conformance to the mobileOK trustmark, which is described in the Mobile Web Best Practices Working Group Charter and is not developed in this document. At the time of writing of this document, documents describing mobileOK and techniques for implementing the Best Practice recommendations are being worked on.

1.2 How the Best Practices are Organized

The document is organized as follows:

1 Introduction. Describes the audience, purpose and scope of the document.
2 Requirements. An illustration of the type of problems that the Best Practices are intended to ameliorate.
3 Delivery Context. Discusses the environment within which mobile access to the Web is realized, with particular reference to adaptation.
4 Structure of Best Practice Statements. A discussion of the organization of the Best Practices, and sources from which they were derived.
5 Best Practice Statements. The statements themselves.
6 Conformance and mobileOK. A brief conformance statement and reference to the mobileOK documentation.

1.3 Audience

Readers of this document are expected to be familiar with the creation of Web sites, and to have a general familiarity with the technologies involved, such as Web servers and HTTP. Readers are not expected to have a background in mobile-specific technologies.

Our intention is to make it clear to all involved what the Best Practices are, and hence establish a common basis of understanding. As a result of wishing to be clear to those not already involved in the development of mobile friendly content, some of our statements may appear to be obvious or trivial to those with experience in this area.

The document is not targeted solely at developers; others, such as interaction and graphic designers are encouraged to read it.

1.4 Scope

The scope of these Best Practices is laid out in "Scope of Mobile Web Best Practices". In summary, this document refers primarily to the extension of Web browsing onto mobile devices.

The Best Practice recommendations refer to delivered content. While they are clearly relevant to the processes of content creation and rendering on devices, they are not intended to be Best Practices for those activities.

As the goal of the document is to specify Best Practices for delivery to mobile devices, statements that do not have a specific mobile aspect are not included. In particular, many Web Content Accessibility Guidelines are general to all forms of Web access and are not repeated here unless they have a specific mobile interpretation. Examples of general good practice which have a specific mobile interpretation include "Error Messages" and "Color".

See **B Related Reading** for information about the related topics of Internationalization, Web Accessibility and Device Independence.

1.4.1 Phasing

As discussed in the Scope document there are many aspects to Mobile Web Best Practices. At present, for example, the design and construction of many Web sites and pages make for a poor user experience when they are viewed on a mobile device.

The quality of the user's Web experience via a mobile device depends significantly on the usability of Web sites, of browsers, and of the device itself. Although browser usability and device usability are important (for reading, navigating, and interacting with content), this document focuses primarily on Best Practices for improving site usability.

In future phases other aspects may be considered, e.g. Best Practices as applied to adaptation and devices. Also in future phases the scope of the recommendations may be extended beyond "Traditional Web Browsing" into fields such as multimodal interaction.

1.5   Relationship to other Best Practices and recommendations

These recommendations are in part derived from the Web Content Accessibility Guidelines. As noted above, WCAG guidelines are supplementary to the Mobile Web Best Practices, whose scope is limited to matters that have a specific mobile relevance.

This document builds on some of the concepts described by the Device Independence Working Group (DIWG) in the Device Independence Principles. The document discusses device and delivery channel characteristics, which the DIWG has named "Delivery Context". In addition, the document uses some terminology from DIWG's Glossary of Terms for Device Independence.

The BPWG is developing a companion document describing techniques by which the Best Practice statements in this document can be implemented.

1.6   Longevity and Versioning

The Best Practices have been written at a level of generality that allows them to be applicable across a range of markup languages. They have been written with enduring properties of mobile access to the Web in mind. While the factors identified in 3.7 Default Delivery Context, such as screen dimensions, will change over time, it seems likely that the distinguishing features of mobile access such as cost and difficulty of input will remain issues.

This document may be reviewed from time to time. When necessary, an updated version will be released with clear documentation as to the changes that have been introduced.

2   Requirements

This section discusses the requirements of the Mobile Web Best Practice statements in section 5. The statement of requirements is intended to be illustrative rather than exhaustive or complete.

2.1   Presentation Issues

Today, many Web pages are laid out for presentation on desktop size displays, and exploit capabilities of desktop browsing software.

Accessing such a Web page on a mobile device often results in a poor or unusable experience. Contributing factors include pages not being laid out as intended. Because of the limited screen size and the limited amount of material that is visible to the user, context and overview are lost.

Because of the limited screen size, the subject matter of the page may require considerable scrolling to be visible, especially if the top of the page is occupied by images and navigation links. In these cases the user gets no immediate feedback as to whether their retrieval has resulted in the right content.

It is particularly important in the mobile context to help the user create a mental image of the site. This can be assisted by adopting a consistent style and can be considerably diminished by an uneven style.

2.2 Input

Mobile device input is often difficult when compared with use of a desktop device equipped with a keyboard. Mobile devices often have only a very limited keypad, with small keys, and there is frequently no pointing device.

One of the difficulties of the mobile Web is that URIs are very difficult to type. Lengthy URIs and those that contain a lot of punctuation are particularly difficult to type correctly.

Because of the limitations of screen and input, forms are hard to fill in. This is because navigation between fields may not occur in the expected order and because of the difficulty in typing into the fields.

While many modern devices provide back buttons, some do not, and in some cases, where back functionality exists, users may not know how to invoke it. This means that it is often very hard to recover from errors, broken links and so on.

2.3 Bandwidth and Cost

Mobile networks can be slow compared with fixed data connections and often have a measurably higher latency. This can lead to long retrieval times, especially for lengthy content and for content that requires a lot of navigation between pages.

Mobile data transfer often costs money. The fact that mobile devices frequently support only limited types of content means that a user may follow a link and retrieve information that is unusable on their device.

Even if the content type can be interpreted by their device there is often an issue with the experience not being satisfactory – for example, larger images may only be viewable in small pieces and require considerable scrolling.

Web pages can contain content that the user has not specifically requested – especially advertising and large images. In the mobile world this extra material contributes to poor usability and may add considerably to the cost of the retrieval.

2.4 User Goals

Mobile users typically have different interests to users of fixed or desktop devices. They are likely to have more immediate and goal-directed intentions than desktop Web users. Their intentions are often to find out specific pieces of information that are relevant to their context. An example of such a goal-directed application might be the user requiring specific information about schedules for a journey they are currently undertaking.

Equally, mobile users are typically less interested in lengthy documents or in browsing. The ergonomics of the device are frequently unsuitable for reading lengthy documents, and users will often only access such information from mobile devices as a last resort, because more convenient access is not available.

2.5 Advertising

Developers of commercial Web sites should note that different commercial models are often at work when the Web is accessed from mobile devices as compared with desktop devices. For example, some mechanisms that are commonly used for presentation of advertising material (such as pop-ups, pop-unders and large banners) do not work well on small devices and are therefore contrary to Best Practice recommendations such as [CENTRAL_MEANING], [LARGE_GRAPHICS] and [POP_UPS].

It is not the intention of the MWI to limit or to restrict advertising; rather it is the intention that the user experience of the site as a whole, including advertising, if any, is as effective as possible.

2.6 Device Limitations

As noted above, the restrictions imposed by the keyboard and the screen typically require a different approach to page design than for desktop devices. As detailed in the Scope document, various other limitations may apply and these have an impact on the usability of the Web from a mobile device.

Mobile browsers often do not support scripting or plug-ins, which means that the range of content that they support is limited. In many cases the user has no choice of browser and upgrading it is not possible.

Some activities associated with rendering Web pages are computationally intensive – for example re-flowing pages, laying out tables, processing unnecessarily long and complex style sheets and handling invalid markup. Mobile devices typically have quite limited processing power which means that page rendering may take a noticeable time to complete. As well as introducing a noticeable delay, such processing uses more power as does communication with the server.

Many devices have limited memory available for pages and images, and exceeding their memory limitations results in incomplete display and can cause other problems.

2.7 Advantages

In discussing the limitations of mobile devices for delivery of Web content it is easy to lose sight of the fact that they are extremely popular and very common.

This popularity largely stems at present from them being:

- personal
- personalizable
- portable
- connected

and increasingly multi-functional beyond their original purpose of voice communications.

In addition to these factors, the advantages of mobile devices will increasingly include:

- location awareness
- one-handed operation
- always on
- universal alerting device

By way of illustration of some of these factors: the Web can go where you go. You do not have to remember to do something on the Web when you get back to your computer. You can do it immediately, within the context that made you want to use the Web in the first place.

Moreover, with mobile devices appearing in all shapes and forms, and with a growing variety of features like location technology, cameras, voice recognition, touch screens, etc., the Web can reach a much wider audience, and at all times in all situations. It has the opportunity to reach into places where wires cannot go, to places previously unthinkable (e.g. providing medical info to mountain rescue scenes) and to accompany everyone as easily as they carry the time on their wristwatches.

Finally, today, many more people have access to mobile devices than access to a desktop computer. This is likely to be very significant in developing countries, where Web-capable mobile devices may play as similar a role in deploying wide-spread Web access as the mobile phone has played for providing "plain old telephone service".

3 Delivery Context

Delivery Context is used with the specific meaning defined in the Device Independence Glossary.

3.1 One Web

The recommendations in this document are intended to improve the experience of the Web on mobile devices. While the recommendations are not specifically addressed at the desktop browsing experience, it must be understood that they are made in the context of wishing to work towards "One Web".

As discussed in the Scope document, *One Web* means making, as far as is reasonable, the same information and services available to users irrespective of the device they are using. However, it does not mean that exactly the same information is available in exactly the same representation across all devices. The context of mobile use, device capability variations, bandwidth issues and mobile network capabilities all affect the representation. Furthermore, some services and information are more suitable for and targeted at particular user contexts (see 5.1.1 Thematic Consistency of Resource Identified by a URI).

Some services have a primarily mobile appeal (location based services, for example). Some have a primarily mobile appeal but have a complementary desktop aspect (for instance for complex configuration tasks). Still others have a primarily desktop appeal but a complementary mobile aspect (possibly for alerting). Finally there will remain some Web applications that have a primarily desktop appeal (lengthy reference material, rich images, for example).

It is likely that application designers and service providers will wish to provide the best possible experience in the context in which their service has the most appeal. However, while services may be most appropriately experienced in one context or another, it is considered best practice to provide as reasonable experience as is possible given device limitations and not to exclude access from any particular class of device, except where this is necessary because of device limitations.

From the perspective of this document this means that services should be available as some variant of HTML over HTTP (see 3.7 Default Delivery Context).

3.2 Background to Adaptation

The widely varying characteristics of mobile devices can make it difficult for a Web site to provide an acceptable user experience across a significant range of devices. For example different devices support different markup features and different screen sizes may demand different sized images. Consequently, it is very common when delivering content to mobile devices to vary the details of the markup, format of images, image sizes, color depths and so on to suit the characteristics of the device in question. The process of altering content to enhance the user experience on particular devices is referred to as *Content Adaptation*.

We do not describe adaptation in detail in this document. For a more detailed description, readers are referred to the Device Independence Principles.

In addition, the sister group of the Best Practices Working Group, the Device Description Working Group, is currently defining requirements for a repository of mobile device characteristics that are relevant to content adaptation.

3.3 Adaptation Implementation Model

There are a number of different implementation models for content adaptation. On the one hand, adaptation may be quite simple and consist of determining the device type and choosing the most appropriate set of previously prepared content to match the device characteristics. At the other extreme it may be carried out in a completely dynamic way, with content formatted at the time of retrieval, taking into account not only statically determined properties, such as screen dimension, but also dynamically determined properties, such as the temporary attachment of a fully featured keyboard.

Adaptation can be carried out in a number of different points in the delivery of content to the device:

Server Side adaptation implies that the content is delivered by the originating content server or application.

In-Network adaptation is where the content is altered as it passes through one or more network components. Some network operators, for example, compress images before they are passed over the air to the mobile device.

Client Side adaptation consists of the device accepting content and displaying it in an appropriate way for its characteristics.

Whatever the adaptation model at work, the process of adaptation should not diminish accessibility.

3.4 Assumptions about Adaptation

In phase 1 (See 1.4.1 Phasing) it is assumed that content adaptation, if any, is carried out Server Side. Future phases may consider the implications of content adaptation elsewhere, especially the issues concerning the granting of authority to third parties to carry out adaptation, prohibiting adaptation and so on. Later phases may also address multiple adaptation, i.e. the possibility that adaptation can be applied at more than one point and that In-Network adaptation may occur more than once.

It is also assumed that it is possible to create a site that is consistent with the Best Practice recommendations without carrying out adaptation at all. However it is likely that a more sophisticated and enhanced user experience will be achieved if adaptation is used.

3.5 Establishing Context

Providing variations on the user experience that are appropriate in different cases requires the content provider to know a significant amount about the characteristics of the device, the properties of the browser in use and the transparency of the network connection to the device.

For simple sites that present an interface which is similar across a broad range of contexts, the need for such information is diminished when compared with a sophisticated site that has an optimized navigation structure, presents different size images or carries out other adaptations to suit the particular delivery context.

There are several methods by which a content provider can discover information about the delivery context, such as CC/PP, UAPROF, CSS Media Queries and various outputs of the Device Independence Working Group. The companion Techniques document describes these methods.

3.6 Choice of User Experience

In the interests of "One Web" (see 3.1 One Web) considerations, the content provider may choose to allow the user to select from broad categories such as mobile or desktop presentation, where these are distinguished in the application. If the presentation option has been determined automatically, the content provider may choose to allow the user to override the automatic determination. Where a choice of presentations is available, it is good practice to record the user's preferences and to allow them to be changed.

Given an appropriate server environment, it is unlikely that the content provider will be unable to find out anything about the delivery context. However, this can happen, either because details of the delivery context are not available in sufficient detail or because the server does not provide the ability to inspect and act on the information provided. In this case a "reasonable default experience" should be provided.

The details of the default experience depend upon a number of factors including, but not limited to, the geographic region in which the service is offered and the primary intention of the service (e.g. considering whether the service is primarily desktop focused vs. primarily mobile focused).

3.7 Default Delivery Context

In order to allow content providers to share a consistent view of a default mobile experience the BPWG has defined the Default Delivery Context. This allows providers to create appropriate experiences in the absence of adaptation and provides a baseline experience where adaptation is used. The Default Delivery Context has been determined by the BPWG as being the minimum delivery context specification necessary for a reasonable experience of the Web. It is recognized that devices that do not meet this specification can provide a reasonable experience of other non-Web services.

It is also recognized that this specification is made against the background of demographic, cultural and economic assumptions. Content providers may choose to provide services that demand a different or lower delivery context specification, but should try to provide an experience that exploits the capabilities of the Default Delivery Context in order to provide the best possible experience for that context.

It is stressed that many devices exceed the capabilities defined by the DDC. Content providers are encouraged not to diminish the user experience on those devices by developing only to the DDC specification, and are encouraged to adapt their content, where appropriate, to exploit the capabilities of the actual device.

In summary, the purpose of defining the DDC is to support the following rules:

- If an adaptation process is used, then information that is known about the actual Delivery Context should (see 5.1.2 Exploit Device Capabilities) be used to vary the delivered content to make it more suitable for that specific Delivery Context or to provide an enhanced user experience.
- If the delivered content does not result from an adaptation process, e.g. the content is statically defined as HTML stored in files, or the details of the Delivery Context cannot adequately be determined, then the delivered content should be suitable for the Default Delivery Context and should comply with the Best Practice statements.

The Default Delivery Context is defined as follows:

Usable Screen Width
    120 pixels, minimum.

Markup Language Support
    XHTML Basic 1.1 delivered with content type application/xhtml+xml.

Character Encoding
    UTF-8.

Image Format Support
    JPEG.
    GIF 89a.

Maximum Total Page Weight
    20 kilobytes.

Colors
    256 Colors, minimum.

Style Sheet Support
    CSS Level 1. In addition, CSS Level 2 @media rule together with the handheld
    and all media types (see CSS 2 Media Types).

HTTP
> HTTP/1.0 or more recent.

Script
> No support for client side scripting.

4 Structure of Best Practice Statements

The Heading
> The functional area that is addressed by the statements.

The Statements
> One or more Best Practice statements, identified in the following way:
> [EXAMPLE] This is a Best Practice statement.

What it means
> An explanation of the significance of the statements under this heading.

How to do it
> A discussion of techniques and some suggestions as to how to implement. The BPWG is
> creating a separate document describing techniques in more detail.

What to Test
> The aspects of the delivered content that an external validator could examine to assess
> conformance with the Best Practice statements. This section is not present for process related
> statements.

> In this section it is noted whether the statement is *Machine Testable* (Automated testing
> is possible) or *Human Testable* (Testing requires human assessment). Some Best Practices are
> partially machine testable, i.e. based on the result of an automated test, some human
> interaction may be required. In such cases both a Machine Testable and a Human Testable
> statement are present.

> Some Best Practice statements use words such as "minimize" and "avoid" which are
> intentionally non-prescriptive. This is in order to provide guidance while leaving room to
> accommodate a wide variety of applications whose requirements cannot be anticipated. It
> also allows creativity and diversity within the same Best Practice framework. More
> prescriptive advice can be found in the Techniques document.

References
> Where appropriate, references to related WCAG points and other immediate references from
> the preceding text.

5 Best Practice Statements

The Best Practice statements are grouped under the following headings

- 5.1 Overall Behavior
- 5.2 Navigation and Links
- 5.3 Page Layout and Content
- 5.4 Page Definition
- 5.5 User Input

5.1 Overall Behavior

There are some general principles that underlie delivery to mobile devices.

5.1.1 Thematic Consistency of Resource Identified by a URI

[THEMATIC_CONSISTENCY] Ensure that content provided by accessing a URI yields a thematically coherent experience when accessed from different devices.

5.1.1.1 *What it means*   This is a realization of the One Web (see 3.1 One Web) principle, whereby content should be accessible on a range of devices irrespective of differences in presentation capabilities and access mechanism. Web sites may paginate their content in various ways corresponding to differences in device characteristics; therefore the navigation structure of the site, and possibly its technical realization, may vary according to the device class that is being served. (See also Section 3.5.1).

A bookmark captured on one device should be usable on another, different type of device even if it does not yield exactly the same experience. If the page that was bookmarked is not appropriate for the device that is now using it, an alternative that is suitable should be provided.

URIs may be decorated to provide session or other information. If a URI is decorated with session information that is no longer current, then the user should be directed to a point in the navigation hierarchy that is appropriate to their device, in order to establish appropriate session and other parameters.

5.1.2 Exploit Device Capabilities

[CAPABILITIES] Exploit device capabilities to provide an enhanced user experience.

5.1.2.1 *What it means*   While encouraging content providers to be sensitive to the needs of the Default Delivery Context, it is not intended that this will result in a diminished experience on

more capable devices. Develop sites that target the Default Delivery Context. In addition, where appropriate, use device capabilities to provide a better user experience on more capable devices.

5.1.3 Work around Deficient Implementations

[DEFICIENCIES] Take reasonable steps to work around deficient implementations.

5.1.3.1 What it means
Just as in the desktop world, there are browsers that do not respect the intentions of the content provider. There are differences in interpretation between browsers and there are also deficiencies in implementation. By deficient we mean non-support of mandatory features of a relevant standard or recommendation and other bugs or errors in implementation.

Because the software in mobile devices is frequently embedded in the device, there is no easy way to correct or enhance it once it is in the field. It is a particular challenge to provide work-arounds for these deficiencies and differences in interpretation. It is recognized that content providers may need to violate specific Best Practices in order to support their intentions on devices that exhibit deficiencies in implementation. If a device is not known to have specific limitations then content providers must comply with Best Practices.

Just as it is not the intention to recommend a least common denominator approach, neither is it the intention to recommend avoiding features that exhibit problems on some class of devices.

It is also not the intention to suggest that content providers should restrict their support to certain device types. Content providers should aim to support as wide a range of device types as is practical.

5.1.4 Testing

[TESTING] Carry out testing on actual devices as well as emulators.

5.1.4.1 What it means
Any Web site should be tested in a range of browsers. Mobile browsers often show markedly different characteristics to desktop browsers. As well as assessing a site's suitability for display in reduced format, content providers are encouraged to test that the features they rely on work in actual devices.

Content providers should also test with specific features disabled, such as using text-only modes and with scripting disabled.

5.1.4.2 How to do it
Many manufacturers provide emulators for their device that can provide a convenient preliminary means of testing. However, in practice, many of the emulators

behave in a different way to the devices they emulate. Consequently testing should be carried out in as wide a range of real devices and specific software versions as is practical.

5.2   Navigation and Links

Because of the limitations in display and of input mechanisms, the possible absence of a pointing device and other constraints of mobile devices, care should be exercised in defining the structure and the navigation model of a Web site.

5.2.1   URIs of Site Entry Points

[URIS] Keep the URIs of site entry points short.

5.2.1.1   *What it means*   Typing URIs on mobile devices can be difficult, and it is expected that users will prefer to use alternative methods of obtaining URIs when available – such as following a hyperlink (from an email, SMS or other Web page), WAP Push, 2D bar code, color bar code, RFID tag and Bluetooth. However, typing a URI may in some cases be the only option available. By keeping site entry point URIs short it is possible to reduce the chance of error and provide a more satisfactory user experience.

5.2.1.2   *How to do it*   When accessing site entry points users should not have to enter a filename as part of the URI. If possible, configure Web sites so that they can be accessed without having to specify a subdomain as part of the URI.

Example: Instead of requiring users to type

"http://www.example.org/index.html"
allow
"http://example.org"
and instead of
"http://www.example.org/example.html"
allow
"http://example.org/example"

5.2.2   Navigation Bar

[NAVBAR] Provide only minimal navigation at the top of the page.

5.2.2.1   *What it means*   Provide basic navigation, which should be placed on the top of the page. Any other secondary navigational element may be placed at the bottom of the page

if really needed. It is important the users should be able to see page content once the page has loaded without scrolling (see 5.3.4 Navigation Bars etc. (Extraneous material)).

5.2.2.2 **How to do it**   Provide the basic links on a single line.

5.2.3 Balanced Structure

[BALANCE] Take into account the trade-off between having too many links on a page and asking the user to follow too many links to reach what they are looking for.

5.2.3.1 **What it means**   The design should aim to provide a balance between having a large number of navigation links on a page and the need to navigate multiple links to reach content.

Scrolling a page when there are many links on it can be very cumbersome, as the scrolling action on many mobile devices selects each link in turn. On the other hand, each retrieval of a navigation page takes time and adds cost, so the number of links on a page should not be minimized at the expense of adding page retrievals.

Design the service so that frequently accessed information is easily reached with a minimum number of page retrievals. Navigation to less frequently accessed information may take more retrievals as a result. A guideline is that users become frustrated if it takes more than four retrievals to reach their objective. Whether this can be achieved depends on the nature of the site and, in particular, how items in menus group together to provide understandable themes.

5.2.4 Navigation Mechanisms

[NAVIGATION] Provide consistent navigation mechanisms.

5.2.4.1 **What it means**   Using the same navigation mechanisms across a service helps users orient themselves and allows them to identify navigation mechanisms more easily.

Users of devices that do not have pointing devices have to scroll between hyperlinks using the keypad. Intelligent grouping, perhaps optimized through adaptation according to usage patterns, can assist usability.

5.2.4.2 **How to do it**   A "drill-down" method, based on major headings, can often provide an effective means of navigation; because of the linearized arrangement of content, small screen size and lack of pointing device, it is often useful to provide a means to jump entire sections of content.

At each target of the drill-down navigation an "up" link should be provided to allow the user to jump up an entire section.

5.2.4.3 *References* This relates to WCAG 13.4.

5.2.5 *Access Keys*

[ACCESS_KEYS] Assign access keys to links in navigational menus and frequently accessed functionality.

5.2.5.1 *What it means* Where there is no pointing device, assigning an access key (keyboard short cut) to a link can provide a convenient way for users to access the link and avoid navigating to the link by repeated pressing of the navigation key.

Provide the same access key for links that are repeated across pages such as links to the home page.

5.2.5.2 *What to test* Machine Test: Test for the presence of the accesskey attribute.

Human Test: Verify the presence of the accesskey attribute on links such as the home page.

5.2.5.3 *References* This relates to WCAG 9.5.

5.2.6 *Link Target Identification*

[LINK_TARGET_ID] Clearly identify the target of each link.

[LINK_TARGET_FORMAT] Note the target file's format unless you know the device supports it.

5.2.6.1 *What it means* Users of mobile devices may suffer undue delay and cost as a result of following links. It is important to identify where a link leads so users can make an assessment of whether following it will be of interest to them. While it is unlikely that the cost in monetary terms of a particular user following a particular link can be specified, it should be possible to give an idea of the size of the resource (in bytes or in an abstract way, e.g. large file).

Links to content that is in a different format or different language to that of the page the link is on (i.e. content that can only be interpreted by other applications or downloads) should be human signposted, so that users are not lead to download content that their device may not be able to use. However, bear in mind that some devices support the rendering of those formats by other applications once downloaded (e.g. music files). Additionally, users may wish to download content for later transfer to other devices altogether. So even if it is known that the user agent does not support a particular content type, that content should still be made available.

5.2.6.2 *How to do it* Use clear, concise, descriptive link text to help users decide whether to follow a link. Identify the implications of following a link if the target is notably large and the user might not anticipate this from the context.

For the Default Delivery Context all formats other than XHTML, GIF and JPG should be noted.

5.2.6.3 *What to test* Human Test: Check for proper descriptions (e.g. no use of "Click here").

Machine Test: Check for links to non-HTML formats.

Human Test: If present check whether there is information about the format of the target of the link.

5.2.6.4 *References* This relates to WCAG 11.3 and 13.1.

5.2.7 *Image Maps*
[IMAGE_MAPS] Do not use image maps unless you know the device supports them effectively.

5.2.7.1 *What it means* Image maps allow fast navigation providing the requesting device can support the image involved and providing there is a means of navigating the map satisfactorily. Up, down, left, right and enter are available on most mobile devices, even if there is no pointing device. This is usually sufficient to allow navigation of the active regions of client-side image maps where they are defined as geometric shapes.

Many mobile devices lack a pointing device and server-side image maps cannot be used on such devices.

5.2.7.2 *How to do it* If only small images can be displayed, break larger images up into smaller sections and deal with them separately.

For the Default Delivery Context, or if a satisfactory image map cannot be displayed, use a list of links with descriptive text instead.

5.2.7.3 **What to test** IMAGE_MAPS Machine Test: Send a request to the site with a device that does not support client-side image maps and check the map element is not present.

5.2.7.4 **References** This relates to WCAG 1.2 and 9.1.

5.2.8 Refreshing, Redirection and Spawned Windows

[POP_UPS] Do not cause pop-ups or other windows to appear and do not change the current window without informing the user.

[AUTO_REFRESH] Do not create periodically auto-refreshing pages, unless you have informed the user and provided a means of stopping it.

[REDIRECTION] Do not use markup to redirect pages automatically. Instead, configure the server to perform redirects by means of HTTP 3xx codes.

5.2.8.1 **What it means** Each of these activities is likely to cause the user confusion, or add cost and delay to their interaction.

Some mobile devices use a separate window for input; this section does not refer to such windows.

Many mobile devices cannot support more than one window and, consequently, attempting to open one will have unpredictable results.

Auto-refreshing pages are widely recognized as presenting accessibility problems. In a mobile environment they may expose the user to undue cost as a result of such a page being left open or put unnoticed into the background. If an auto-refreshing page is demanded by the application, always provide a means of ceasing the refresh and always inform the user that the page will refresh and may expose them to higher usage costs.

While redirection is a commonly employed mechanism, it must be remembered that redirection usually requires a round-trip to the browser. This adds to delay on slow links; so use a maximum of one redirect per page and limit the number of pages that are redirected.

5.2.8.2 **What to test** POP_UPS Machine Test: Look for the target attribute on links and if present check to see if it has a value different from _self, _parent or _top.

AUTO_REFRESH Machine Test: Check whether meta http-equiv="refresh" content="<the same URI>" is used.

AUTO_REFRESH Human Test: If auto-refresh is used, check that options are provided to stop any page using auto-refresh.

REDIRECTION Machine Test: Check whether meta http-equiv="refresh" content="<a different URI>" is used.

5.2.8.3 *References* This relates to WCAG 7.4, 7.5 and 10.1.

5.2.9 *Externally Linked Resources*
[EXTERNAL_RESOURCES] Keep the number of externally linked resources to a minimum.

5.2.9.1 *What it means* Each linked resource (images, style sheets and other objects) requires a separate request across the network. This may add significantly to the load time of the page in the mobile context.

5.2.9.2 *How to do it* Minimize the number of images on a page and consolidate style information into a single sheet per page (see also 5.4.9 Style Sheets).

5.2.9.3 *What to test* Machine Test: Count the number of linked images, style sheets and other linked items.

Human Test: Review whether a similar effect could be obtained using fewer links.

5.3 Page Layout and Content
This section refers to the user's perception of the delivered content. It concentrates on design, the language used in its text and the spatial relationship between constituent components. It does not address the technical aspects of how the delivered content is constructed, which is discussed in 5.4 Page Definition.

5.3.1 *Page Content*
[SUITABLE] Ensure that content is suitable for use in a mobile context.

[CLARITY] Use clear and simple language.

[LIMITED] Limit content to what the user has requested.

5.3.1.1 **What it means** Users in a mobile context are often looking for specific pieces of information, rather than browsing. Content providers should consider the likely context of use of information and, while providing the option to access all information, should offer appropriate information first. See also discussion under 2.4 User Goals and 3.1 One Web.

The general prescription to use clear language is of particular importance for mobile delivery, where brevity and directness are generally more desirable than a discursive style.

Writing content in the traditional journalistic "front loaded" style can assist users determining whether information is of interest to them and allow them to skip it more easily if it is not. Placing distinguishing information at the beginning of headings, paragraphs, lists, etc. can also help the user contextualize when using devices with limited screen area. See also 5.3.4 Navigation Bars etc. (Extraneous material) for a discussion of making sure that the subject matter of the page is near the top.

Mobile users often pay for bandwidth, so offering them content that is extraneous to their needs, especially advertising, costs them time and money and contributes to an unsatisfactory experience. In general, the user's consent should be sought before initiating the download of content.

5.3.1.2 **What to test** Human Test: Examine content to determine if, given the subject matter, it is appropriate in a mobile context.

5.3.1.3 **References** This relates to WCAG 13.8 and 14.1.

5.3.2 Page Size

[PAGE_SIZE_USABLE] Divide pages into usable but limited size portions.

[PAGE_SIZE_LIMIT] Ensure that the overall size of page is appropriate to the memory limitations of the device.

5.3.2.1 **What it means** If pages are too big they may take an unduly long time to load. In addition, mobile devices typically have restrictions on the largest page they can accommodate.

On the other hand, if pages are too short then the user will be required to make multiple requests to read the relevant information. This can lead to an unnecessary delay, since each request typically takes a measurable time to complete.

The balance between pagination and scrolling is partly a matter of taste and partly a matter of necessity. Devices with severe memory restrictions can only have small pages delivered to them. Equally some devices offer a poor scrolling experience and a better page retrieval experience.

Some studies have been carried out in this area to test for user preferences. Some of these indicate that users prefer scrolling to click-throughs and some indicate the contrary. More research is likely to be needed in this area.

5.3.2.2 How to do it

For the Default Delivery Context assume the limits specified in 3.7 Default Delivery Context.

5.3.2.3 What to test

PAGE_SIZE_USABLE Machine Test: Measure the total size of the markup for a page; check that it does not exceed 10 kilobytes for the Default Delivery Context.

Human Test: Check that the page is still usable (e.g. not cut in the middle of a sentence, just before the end of a section, and so on).

PAGE_SIZE_LIMIT Machine Test: Measure the total size of markup and images for a page; check that it does not go over the allowed size for the device – 20 kilobytes for the Default Delivery Context.

5.3.2.4 References

This relates to WCAG 12.3.

5.3.3 Scrolling

[SCROLLING] Limit scrolling to one direction, unless secondary scrolling cannot be avoided.

5.3.3.1 What it means

The page should lay out so that simple repeated scrolling in the same direction (axis) allows the user to experience all its content. However some content (such as maps and other images) cannot be displayed without secondary scrolling.

If some element on the page requires secondary scrolling it must not cause the remainder of the page to require this. For example, if an object causes subsequent text to lay out with a significant margin to its left, then this text may not be visible once a user has scrolled past the object.

Equally, if the presence of such an object causes text to render beyond the right boundary of the page then the user will be required to scroll to read each line of text.

5.3.3.2 How to do it If it is not possible to avoid presenting images that are larger than the screen size, then consider providing these images on a separate page with a link back to the main content.

In the Default Delivery Context assume a width of 120 pixels.

5.3.3.3 What to test SCROLLING Machine Test: Check for width attributes and width style properties wider than the screen size – for the Default Delivery Context, 120 pixels.

Human Test: If it is wider than the screen size, check that the use case warrants it (e.g. maps).

SCROLLING_LIMIT Human Test: Browse URIs within a site with a mobile device and observe that on pages with elements that require secondary scrolling only those elements require it, and the rest of the page requires only primary scrolling.

5.3.4 Navigation Bars etc. (Extraneous material)

[CENTRAL_MEANING] Ensure that material that is central to the meaning of the page precedes material that is not.

5.3.4.1 What it means Many Web pages are designed with significant navigational and other elements at the top of or to the side of the page (e.g. Menu Bars, Breadcrumb Trails and Search Functions). This provides a convenient and well-understood navigational metaphor on large displays. However, on small displays this can result in the navigation appearing instead of the actual content of the page when the page is first retrieved.

Because it is important for the user to gain an idea of the content of the page on initial view, there should be a minimum amount of clutter preceding this – including navigation, decorative images, advertising and other material that is not central to the user's experience of the page. The user should not have to scroll significantly to find the primary content of the page.

See also 5.3.1 Page Content for a discussion of how writing style can help the user identify meaning.

5.3.4.2 How to do it Menu selections can be placed away from the top of the page with a simple link to the selection at the top of the page. Alternatively, use meta navigation on top of the page with simple text links to major sections of the Web site.

5.3.4.3 What to test Human test: Browse URIs within a site with a mobile device and observe that the most important/relevant information is conveyed first.

5.3.4.4 *References* This relates to WCAG 13.5.

5.3.5 *Graphics*
[GRAPHICS_FOR_SPACING] Do not use graphics for spacing.

[LARGE_GRAPHICS] Do not use images that cannot be rendered by the device. Avoid large or high resolution images except where critical information would otherwise be lost.

5.3.5.1 *What it means* The popular mechanism of using a 1 pixel graphic for absolute positioning does not work on a variety of screens.

Graphics that are larger than necessary, for example by having a higher resolution than is displayable on the device or by having too many colors, waste bandwidth.

5.3.5.2 *What to test* GRAPHICS_FOR_SPACING Machine Test: Check for very small and/or transparent graphics.

LARGE_GRAPHICS Machine Test: Check dimensions of graphics.

5.3.6 *Color*
[USE_OF_COLOR] Ensure that information conveyed with color is also available without color.

[COLOR_CONTRAST] Ensure that foreground and background color combinations provide sufficient contrast.

5.3.6.1 *What it means* Mobile devices often do not have good color contrast and are often used in less-than-ideal lighting conditions. Hence information highlighted in color may not be visible to users. If color is used to indicate a feature then that feature should generally also be indicated in a way that is not color dependent. In particular, do not use blue or purple text, as this may be confused with hyperlinks, especially on devices that do not underline links.

5.3.6.2 *What to test* USE_OF_COLOR Human Test: Browse the page in a monochrome environment.

COLOR_CONTRAST Human Test: Browse the page under a strong light parallel to the screen.

Machine Test: There are automatic tools to test color contrast.

5.3.6.3 References This relates to WCAG 2.1 and 2.2.

5.3.7 Background Images

[BACKGROUND_IMAGE_READABILITY] When using background images make sure that content remains readable on the device.

5.3.7.1 What it means Images that are used indiscriminately can lead to content that is hard to view, particularly with the limited contrast often found on mobile devices and in the hostile viewing conditions in which mobile devices are frequently used.

Before using background images, consider carefully your objectives for doing so and try to use alternative techniques to achieve similar objectives. If you use a background image ensure that the content is readable with and without the background image for devices that do not support them.

5.3.7.2 What to test Machine Test: Test for the presence of a background image.

Human Test: Test readability both on devices that support them and devices that do not.

5.4 Page Definition

5.4.1 Title

[PAGE_TITLE] Provide a short but descriptive page title.

5.4.1.1 What it means Provide a descriptive title for the page to allow easy identification. Keep the title short to reduce page weight, and bear in mind that it may be truncated.

Many mobile browsers do not display the title of a page. Where the title is displayed the available space may be limited.

The device may use the page title as the default label for bookmarks. Again, space may be limited, so use it to help identify the content and not for other purposes.

5.4.1.2 What to test Machine Test: Test for presence of the title element.

Human Test: Test that the title is descriptive of content.

5.4.2 *Frames*

[NO_FRAMES] Do not use frames.

5.4.2.1 *What it means* Many mobile devices do not support frames. In addition, frames are recognized as being generally problematic.

5.4.2.2 *What to test* Machine Test: Test for presence of frame related elements – check for frameset and iframe elements.

5.4.2.3 *References* See http://www.w3.org/TR/xframes/#s_intro for a discussion of problems with frames.

5.4.3 *Structural Elements*

[STRUCTURE] Use features of the markup language to indicate logical document structure.

5.4.3.1 *What it means* It is good practice for all but the simplest documents to indicate their structure through headings and sub-headings. Using structural markup, rather than formatting effects, allows easier adaptation of content where it needs to be divided into several pages, as well as potentially facilitating access to the sections of the document that a user is interested in.

Where headings are used they should be used in accordance with the specification, i.e. they should be properly nested according to their level.

Structural markup must not be used solely to create a font effect (see also 5.4.3 Structural Elements).

5.4.3.2 *How to do it* Markup languages like HMTL contain many constructs to indicate structure.

5.4.4 *Tables*

[TABLES_SUPPORT] Do not use tables unless the device is known to support them.

[TABLES_NESTED] Do not use nested tables.

[TABLES_LAYOUT] Do not use tables for layout.

[TABLES_ALTERNATIVES] Where possible, use an alternative to tabular presentation.

5.4.4.1 What it means   Tables do not work well on limited size screens and may result in the user having to scroll horizontally to read them. Putting navigational links into tables may result in the user having both to scroll horizontally and vertically to see possible navigational choices.

5.4.4.2 What to test   TABLES_SUPPORT Machine Test: Send a request to the site with a device that does not support tables and check the table element is not present.

Machine Test: Check that there are no nested tables.

TABLES_LAYOUT Machine Test: Check that no column or row in a table is empty or contains only a 1×1 transparent GIF.

Machine Test: If there is a table element, check to see whether there is rendered content outside the element. If there is not then it is likely that the table is being used for layout.

5.4.4.3 References   This relates to WCAG 5.1, 5.2, 5.3, 5.5 and 5.6.

5.4.5 Non-Text Items

[NON-TEXT_ALTERNATIVES] Provide a text equivalent for every non-text element.

[OBJECTS_OR_SCRIPT] Do not rely on embedded objects or script.

5.4.5.1 What it means   A *non-text item* is defined by Non-text content in the WAI Glossary.

Downloading images to a mobile device adds to the time to display an image and the cost of displaying the page. Making the page readable in text-only mode can help the user assess its usefulness before images arrive.

Many mobile devices do not support embedded objects or script and in many cases it is not possible for users to load plug-ins to add support. Content must be designed with this in mind.

Even where a device does support scripting, do not use it unless there is no other way of accomplishing your objectives. Scripting increases power consumption and so decreases battery life.

5.4.5.2 How to do it   Design pages so that they are useful when rendered as text-only. See also 5.1.4 Testing.

Always use features of the markup designed to support alternate rendering such as the longdesc and alt attributes in XHTML.

Use only features from the markup that are known to be supported by the device in question.

Avoid things like CSS image replacement and pictures of words.

If scripting is used, do not use onmouse and onkey triggers, use onclick.

5.4.5.3 *What to test*

NON-TEXT_ALTERNATIVES Machine Test: Test for presence of alt attribute on images and text content on objects.

Human Test: Check the relevance of the meaning of the content of alt attributes.

OBJECTS_OR_SCRIPT Machine Test: Test for the presence of object or script elements in content delivered to a device that does not support them.

Human Test: If present, test that the user experience is acceptable.

5.4.5.4 *References*

This relates to WCAG 1.1, 3.1, 6.2, 6.3, 6.5 and 9.2.

5.4.6 *Image Size*

[IMAGES_SPECIFY_SIZE] Specify the size of images in markup, if they have an intrinsic size.

[IMAGES_RESIZING] Resize images at the server, if they have an intrinsic size.

5.4.6.1 *What it means*

Images such as bitmaps have an intrinsic size. Telling the browser in advance what the size is avoids it having to re-flow the page when it receives it. Resizing images at the server reduces the amount of data transferred and the amount of processing the device has to carry out to scale the image.

Note that this recommendation contrasts with 5.4.8 Measures, which recommends using relative measures where possible.

5.4.6.2 *What to test*

IMAGES_SPECIFY_SIZE Machine Test: Test for presence of width and height attributes on img elements.

IMAGES_RESIZING Machine Test: Check width and height attributes are equal to image dimensions.

5.4.7 Valid Markup

[VALID_MARKUP] Create documents that validate to published formal grammars.

5.4.7.1 What it means
If the page markup is invalid this will result in unpredictable and possibly incomplete presentation.

5.4.7.2 What to test
Machine Test: Validate documents.

5.4.7.3 References
This relates to WCAG 3.2, 11.1 and 11.2.

See http://www.w3.org/QA/Tools/#validators.

5.4.8 Measures

[MEASURES] Do not use pixel measures and do not use absolute units in markup language attribute values and style sheet property values.

5.4.8.1 What it means
Avoiding pixel and absolute measures allows the browser to adapt content to fit the display. An exception to rule is where an image has been specifically sized for a particular display (see 5.4.6 Image Size). In this case references to the image in markup may specify the exact dimensions of the image in pixels, in order to help the browser to flow the page and avoid re-flowing it after the page has been retrieved. Devices may realize the intentions of authors more accurately if margins, borders and padding are specified in pixels.

5.4.8.2 How to do it
Use percentage and relative measures such as em, ex, bolder, larger and thick.

5.4.8.3 What to test
Machine Test: Send a request to the site with a device that supports relative measures correctly and check the values of font-size are not absolute or pixels.

5.4.9 Style Sheets

[STYLE_SHEETS_USE] Use style sheets to control layout and presentation, unless the device is known not to support them.

[STYLE_SHEETS_SUPPORT] Organize documents so that if necessary they may be read without style sheets.

[STYLE_SHEETS_SIZE] Keep style sheets small.

5.4.9.1 *What it means*

Style information may be contained in an externally linked style sheet or, in HTML, may be contained either in a style element or in a style attribute on specific elements.

Mobile devices offer varying support for style sheets. Some provide full implementations, including caching of external style sheets; some do not cache external style sheets; some do not support the style element; some implementations do not support more than one style sheet and some do not support style sheets at all.

If style sheets are turned off or not supported, content will be rendered in document order, so it is important that the content makes sense when read in document order.

5.4.9.2 *How to do it*

It is preferable to share style information between pages, but if the device does not support caching of style sheets then this approach would result in the same style sheet being retrieved for each page. Consequently, in order of preference: if the device caches style sheets, put style information in a single external style sheet (see also 5.2.9 Externally Linked Resources); if the device supports the style element, use it; otherwise use an external style sheet.

Optimize style information so that only styles that are used are included.

When creating style sheets, take advantage of the CSS media types (these may be used both in the CSS @media rule and in the media attribute of the link element) to specify styles that apply to handheld rendering. The CSS Media types that apply are "handheld" and "all". If handheld rendering is not specified, browsers may download other style sheets even if they are identified as applicable to non-handheld rendering.

5.4.9.3 *What to test*

STYLE_SHEETS_USE Machine Test: Send a request to the site with a device that supports CSS and check that style sheets are used and that the page does not use formatting tags (e.g. font).

STYLE_SHEETS_SUPPORT Human Test: Disable style sheets and check that the page is still readable.

STYLE_SHEETS_SIZE Machine Test: Check that the elements in a style sheet are used in at least one of the pages that reference it.

5.4.9.4 References This relates to WCAG 3.3 and 6.1.

5.4.10 Minimize
[MINIMIZE] Use terse, efficient markup.

5.4.10.1 What it means Content which is marked up in languages such as XML can often be made smaller while preserving exactly the same semantics merely by removal of redundant white space (i.e. spaces and new lines).

Marking fonts, colors and other stylistic effects in-line can cause considerably larger page sizes when compared with using logical markup, and use of the HTML class attribute for application of style (see also 5.4.9 Style Sheets).

5.4.10.2 How to do it While it is not intended that authors should create their content in a single line to remove white space altogether, it is suggested that authors should not contribute to page weight by introducing unnecessary white space. Note that "pretty printing" (the formatting of markup with indentation) can generate large amounts of white space and hence add to page weight.

If "pretty printing" is an important part of the authoring process, then try to arrange that redundant white space is stripped when serving a page.

Even though some network proxies strip white space that they think is redundant, not all do so, so it is not best practice to rely upon this behavior.

Use of structural markup (see 5.4.3 Structural Elements) contributes to minimizing the size of the markup on a page, as does centralizing the style descriptions using CSS.

5.4.10.3 What to test Machine Test: Count the number of non-significant white space characters in the document.

5.4.11 Content Types
[CONTENT_FORMAT_SUPPORT] Send content in a format that is known to be supported by the device.

[CONTENT_FORMAT_PREFERRED] Where possible, send content in a preferred format.

5.4.11.1 What it means Transferring content that a device cannot display wastes users' time and money. A device may express a preference for formats. In this case it is good practice to respect the device's preference, as it may have a fuller implementation of those formats.

5.4.11.2 How to do it To determine what formats a device supports, Web sites may use any combination of device profile information such as the HTTP User-Agent header, HTTP Accept headers and UAProf.

There are problems with using any one approach to the exclusion of the others. Some issues that have been noted by the BPWG in this context are:

- Some devices do not supply accept headers;
- Some devices mis-state their capabilities;
- Some operator gateways supplement the accept headers to include formats that they adapt;
- User agent headers do not always uniquely identify the device;
- UAProf information may not be available or may be incomplete.

5.4.11.3 What to test CONTENT_FORMAT_SUPPORT Machine Test: Check MIME types of content with various devices.

CONTENT_FORMAT_PREFERRED Machine Test: Check MIME types of content with various devices and check that the preferred format is sent or that the format is compatible with the Default Delivery Context.

5.4.12 Character Encoding

[CHARACTER_ENCODING_SUPPORT] Ensure that content is encoded using a character encoding that is known to be supported by the device.

[CHARACTER_ENCODING_USE] Indicate in the response the character encoding being used.

5.4.12.1 What it means As in the previous section, content should not be sent to a device if it can not use it.

5.4.12.2 How to do it The supported character encodings for a device may be obtained either from a device profile or by examining the value of the HTTP Accept-Charset header.

The character encoding being used in a response may be indicated using the HTTP Content-Type header.

Example:

```
Content-Type: text/html; charset=utf-8
```

Additionally for XML documents the character encoding may be indicated in the encoding declaration, although this will generally be ignored if an HTTP Content-Type header is present.

Example:

```
<?xml version=''1.0'' encoding=''UTF-8''?>
```

Encoding of the content to a desired character encoding is dependent on the authoring tools being used, Web server configuration and the server side scripting technology being used (if any). For a discussion of this see [CHARSET1] and [CHARSET2].

Unicode is a good choice for representing content when served in multiple languages. The amount of bandwidth required to transmit content can vary significantly depending on the character encoding used. Text consisting principally of characters from the Latin alphabet will encode more efficiently in UTF-8, whereas text consisting principally of characters from ideographic scripts will encode more efficiently in UTF-16. When choosing a character encoding, consider the efficiency of the available encodings.

Since the Default Delivery Context specifies use only of UTF-8, all applications should support UTF-8.

5.4.12.3 What to test Machine Test: Check that the encoding is declared in some way and is supported. The content type may be declared in one or more of the following ways: The Content-Type HTTP header, the XML declaration for XML-based content, the CSS @charset rules for CSS, the Content-Type Meta element for HTML content.

5.4.12.4 References See Character Encoding in Entities for a discussion of character encoding in XML documents.

5.4.13 Error Messages
[ERROR_MESSAGES] Provide informative error messages and a means of navigating away from an error message back to useful information.

5.4.13.1 What it means It is inevitable that, on occasions, a mobile user will not be successful in accessing the content or information they sought. Providing easy navigation away from the error is particularly important in the mobile arena, where browsers may not have an easy-to-find "back" button, where contextualization is frequently difficult and where re-entry of URIs as a means of error recovery is particularly difficult.

It is noted that errors due to networking, connection and some kinds of mistyping of URIs are not within the control of the content provider, which has no way to influence how such errors are presented to the user. However, where errors are within the control of the content provider the user should be provided with clear information regarding the fault they have experienced. This should help them to understand whether the fault was temporary or permanent, whether they should retry the attempt to access the content and how they may be able to escalate the problem.

It should also be possible for the user to escape from the error condition. They should either be able to return to the page they were on prior to the error, or to be able to move onwards to a convenient part of the service from where they can retry or alter the transaction they were attempting.

5.4.13.2 How to do it It is noted that many Web servers provide a default error page, especially in the event of a request for a non-existent page (404) or an internal error (500). Where possible, applications should trap all error conditions by overriding the default pages if necessary, and handle them in a user-friendly, and graceful, way.

Error messages should be provided in the same language as the application that was being used. They should be clear and concise, adhering to the same Best Practices as the rest of the application. They should be provided in a format that the device can handle.

The error message should detail whether the issue is likely to be temporary or permanent, whether the user may be able to solve the issue themselves (for example, by changing input data or a handset setting), or whether it is an issue that can be escalated to the content provider or network operator. In the latter case, contact details, such as an SMS address or a support line number, might be appropriate.

The error message should provide one or more of the following navigational constructs:

1 A "back" link to return to the previous page (particularly for devices that do not have an easy-to-find back button);
2 A "retry" link to attempt the relevant part of the transaction again (note that this may not be equivalent to a page "refresh");
3 A "home" link to allow the user to return to the main part of the application.

The error message can provide an error code to be used for diagnosis of the issue. However, the use of an error code is not a substitute for a human-readable message. While some users may understand "404" to mean "page cannot be found", this must not be assumed to be true for all users.

5.4.13.3 What to test   Enter an extraneous URI, known not to represent an actual resource on the site, and check that a HTTP 404 error response is accompanied by a page whose markup is appropriate for the requesting device, or the default context.

Human Test: Check that the page returned contains an explanation of the error and appropriate corrective actions, without assuming any technical knowledge on the part of the end user.

5.4.14 Cookies
[COOKIES] Do not rely on cookies being available.

5.4.14.1 What it means   Cookies are frequently used to carry out session management, to identify users and to store user preferences. Many mobile devices do not implement cookies or offer only an incomplete implementation. In addition, some gateways strip cookies and others simulate cookies on behalf of mobile devices.

5.4.14.2 How to do it   Test that cookies are supported by the device on its current access path. If they are not supported, use URI decoration for session management, being careful not to exceed the device's maximum length for such strings. Some gateways provide user identification without setting cookies.

5.4.14.3 What to test   Machine Test: Check that an alternative to cookies is used for session management when they are not available.

5.4.15 Cache Headers
[CACHING] Provide caching information in HTTP responses.

5.4.15.1 What it means   Limited bandwidth and high latency can reduce the usability of Web sites on mobile devices. Using caching information effectively can reduce the need to reload data such as style sheets, images and pages, thus improving performance and reducing cost of use. It can also prevent the re-use of content where this is not appropriate, for example content that is adapted for one device should not be re-used by different devices. Devices and network caches are both affected by caching information.

5.4.15.2 How to do it   Set expiry times in a way that is appropriate to your application. Consider using Cache-Control: public to allow sharing of pages between devices, Cache-Control:

private to allow re-use but only by the requesting device and Cache-Control: nocache to prevent caching.

The HTTP 1.1 specification and Techniques document contain discussions of caching.

5.4.15.3 *What to test* Machine Test: Check for the presence of cache headers on the HTTP response.

5.4.15.4 *References* Section 13 Caching in HTTP discusses caching.

5.4.16 *Fonts*
[FONTS] Do not rely on support of font related styling.

5.4.16.1 *What it means* Mobile devices often have few fonts and limited support for font sizes and effects (bold, italic etc.). As a result of this, the use of font size, face or effect, for example to highlight an answer or a stressed word, may not achieve the desired effect. See also 5.4.3 Structural Elements.

5.4.16.2 *How to do it* For the Default Delivery Context do not use font related styling.

5.4.16.3 *What to test* Machine Test: Check for the presence of font related styling in an environment that does not support it.

Human Test: If present, ensure that the author's intentions remain clear.

5.5 User Input
This section contains statements relating to user input. This is typically more restrictive on mobile devices than on desktop computers (and often a lot more restrictive). For example, mobile devices may lack pointing devices and often do not have a standard keyboard for text entry.

5.5.1 *Input*
[MINIMIZE_KEYSTROKES] Keep the number of keystrokes to a minimum.

[AVOID_FREE_TEXT] Avoid free text entry where possible.

[PROVIDE_DEFAULTS] Provide pre-selected default values where possible.

[DEFAULT_INPUT_MODE] Specify a default text entry mode, language and/or input format, if the device is known to support it.

5.5.1.1 *What it means*   Given the typical input limitations of a mobile device, the interface must as far as possible minimize user input. Where possible, use selection lists, radio buttons and other controls that do not require typing.

Some markup languages allow the specification of an input mode, which is particularly useful in cases where user input is to be restricted, for example to numeric only. It is anticipated that XHTML-Basic will support this functionality in the future.

5.5.1.2 *How to do it*   There are a number of techniques available for this, including:

- Where possible use previous entries as defaults.
- Make it possible to select items using navigation keys and/or numeric input.

5.5.1.3 *What to test*   AVOID_FREE_TEXT Machine Test: Check whether input type="text" and textarea are used.

Human Test: If one of them is used, check whether it can be replaced by a pre-determined entry.

PROVIDE_DEFAULTS Machine Test: Check if there is a pre-selected value in controls (selected or checked attribute set).

Human Test: If not, check if there could be sensible pre-selection in the context (e.g. most common choice).

DEFAULT_INPUT_MODE Machine Test: Send a request with a device known to support the inputmode attribute and if the response is in a language that supports this attribute, check that it is present on input type="text" and textarea elements.

5.5.1.4 *References*   This relates to WCAG 10.4.

5.5.2 *Tab Order*
[TAB_ORDER] Create a logical order through links, form controls and objects.

5.5.2.1 *What it means* It is important that as the user navigates through the page the various fields and objects are presented in a logical order, especially as many of them will not be visible at the same time as the focus item.

5.5.2.2 *How to do it* Use document order to control layout and tab order.

5.5.2.3 *What to test* Machine Test: Check that there are no tabindex attributes or layout effects that affect the order of presentation.

If there are tabindex attributes check that all controls have a tab index and that they are used consistently.

Human Test: If there are either tabindex attributes or layout effects that might affect the order of presentation, then check that the order is usable.

5.5.3 Labels for Form Controls

[CONTROL_LABELLING] Label all form controls appropriately and explicitly associate labels with form controls.

[CONTROL_POSITION] Position labels so they lay out properly in relation to the form controls they refer to.

5.5.3.1 *What it means* This means use the label element in HTML, or its equivalent in other languages. Make sure that where the label goes is consistent and close to the form control so re-flowing or adapting the content intelligently will always recognize label controls and keep them together.

5.5.3.2 *What to test* Machine Test: Check if the label element is used in forms.

Human Test: Check whether the labels are properly positioned with regard to the controls.

5.5.3.3 *References* This relates to WCAG 10.2 and 12.4.

6 Conformance and mobileOK

The Best Practice statements are intended to be capable of having conformance statements constructed around them in support of the mobileOK trustmark and for other purposes.

Work on the mobileOK trustmark will develop specific recommended requirements for a trust-mark, which will be based on some profile, or subset, of the Statements in this document.

As such, the mobileOK trustmark will serve as the main conformance claim for the Best Practices document.

All of the Best Practice statements have a fragment identifier to allow formal reference to them and allow the construction of compliance claims that refer to them.

6.1 Classes of Products

This specification applies to one class of product: content delivered to a mobile device, including the metadata transferred as part of the delivery protocol.

6.2 Extensibility

This specification may be compatible with other specifications that describe a different set of requirements for content, insofar as such requirements do not conflict with the current specification.

Appendix B

404: The server will generate a 404 error when a visitor attempts to view a page that is unavailable.

Ad inventory: The number of page views a site has available for advertising.

Adult words: Words that are censored by search engines. Adult words are called STOP WORDS by the search engines because the indexer stops when it finds one.

Affiliate: Someone who sets up a business that is in between the original manufacturer and the end customer.

Algorithm: The way a search engine decides where a site is ranked for a particular search. Each search engine uses a different set of algorithms; factors such as a site's title, body copy, META tags and link popularity are all important.

Altavista: One of the most popular search engines, found at www.altavista.com.

ALT tag: An HTML tag that allows a browser to display text instead of a graphic. As spiders cannot read graphics, ALT tags should be used to give the spider something to read.

Apache web server: Web server software.

Ask Jeeves: A search engine that accepts queries phrased as questions, found at www.askjeeves.com.

ASP: Active Server Pages — a scripting language that provides dynamic content for database-driven websites.

B2B: Business to business. Products and services for other businesses.

B2C: Business to consumer. Products and services for the general public.

BBS: Bulletin Board System — an online text exchange.

Boolean search: The search operators AND, OR, and/or NOT, that can be used to refine a search.

Bridge page: Another name for a doorway page.

CGI: Common Gateway Interface. CGI programs are used to generate web page content dynamically.

CGI-BIN: A directory on a web server that contains CGI files. These directories usually have much tighter access privileges than normal files.

Click-through: This is what happens when a user selects a link on a web page. The click is the noise of the mouse being pressed, and the 'through' is the act of passing from one page to another. Many advertising systems are based on the number of click-throughs a banner ad has.

Client: A browser is a client, and a web server is a server. The client computer gets information from the server computer.

Cloaking: A way of hiding code or content from a user or search engine spider. There are three types of cloaking: IP based, user-agent based, and a combination of the two.

Clustering: The process that some search engines use to cluster pages from the same website in groups in order to keep any one site from dominating the top results with more than one listing.

Counter: A counter counts hits on a website and reports the results back to the webmaster.

CPC: Cost Per Click. Search engines such as Overture.com charge sites for the number of users sent to them, depending on how many times the sites listing is clicked on.

Crawler: Also known as *robots* or *spiders*, these are the tools that search engines send out to find websites, record them, and index them within their databases. They also follow links between websites, which is why it's good to have a high 'link popularity'. Different crawlers crawl in different ways, depending on the engines they have come from.

Cross linking: Linking to content from within the same site.

Dead link: An HTML link that does not point anywhere, as the destination page does not exist. Dead links used to be a serious problem on search engines, but spiders can now check to see whether a link is dead.

Deep linking: Linking to content buried deep within a website — more than a couple of directories into the hierarchy of a site.

Directory: A web search tool compiled manually by human editors. Websites are submitted with a title and description, and are then assessed by an editor and listed under one or more subject categories if accepted. Good examples of directories are Yahoo! and the Open Directory Project. Users can browse through the directory of websites, which is organized in a hierarchical manner.

Domain: Domain is a generic term to describe a level of domain. Domain names can play an important part in determining a site's rankings on the search engines. There are top level domains (such as .com, .net, or .co.uk), and then there are midlevel domains such as Ford (ford.com, ford.net or ford.org).

Domain name registration: The act of registering a domain name with an approved registrar.

Doorway domain: A domain designed to redirect traffic to another page that is located on a different domain.

Doorway page: A page designed as an entrance to a website, which is located on a different page. Many doorway pages are specifically created to rank high on a search engine. Also known as a bridge page.

Downloading: The process of retrieving information.

Dynamic content: A page that is generated just as the user views it. The content delivered to the user is often updated on-the-fly, out of a database of content.

Entry page: A specific entry page to a website, which may take the form of a single page with a logo and 'click here' to enter.

Error log file: Web servers run separate logs that show website errors, which can then be viewed at a later date.

Excite: One of the original major search engines, found at www.excite.com.

FFA: Free-For-All sites are often included within the lists used by some companies or software, offering submission of your website to 'thousands of sites'. Submissions to FFA sites will usually result in your website only being listed for a short time, and in return your email address will receive hundreds of 'junk' marketing emails, many of which will require a manual opt-out. FFAs are not worth using.

Frames: This is the HTML technique that creates a static area on a web page, usually containing navigation buttons and a title bar. Frames can cause problems for search engine optimization, as they restrict the ability of some crawlers to index the site.

Gateway domain names: A domain name the purpose of which is to direct traffic to a main site.

Gateway pages: These pages are also known as *bridge pages* or *doorway pages*, and are submitted to search engines separately from the main site. They are used for a variety of reasons, such as to emphasize particular keywords or phrases or to target the optimization requirements of a specific search engine. They can also be used as a way to submit a site that has database-driven pages or that uses Flash. They can be viewed as being spam if used incorrectly, so should be prepared carefully.

Google: Now the most widely used search engine on the Web, found at www.google.com.

Heading tag: An HTML tag of six sizes. It is possible that search engines rank a keyword higher if it appears in a larger heading.

Hidden text/tiny text: Placing coloured characters on the same-coloured background causes them to be hidden. This technique was popular for a while to increase keyword coverage on a site, but has been identified now and is viewed as spam.

Hit: A request for a file on a web server. If someone visits your page, it is a 'hit' on that page.

HotBot: Another popular and powerful search engine, located at www.hotbot.com.

HTML: HyperText Markup Language — the programming language of tag commands used in web pages, which web browsers read in order to present pages to a web user.

HTML link: A hyperlink within a web page.

HTTP: HyperText Transfer Protocol — the standard system to transfer data between a web server and a web browser.

Image map: A system of associating parts of an image with hyperlinks. Pictures can be split into specific areas that then link to different pages on a site.

Inbound link: Links pointing to a website. When a user arrives at a website from another site, that link is called an inbound link.

Indexer: The part of a search engine that is responsible for processing pages that a spider has visited. It will store any pages in the searchable database.

Infoseek: An older but still popular search engine, found at www.infoseek.com and now owned by Disney and the Go.com group.

Inktomi: A search engine database of sites that just services other search engines, providing search results. Inktomi provides more searches per search engine than any other site on the Internet, and can be found at www.inktomi.com.

Invisible web: The group of dynamic or large database sites and online documents that search engines will not index.

IP address: Whenever you connect to the Internet, you are giving a unique four-number Internet Protocol address (IP address). If your IP address stays the same from connection to connection you have a static IP address. If it changes each time you connect, you have a dynamic IP address. IP addresses let search engines know where you are coming from; they can then deliver customized content depending on your location (Yahoo! does this).

IP delivery: The process of delivering customized content based upon the user's IP address.

ISP: Internet Service Provider — the name designed by a Madison Avenue advertising and marketing firm for Internet point-of-access sellers.

Java: A computer language designed to be delivered from websites to a user's browser. Small programs written in Javascript can be run from within the browser window.

Javascript: A language embedded within HTML that is executed after a page of HTML has been transferred to a user's browser, and adds extra functionality to a web page.

Keyword: A singular word or phrase that is typed into a search engine. Mainly refers to popular words that relate to any one website.

Keyword density: A percentage measure of how many times a keyword is repeated within the text of a page — for example, if a page contains 100 words and 10 of those words are 'house', then 'house' is said to have a 10 per cent keyword density.

Linkage: A count of the number of links pointing (inbound links) at a website. Many search engines, most notably Google, now count linkage in their algorithms.

Link farm: Otherwise known as free-for-all links. These are places that allow anyone to add a link.

Link popularity: The term used to describe the number of hypertext links coming into a website from other websites. Building link popularity is a great way to get a higher listing on many search engines. Google is the most high profile engine to place a large emphasis on link popularity.

Logger: A program that logs web page views.

LookSmart: One of the largest directories on the Internet, found at www.looksmart.com.

Lycos: A large search engine, found at www.lycos.com.

Metasearch: A process of searching several databases simultaneously and combining the results.

Metasearch engine: A type of search tool that conducts a search across a number of search engines and directories in one go; it does not hold its own index.

META tag: Author-generated HTML commands that are placed in the head section of an HTML document. The META keywords and META description can affect a site's listing on most major search engines. The Robots META tag is used to control certain aspects of how a search engine indexes the page, and can stop a spider from indexing certain parts of it.

Mirror site: A duplicate copy of a website at a different address, which allows websites to spread their resources. Search engines view the multiple duplicate pages of mirror sites as spamming.

Misspellings: The technique of making a spelling mistake in META keywords or META tags to catch search engine users who also misspell words when searching.

Multiple keyword tags: Using two or three keyword META tags to increase the relevancy of a page. This technique is considered spam by most search engines, and should be avoided.

Obfuscation: The act of misrepresenting META tags or content. The user is presented with a page that looks normal, but it is not the page submitted to search engines.

Open Directory Project: The Open Directory Project (ODP) is a site directory run by volunteer editors, and found at www.dmoz.org.

Optimization: Creating a page that is specifically intended to rank well at search engines. Basics optimization includes keywords and a description paragraph, no frames, and making sure that keywords are repeated across the page (e.g. in alt tags).

Opt-in: A program that gives the user the choice of whether to participate.

Opt-out: Any program or process that requires a user to take action to stop being included in some action — e.g. opt-out email lists.

Outbound link: A link that points away from your website.

Overture: A search engine that sells keywords via auctions, found at www.overture.com.

Page view: The number of times a page is viewed.

Perl: One of the main CGI programming languages, which has an easy-to-use syntax built from several common languages.

Pigeon ranking: Web searching in clusters — the name comes from the way pigeons scavenge for food. Google uses this technique to index sites.

Pop-up: An ad that opens in a new browser window.

Portal: A once popular term to refer to a site that is an entry point to other sites on the Internet. Portals are also known as online communities, and usually offer a range of services. Yahoo! could be described as a portal.

Positioning: The position of the site's entry in the results list returned by a search engine query.

PPC: Pay Per Click. A pay-per-click search engine charges websites on a per-click basis. Charges operate on an auction-style basis.

Proximity search: Defines how close words are together in any search query result.

Query: The act of typing search terms or keywords into a search engine in order to get a result. A single search of the search engine's database is called a query.

Ranking: In the context of search engines, it is the position of a site's entry in a search engine results screen.

Reciprocal link: When two websites swap links so they point at each other.

Referrer: The address of the Web page from which a user came to another site. Referrer strings can report where a visitor to your site has come from, and record what a user has typed into a search engine to get your site.

Refresh tag: The META refresh tag reloads a page at a set time.

Registration: The act of submitting a website to a directory for inclusion (such as registering with Yahoo!).

Relevancy: The accuracy of results that a search engine returns.

Results page: A page at a search engine that displays the results of a search. This is the page that appears after the user has typed a search query into the engine. The order the results are presented in is called the rankings.

Robot: In the context of search engines, robots are the programs that go out onto the Web and follow links to record web pages, which are then stored in the search engine's database. A spider is a type of robot.

robots.txt: A file in the root directory of a website that is used to control which pages spiders can access. When a spider or robot connects to a website, it checks for the presence of a robot.txt.

ROI: Return On Investment. In relation to search engine advertising, this refers to the amount of return in relation to the amount of money invested in a particular campaign. This can be hard to measure in relation to search engine optimization.

Search engine: A web-based search tool that visits websites and records and indexes them to its database. It then uses this database to provide results based on user queries. Examples of search engines are Google and AltaVista.

Search engine marketing: SEM is the term used to describe the process of making a website visible on search engines and directories so that it will attract more visitors. There are a number of different techniques, including site optimization, submission to directories and search engines, and the use of pay-per-click services.

Search engine optimization: SEO is the term used to describe the preparation of a website in order to improve its chances of being ranked highly in search engine listings.

Search terms: The words that are typed into a search engine search box. Also called search words, keywords, and queries.

SEO: Search engine optimization, the act of preparing a website for search engine submission.

Server: A computer that is designed to provide information for clients' computers. Servers store documents, which are then supplied to the client computer.

Spamdexing: The submission of pages that have been modified in an unethical way to rank highly. Techniques include submitting hundreds of different pages designed to rank high, or small invisible text to increase the keyword count of a page.

Spamming: See spamdexing. A broad term mainly used to describe unsolicited junk email.

Spider: The main program used by search engines to retrieve web pages to include in their database (see Robot).

Spidering: The process of a spider downloading a web page. Most modern spiders download pages and store them raw in a database. Different search engines use different custom spiders.

Static IP address: An IP address that remains the same each time a person logs on to the Internet.

Stop words: A stop word is a word that causes an indexer to stop indexing in the current procedure and do something else — most commonly when an indexer encounters an Adult word.

Submission: The act of submitting a web page to a search engine, or a website to a directory.

Submission service: A service that will automatically submit your page or website to many search engines at once. These were once popular, but many search engines now ban these types of services. One that is still widely used is Submit It, part of Microsoft's bCentral suite.

Theme engine: A theme engine is a search engine that indexes entire sites as one giant page. Theme engines then use only the most relevant keywords found to determine your site's theme. By determining a theme, search engines hope to return more accurate results.

Title: The part of an HTML page that is displayed on a browser title line. The text of a title is important, as it is the text displayed on the search results page as the link to that page.

Traffic: The number of visitors a website receives.

Unique user: A single individual website visitor. Unique users are important, as these give an indication of success of a website. If you have a high unique user count but a low hit count this means people are not staying on your site; the opposite would mean less people are visiting your site, but they are staying on it longer and looking at more pages.

Upload: The process of retrieving information from any computer is called downloading. When one computer sends information to another, it is called uploading.

URL: Universal Resource Locator. URLs form the basis of how we find websites; your URL is basically a web address, and by typing it into a web browser you will be taken to that page.

URL submission: The process of submitting a web page to search engines.

Yahoo!: One of the oldest site directories on the Internet, found at www.yahoo.com.